The Dark Side of
the Internet

The Dark Side of the Internet

Protecting Yourself and
Your Family from Online Criminals

Paul Bocij

PRAEGER

Westport, Connecticut
London

Library of Congress Cataloging-in-Publication Data

Bocij, Paul.

The dark side of the internet : protecting yourself and your family from online criminals / Paul Bocij.

p. cm.

Includes bibliographical references and index.

ISBN 0-275-98575-X (alk. paper)

1. Computer crimes. 2. Cyberterrorism. I. Title.

HV6773.B633   2006

005.8—dc22   2006026800

British Library Cataloguing in Publication Data is available.

Library of Congress Catalog Card Number: 2006026800

ISBN: 0–275–98575-X

First published in 2006

Praeger Publishers, 88 Post Road West, Westport, CT 06881

An imprint of Greenwood Publishing Group, Inc.

www.praeger.com

Printed in the United States of America

The paper used in this book complies with the Permanent Paper Standard issued by the National Information Standards Organization (Z39.48–1984).

10 9 8 7 6 5 4 3 2 1

To my children, Tomasina, Peter, and Donna

Contents

PART 3: IDENTITY THEFT AND FRAUD

Acknowledgments

I would like to thank my wife, Helen Bocij, for her help and advice.

Many thanks also to Suzanne Staszak-Silva, my editor at Greenwood Publishing. Without Suzanne's patience, understanding, and encouragement, this book would not exist. I would also like to thank the copyeditor, Victoria Keirnan, and Apex Publishing.

The publisher and the author acknowledge the intellectual rights of others, including all trademarks and registered designs.

Introduction

The Internet has enriched the lives of millions of people around the world: Chat rooms allow us to find companionship; webcams and instant messaging let us keep in touch with relatives on the other side of the world; and online encyclopedias help our children complete their homework. We can entertain ourselves by playing online games, watching movies, or listening to Internet radio. We can also make tedious tasks a little quicker and easier for ourselves. For instance, Internet banking lets us manage our finances without standing in line and allows us to avoid filling in deposit or withdrawal slips; of course, the bank is also open 24 hours a day, every day. We can shop online, look for a job, research our family tree, take a virtual tour of an art gallery, and even find out what became of the people we went to school with.

But the Internet also has a darker side. By making it part of our daily lives, we run the risk of allowing thieves, swindlers, and all kinds of deviants directly into our homes. Armed with a personal computer, an Internet connection, and just a little knowledge, a thief can easily access confidential information, such as details of bank accounts and credit cards. Add a little knowledge of psychology, and a con man can start to manipulate us in different ways. For instance, a potential romantic partner might quickly become a blackmailer or a cyberstalker.

These examples illustrate two main points. First, anyone who uses the Internet at home, school, or work is vulnerable to the different kinds of criminals and deviants who populate the Internet. Second, there are many different kinds of Internet predators that we should beware of. With regard to the seriousness of their behaviors, we can think of these people as being on a continuum. At one end are the people who simply want to cause a little mischief, for example by spreading a rumor or causing an argument. At the other end are the most serious criminals in society, such as sexual deviants and serial killers.

This book aims to help people avoid harm at the hands of those who inhabit the less pleasant parts of the Internet. It offers a guided tour of some of the most dangerous areas, protected by a guide who explains who the predators are and discusses their motivations, how they operate, and how to protect against them.

Instead of concentrating on technology, the material focuses on people—their behaviors and the motives behind them. Each section tries to answer some basic questions about those being discussed: What do they do? How do they do it? Why do they do it? How do I protect myself against them?

Another important aim of the book is to correct some of the misconceptions that readers may have. For instance, there is a common misconception that computer viruses can only be created by experts with superb technical skills. In reality, "virus construction kits" mean that new computer viruses can be created by almost anyone who can operate a Web browser and a mouse. It is also commonly believed that virus writers are motivated by a desire for money or notoriety or a psychological need to cause widespread destruction. Again, the reality is somewhat different: Many viruses are created for fairly mundane reasons, perhaps as programming experiments or from a desire for revenge against a single, specific individual (such as a girlfriend or a colleague).

Of course, a further aim is to entertain the reader. Every section contains numerous examples, statistics, and facts that I hope will amuse—and sometimes shock—readers.

Before describing the overall content and structure of the book, a few comments need to be made.

Many of the explanations given in the text have been simplified in order to aid understanding. Since this book is about the social effects of technology, rather than the technology itself, some explanations may contain minor technical inaccuracies. These are deliberate and have been introduced when the need for straightforward explanations has outweighed the need for technical accuracy.

For the sake of clarity, the text refers to criminals and deviants as male, while victims are usually referred to as female. This should not be taken as evidence of gender bias, since it is merely a reflection of the fact that many of the crimes discussed are carried out by men against women. Despite this, I have not adhered to this convention strictly, especially since there are places where it is more appropriate to refer to women as wrongdoers.

On many occasions I have chosen to refer to deviance rather than criminality. This is because many of the acts we find deplorable are not considered crimes. Furthermore, what may be a criminal act in one country might be perfectly legal in another. There are also a number of grey areas where it is unclear whether a certain act constitutes a crime.

Where possible, I have avoided using what is often called *technobabble*. Technical terms are used only where necessary. Where they are used, they are normally explained within the text and are included in the glossary.

Structure and Overview

I have written this book to be accessible both to those with a professional interest in Internet crime, such as teachers, students, and police officers, and to those who simply have an interest in the topic. No prior technical knowledge is needed, except for a basic understanding of how people use the Internet. While it may be helpful if readers know what Web browsers, e-mail, and chat rooms are, they need not know the inner workings of computer viruses, how *anonymous e-mail* works, and firewalls. It may be helpful to make use of the glossary of technical terms provided at the end of the book.

The Internet plays host to an enormous variety of deviant behaviors. This has meant making a choice between offering readers superficial coverage of a huge number of areas and writing in more depth about selected topics. I have tried to achieve some kind of balance by dividing the book into four broad sections, then selecting specific topics for each section. Inevitably, it has been necessary to discard some topics so that more attention can be paid to others. In doing this, I have tried to retain areas not normally dealt with in books of this kind by discarding topics that have been covered extensively elsewhere. Hacking, for instance, receives little attention so that cyberterrorism can be discussed in depth.

As mentioned, the book has been divided into four major sections.

- The first section focuses on cyberterrorism and information warfare, explaining how terrorists use the Internet and examining the risk posed by cyberattacks.
- The second section concentrates on malware (malicious software), examining the motives behind the creation of computer viruses and other destructive software.
- The third section deals with identity theft, covering areas such as phishing, e-mail fraud, and auction fraud.
- The final section focuses on online relationships, discussing topics such as cyberstalking, suicide clubs, and hate speech.

Additional Resources

Additional resources supporting this book and more information about the author are available from www.pbocij.com.

A Final Note

Anyone reading this book is likely to gain the overwhelming impression that the Internet is populated solely by blackmailers, perverts, thieves, and murderers. Readers should keep in mind that the deviants described in this book represent a minority, and that the majority of the Internet is populated by normal, everyday people. The Internet can be dangerous, but with a little caution, the benefits it brings easily outweigh the potential risks.

Part 1

Cyberterror and Information Warfare

Cyberterror

In the 1995 movie *Hackers,* an ecoterrorist threatens to unleash a computer virus that will capsize a fleet of oil tankers and cause a worldwide ecological disaster. Only a group of teenage computer hackers stands in the way of this terrible plan. The movie—which helped to make stars of Angelina Jolie, Matthew Lillard, and Jesse Bradford—shows hackers breaking into some of the most secure systems in the world with ease. Armed with technology that would be considered laughable by today's standards, the hackers are able to uncover passwords and decipher encrypted data in seconds. More impressive is the ability of the terrorist, called "The Plague," to take complete control of a supertanker through the use of a computer virus.

Although criticized for its lack of realism and the way in which hackers are portrayed, the movie helped to highlight some of the fears associated with technology. In particular, the movie dealt with a question that continues to worry many people today: Does our ever-increasing reliance on technology expose us to danger? For instance, could a hacker or terrorist take control of a critical computer system and cause widespread damage, possibly resulting in the loss of lives?

The threat posed by terrorists making use of sophisticated technology is often called *cyberterrorism.* The National Infrastructure Protection Center (NIPC) defines cyberterrorism as "… a criminal act perpetrated through computers resulting in violence, death and/or destruction, and creating terror for the purpose of coercing a government to change its policies."[1] Many people agree that three elements need to be present in order for an action to be classed as cyberterrorism: There must be a criminal act carried out using technology, the act must be politically motivated, and there must be a threat of violence, death, or destruction. These conditions help to distinguish between genuine terrorist actions and other malicious acts. Well-known security expert Bruce Schneier calls these other kinds of acts *cyberhooliganism*.[2] For instance, disseminating a computer virus or defacing a Web site are malicious and destructive actions, but they are not necessarily terrorist acts (unless carried out for political reasons).

Some experts[3] have played down the danger posed by cyberterrorism.[4] For instance, at an international security conference in 2005, Schneier said, "Nobody's getting blown to bits. I don't think that cyberterrorism exists—if you add 'terrorism' to things, you get more budget. If you can't get e-mail for a day, you're not terrorized, you're inconvenienced."[5] This view has some superficial plausibility, especially when it is pointed out that not even a single instance of cyberterrorism has ever been recorded.[6] However, this "fact" relies on a fairly strict definition of cyberterrorism in order for it to be true. In addition, it ignores the fact that terrorists *do* use the Internet to support their activities and that many of these activities can result in serious harm. Some of these activities will be looked at in more detail later on.

But why do some experts believe that there is little to fear from cyberterrorism? There are two major arguments put forward by writers such as Schneier and Denning. Schneier's view is that terror threats have been exaggerated in order to sell security products and justify all kinds of increased expenditure. Fear is used to excuse many costly actions, from hiring more staff and buying new firewall software to pushing through major technology projects and increasing defense budgets. Security companies, defense contractors, consultants, and others have a financial interest in overstating the threat of cyberterrorism; the more worried people become, the higher revenues climb.

A DIGITAL PEARL HARBOR?

A common justification for increased expenditure is the notion of a *digital pearl harbor*, an unexpected attack on computer systems that causes a huge amount of damage.[7] This term was first used in 1991 by James Bidzos, president of security company RSA, but became popularized in the late 1990s as Internet use grew and concerns over computer security increased. Over time, the meaning of this term has gradually altered. At first, it came to mean an attack on important computer systems that results in extensive damage, such as power blackouts. Today, it is often used to describe an attack intended to disrupt the Internet.

Many people believe that it would be extremely difficult, if not impossible, to mount a devastating attack on the Internet. Although it may seem quite fragile at times, it is worth remembering that the Internet was designed to allow communication even in the event of a nuclear war. This means that the technology used to shuttle data around the globe is fairly robust and reliable. From the very beginning, the Internet was designed as a distributed network that did not rely on any one computer system for its operation. In a war, this was intended to prevent an enemy from crippling government communications by destroying a single computer system or attacking a single location.

It might be helpful to compare the Internet to a network used within a typical office. If a single terminal or printer breaks down, only a very small number of workers will be affected. The majority of network users will be unaffected and may not even be aware that a fault has developed elsewhere in the building. In the same way, the effect of destroying a handful of systems connected to the Internet is likely to be negligible. Although services might be disrupted locally, it is unlikely that all communications traffic would grind to a halt.

Another argument suggesting that fears about cyberterrorism may have been overstated has been put forward by Professor Dorothy Denning, arguably one of the world's leading authorities on matters such as *information warfare*. She argues that terrorists are likely to be reluctant to use cyberterrorism for a number of different reasons.[8] Essentially, cyberterrorism is less attractive to terrorists because it has less of an impact than traditional methods, such as bombings. Not only is it difficult to cause significant damage—such as casualties—but it is also less newsworthy. Denning explains her view as follows:

> Cyberterrorism ... has its drawbacks. Systems are complex, so it may be harder to control an attack and achieve a desired level of damage than using physical weapons. Unless people are injured, there is also less drama and emotional appeal. Further, terrorists may be disinclined to try new methods unless they see their old ones as inadequate, particularly when the new methods require considerable knowledge and skill to use effectively. Terrorists generally stick with tried and true methods. Novelty and sophistication of attack may be much less important than assurance that a mission will be operationally successful. Indeed, the risk of operational failure could be a deterrent to terrorists. For now, the truck bomb poses a much greater threat than the logic bomb.[9]

INFORMATION WARFARE

Although experts like Schneier seem to feel that the Internet is of little value to terrorists, many others disagree.[10] Even Denning[11] recognizes that modern technology can support terrorism in many ways. Given opposition to the use of the term cyberterrorism, it is perhaps better to discuss how terrorists use technology in terms of information warfare. Dr Ivan Goldberg, Director of the Institute for the Advanced Study of Information Warfare (IASIW),[12] defines information warfare as "... the offensive and defensive use of information and information systems to deny, exploit, corrupt, or destroy, an adversary's information, information-based processes, information systems, and computer-based networks while protecting one's own. Such actions are designed to achieve advantages over military, political or business adversaries."

This kind of approach sees technology as an enabler, that is, as a tool or aid that supports a larger objective. In some cases, it may not be possible to achieve the objective at all without the help of enabling technology. If this seems a little unclear, imagine a robber planning to hold up a store. If he enters the store without any weapon at all, any threat he makes to the owner is unlikely to be taken seriously. The robber's aim—stealing money—will only be achieved if he can frighten the owner of the store into handing over the contents of the cash register. In order to make his threats more convincing, the robber is likely to need a weapon, such as a gun or knife. In this way, the use of a weapon enables the robber to achieve his objective of holding up the store and stealing some money.

This idea can be applied to the use of the Internet and other technology by terrorists. Even if a terrorist group is incapable of causing significant death or destruction directly through technical means, technology can cause indirect injury. In some cases, mounting an attack might not be possible at all without the use of technology in one form or another. As an example, Al Qaeda is known to have used computers to help plan and prepare attacks as early as 1993. According to the National Commission on Terrorist Attacks upon the United States,[13] both the 1993 and 2001 attacks on the World Trade Center made use of computers in various ways, from managing communications to helping plan the attacks in depth. Four years later, the Al Qaeda terrorists responsible for the attack on London in July 2005 also made use of computers, relying heavily on the Internet to support their communications and avoid detection.[14]

TERRORIST USES OF TECHNOLOGY

Discussing how terrorists make use of technology could easily fill a whole book. For this reason, this section can offer only an overview. The material will, however, address a number of basic questions. For instance, is it possible for a terrorist group to inflict casualties from a distance, perhaps by taking control of a plane or by causing a nuclear reactor to melt down?

In general, the Internet and associated technologies can be used to support the activities of terrorist groups in a number of broad areas:

- Command and control
- Propaganda and psychological warfare
- Alliances
- Information gathering and training
- Fundraising
- Recruitment
- Intelligence gathering

Although there are likely to be many more applications for technology, the items listed here are most common and are likely to be of most importance to terrorist groups.

COMMAND AND CONTROL

Command and control involves organizing and directing people, equipment, and resources in order to accomplish a task. For a group planning an attack, this will involve moving personnel into position, issuing orders, moving weapons and other supplies to where they are needed, supplying funds, receiving progress reports, and so on.

Imagine the ease with which many of these tasks can be carried out with the help of the Internet. As an example, money can be transferred around the world in a matter of seconds using the online services offered by banks and other institutions. It is even feasible that services such as PayPal could be used to move small amounts of money around. The Internet can also help to obscure the source and destination of the money by using various techniques. For instance, money-laundering rules mean that banks and other institutions scrutinize any transactions over a certain limit. An attempt to transfer, say, $500,000 from one country to another is likely to draw quite some attention. However, technology makes it a fairly simple matter to use a number of smaller, less conspicuous transactions. A large sum could be moved from one place to another in stages by using a number of bank accounts located at several different banks to make dozens of transactions—each for different amounts—over a period of several months.

The Internet has also made it easier for terrorists to communicate with each other. Before encryption and e-mail, instructions and other information needed to be passed on in person, by telephone, or in some written form. Each method exposed operatives to risk—people could be followed, telephones could be tapped, and written messages could be read by outsiders. As the popularity of e-mail grew, groups such as Al Qaeda were quick to see how it could be used to provide a means of fast, secure communication with their operatives around the world.

Although modern industry was eager to obtain the productivity increases promised by e-mail, there were fears that valuable business secrets might be stolen by competitors intercepting e-mail traffic. This created a demand for powerful encryption software that could be used to encode important information. Even if a competitor managed to intercept an encrypted e-mail message, the information it held would appear as meaningless garbage and be completely useless.

Government agencies around the world had been using encryption software for many years and were well aware of its value as a means of keeping secrets safe. Governments also had the resources to deal with the relatively feeble encryption techniques being used by businesses, terrorist groups, and some rival governments. However, the situation changed as the demand stimulated by the business world quickly resulted in extremely powerful encryption programs that could be bought off the shelf. Messages encoded using these modern techniques suddenly required a huge amount of time, effort, and expense to decrypt. Today, some encryption algorithms are considered so powerful that they are impossible to "break."

WHAT IS ENCRYPTION?

In some ways, *encryption* can be thought of as translating a message from one language into another, for instance from English to French. The data to be encrypted is usually known as *plain text*, and the encrypted text is usually called *cipher text*. Encryption turns plain text into cipher text.

Messages are encrypted using a special key, password, or pass phrase. Effectively, the *key* explains how to convert the message from one form to another. Once encrypted, a message appears as a meaningless jumble of characters.

The length of the key determines how difficult it is to crack the code used. For instance, it is possible to "break" encryption methods that use a very short key using a home computer. On the other hand, even a supercomputer may not be able to defeat an encryption method that uses a very long key.

For further information, see http://en.wikipedia.org/wiki/Encryption

Not surprisingly, governments around the world became fearful that terrorist groups would begin to use encryption in order to safeguard their communications. In an attempt to stop this from happening, some governments placed export restrictions on certain kinds of encryption software. Unfortunately, this did little to prevent almost anyone from obtaining software, since they could buy it from abroad or even obtain illegal copies via the Internet.

The availability of powerful, low-cost encryption software poses two major problems for the security services: cost and time. In general, decoding an encrypted message requires a huge amount of computing power. The more powerful the computer, the faster the message can be decoded. However, the sheer power needed to decode a message within a reasonable period of time is extremely expensive in terms of equipment, personnel, specialized software, training, and so on. It would not be unusual, for instance, to find that the cost of decoding even a single message might fall between $100,000 and $1 million. With some agencies needing to process thousands of messages each day, one can only imagine the overall cost of monitoring the communications of terrorist groups and others.

In business, the decision to invest resources in decrypting a competitor's communications is a simple one: Is the content of the message likely to be worth more than the cost of decrypting it? However, a government agency cannot use a simple cost-benefit analysis to decide how to use its resources. A mistake or omission might cost innocent lives, so financial considerations must become secondary. Obviously, this places tremendous pressure on these agencies.

CRACKING THE CODE

The method or approach used to encrypt data is normally known as an *algorithm*. The art of "breaking" an algorithm is known as *cryptanalysis*. An attempt to defeat an algorithm is usually called an *attack*. Attacks are typically based around two main approaches: *analytical* and brute force.

The *brute force attack* approach involves trying every single permutation in order to discover the key. The longer the key, the greater the possible combinations. This means that when a key approaches a certain size, it may take years to work through every possible combination.

A simple example can be used to give some idea of the difficulty involved in using a brute force attack. Imagine a key made up of just three characters from the alphabet (a ... z and A ... Z) and the digits 0 ... 9. In all, this gives 26 + 26 + 10 = 62 characters that can be used in the key. In turn, this gives 62 X 62 X 62 = 238,328 possible combinations for the key. If the length of the key is increased just four characters, the number of possible combinations suddenly leaps to 14,776,336. An even more impressive example is offered by the National Institute of Standards and Technology,[15] which states:

> In the late 1990s, specialized "DES Cracker" machines were built that could recover a DES [Data Encryption Standard] key after a few hours. In other words, by trying possible key values, the hardware could determine which key was used to encrypt a message.
>   Assuming that one could build a machine that could recover a [56-bit] DES key in a second ... then it would take that machine approximately 149 thousand billion (149 trillion) years to crack a 128-bit AES [Advanced Encryption Standard] key. To put that into perspective, the universe is believed to be less than 20 billion years old.

Of course, an element of luck may sometimes be involved in a brute force attack. Although very unlikely, it is possible that the key might be discovered early on. However, it is equally possible that the key might not be discovered until almost every combination has been tried.

The *analytical attack* approach relies on the fact that languages are based on rules and have certain features. Where the brute force approach might involve trying billions of possible combinations to discover the key, the analytical approach attempts to reduce the number of possible keys to a more manageable figure. For instance, if it is known that the key is based on a password or pass phrase, it is likely to consist of words that can be found in a dictionary. Depending on the language (and the dictionary) used, this might reduce the number of items that need to be tested to around 30,000.

The need to decode messages quickly also places pressure on the security services. Information gathered from e-mail messages and other communications becomes less valuable as time goes on. Knowing when and where a terrorist attack will take place is of little use if the knowledge only becomes available a few minutes before the attack. As mentioned, decoding messages quickly means investing in expensive equipment. However, it also means making difficult decisions, such as deciding which messages need to be given the highest priority.

As terrorists have become more educated and more sophisticated in their use of technology, they have been able to devise ways in which to work around the electronic eavesdropping methods used by the security services. An investigation into the Al Qaeda attacks on London in July 2005, for example, found that although the terrorists were using e-mail, they were using it in an unusual way.[16] Hotmail and Yahoo! e-mail accounts were used to compose messages that were saved as drafts and never sent. Anyone who knew the username and password for the account could log in from anywhere in the world, read any messages left, and then compose a reply. Since the messages were never sent out, they could never be intercepted. In this way, the terrorists reduced the need for encryption or other technological security measures.

In terms of command and control, this example highlights a number of important points. First, the method adopted by the terrorists was quick and easy to use. Operatives would need little, if any, training and could use the same basic method almost anywhere in the world. It would also be quick and easy to set up new accounts should the original become compromised. Second, this approach cost very little and required no special equipment. Free e-mail accounts are widely available, as is free or low-cost access to computers and the Internet. Virtually anyone can access the Internet through universities, cybercafés, schools, friends, relatives, and libraries. Third, this technique offered a very high level of security and made it extremely difficult for the security services to intercept communications.

All of this illustrates some of the difficulties faced by the security services in attempting to disrupt terrorist command and control functions. As this particular case shows, a government's multibillion-dollar investment in the hardware, software, and personnel used to monitor communications and decrypt messages was rendered virtually useless by little more than the use of a free e-mail account—the terrorist group did not even have to bear the expense of buying a computer.

Researchers Ballard, Hornik, and McKenzie[17] dispel any remaining doubts about the use of encryption by terrorists and the difficulties faced by the security services by stating:

> ... counterterrorism professionals have recently been faced with the reality of terrorists using advanced technology to hide their communications from prying eyes ... The prospect that terrorist organizations or in fact any group that could

potentially evolve into a violent political movement could be using the Internet to advance their cause is not science fiction but reality. The reality is also that counterterrorism agencies are not organizationally prepared to defend against such advances in technology.

PROPAGANDA AND PSYCHOLOGICAL WARFARE

As far back as World War II, the United States recognized the importance of psychological warfare and how it could influence the outcome of entire wars. At the end of the World War II, General Dwight D. Eisenhower (1890–1969) said:

> In this war, which was total in every sense of the word, we have seen many great changes in military science. It seems to me that not the least of these was the development of psychological warfare as a specific and effective weapon.

Although psychological warfare may be waged in pursuit of a number of objectives, it is perhaps most often used to damage the morale of an enemy. While civilians might underestimate the importance of morale, military leaders understand that victory often depends on ensuring that their forces are in good spirits. Eisenhower clearly understood this when he stated: "Morale is the greatest single factor in successful wars."

Zimm[18] outlines what can happen when morale is reduced:

> Degraded morale impairs cooperation, fighting spirit and command processes and can cause:

- Reduced unit effectiveness.
- Friction.
- Induced behavior such as forcing the enemy to retreat from a defensive position.
- Denied behavior. The force cannot complete tasks, for example.
- Goal displacement; that is, individual goals such as survival become more important than unit objectives.
- Catastrophic collapse; for example, soldiers desert or refuse to use weapons, units lose tactical stability, and unit organizations fail.

The Iraq conflict has brought with it a new form of psychological warfare based around atrocities committed against soldiers and civilians from a number of different countries. The most shocking incidents have involved the murders of civilian hostages that have then been broadcast via the Internet. These gruesome images showed hostages from a number of different countries, including the United States, the United Kingdom, and South Korea, being beheaded by masked terrorists.

Clearly, these atrocities were calculated to damage the morale of the coalition forces and civilian contractors in Iraq. In the case of the soldiers, it is easy to imagine how the fear felt by some might result in some of the effects described by Zimm. It is also easy to see how civilian contractors might be discouraged from working with the Iraqi people. In this way, each murder not only affected military operations but also obstructed civilian efforts to rebuild Iraq's industries, stabilize its economy, and improve services for the population.

The murders also served a political purpose. For the United States and coalition governments, the beheadings helped stimulate opposition to the military presence in Iraq. This seems understandable given that the parents, relatives, and friends of those serving in Iraq now had to fear that their loved ones might be abused and murdered as many others were. For terrorist groups, the murders served as a kind of commercial that showed how even the most powerful nation on earth can be vulnerable to acts of terror. In addition to improving morale, such a commercial undoubtedly brought other benefits: It might become easier to recruit new members; donations of money and materiel could be solicited from sympathizers; and other terrorist groups could be encouraged to launch their own attacks.

Only the Internet could have been used to distribute these video clips worldwide—certainly, no responsible television station would have shown the whole of each video clip. Within hours of release, each video clip traveled around world and was downloaded millions of times. People began to e-mail copies of each clip to friends, family, and colleagues. FTP sites made copies of the clips available for download, as did a number of Web sites.

These Web sites continue to allow the clips to be downloaded.[19] In addition, some of these video clips are now included in special collections that can be downloaded or purchased on DVD. These collections contain dozens of clips of people being murdered or killed in accidents. An example of such a collection is called *Faces of Death* and is widely available via various underground Internet sites. One of the consequences of releasing this material on the Internet is that the clips will remain available for download for many years. This means that the message being promoted by terrorists will be available any time of day or night, anywhere in the world.

It is also important to consider the harm that this material might cause to children and other vulnerable members of the population. For instance, having already been traumatized by the murder of a loved one, the families of victims are likely to be re-traumatized each time one of these clips resurfaces.

ALLIANCES

An increased use of technology has enabled many terrorist groups to reorganize, adopting new control structures that provide more autonomy and increased security. Many groups have moved away from a hierarchical structure towards a network design.[20] In practical terms, this means that groups are organized into smaller, interconnected "cells," and there is less need for a centralized command structure. Technology—especially e-mail—allows these cells to communicate with each other and coordinate their activities.

Weimann[21] provides an example of how the Internet allows terrorist groups to support each other:

> The Internet connects not only members of the same terrorist organizations but also members of different groups. For instance, dozens of sites exist that express support for terrorism conducted in the name of jihad. These sites and related forums permit terrorists in places such as Chechnya, Palestine, Indonesia, Afghanistan, Turkey, Iraq, Malaysia, the Philippines, and Lebanon to exchange not only ideas and suggestions but also practical information about how to build bombs, establish terror cells, and carry out attacks.

As well as creating new opportunities for terrorist groups to collaborate with one another, it is worth remembering these new control structures also bring other advantages for these groups. For instance, each group as a whole becomes more resistant to attack. Without a specific leadership or headquarters to target, a "cut off the head and the body will die" strategy will simply fail.

INFORMATION GATHERING AND TRAINING

Thanks to the Internet, the need for would-be terrorists to attend training camps in remote locations has been reduced significantly. Terrorists can obtain much of their training via e-mail, *instant messaging,* and the World Wide Web. Much of the information they need, such as how to manufacture explosives, is freely available for download. Any other information needed, such as details of the vulnerabilities of a specific target, can be obtained easily via other means, like e-mail.

The use of distance-learning techniques has many advantages for terrorist groups in addition to those usually associated with computer-based learning. For instance, as well as making it easier to ensure that all recruits receive the same level of instruction, these methods also help to improve security. Since senior members of the group do not need to travel around in order to train recruits, there is less chance of arrest. In addition, since fewer training camps are needed, antiterrorist forces have fewer targets to engage and less chance of capturing large groups of terrorists and their leaders.

The use of technology, and in particular the Internet, as a means of training terrorists must not be underestimated. It was mentioned earlier that technology often serves as an enabler, allowing people to accomplish tasks that would normally be difficult or impossible for them to complete. Information gathered via the Internet can help terrorists to create bombs, learn how to obtain fake documents, make or modify weapons, locate potential targets, and so on. It is even possible for these groups to familiarize themselves with the tactics likely to be used by the antiterrorist forces opposing them.

The terrorist attacks on New York and Washington in September 2001 provided a concrete example of the Internet's importance in planning and preparing an attack. Without the information obtained via the Internet, it could be argued that the attacks might not have taken place, or that they might not have resulted in so much destruction and so many casualties.

The 9/11 Commission Report found that the terrorists responsible for hijacking the aircraft employed in the attacks used computer games as training aids. Flight simulator programs, which were sold as computer games, were used to "… increase their familiarity with aircraft models and functions, and to highlight gaps in cabin security."[22] The terrorists were also able to buy a more sophisticated flight simulation package via the Internet, allowing them to study the Boeing 747-400 in detail.

The Internet was also used to research flight schools so that the terrorists could take lessons in preparation for the attack. Other research was also carried out via the Internet—one terrorist even attempted to find a wife online.[23]

The example of 9/11 showed Al Qaeda how the Internet could provide members with task-specific training quickly, cheaply, and with a high level of security. This lesson was clearly taken to heart, since the group created and released an online terrorist training manual in early 2004.[24]

The sheer quantity of information that might be of value to terrorists is difficult to measure. It is also difficult to explain how easily such information can be found. Even a cursory search using a search engine such as Google will return literally thousands of documents if the correct search terms are used. More skilled computer users can search other resources, such as Usenet, in order to locate even more information.

In an attempt to determine how easy it would be for a terrorist group to locate some of the information needed to stage an attack similar to 9/11, I carried out a simple experiment. Relying only on a search engine and a newsreader program, a number of simple searches was carried out.[25] In less than an hour I was able to locate:

- Several computer-based training packages intended to help pilots learn to handle large passenger jets
- Various technical manuals providing extremely detailed information about aircraft in service today, including plans, catalogs of parts, maintenance guides, and so on
- Almost three million pages explaining how to make explosives, including nitroglycerine, plastic explosives, and other compounds that can be made from household chemicals
- Instructions on how to create a wide variety of bombs and weapons, including guns, timed explosives and even homemade napalm
- Instructions on how to create various poisons, ranging from cyanide to sarin (sarin was used to kill 12 people and injure 6,000 more when members of a religious group called Aum Shinrikyo launched a series of attacks on the Tokyo subway in 1995)
- Operator's manuals for various weapons (outlining how to use and maintain the weapon)
- Instructions on how to obtain false documents, such as passports

It is worth noting that some experts on security are skeptical of the accuracy of information obtained via the Internet. As an example, Smith[26] argues that some "recipes" for deadly poisons may have some superficial plausibility but could never be used to create a real weapon. It is the grain of truth contained within each of these recipes that convinces some people to take them seriously. Smith supports his argument by examining a recipe for ricin—a deadly poison— that has been circulating around the Internet for a number of years and has been the subject of numerous newspaper stories. The recipe has also been the subject of government reports and has been examined by several government agencies, including the Department of the Treasury and the Drug Enforcement Administration. Our continued belief, Smith argues, that a recipe published via the Internet gives almost anyone the power to create a powerful toxin

> ... requires that everyone swallow that some anonymous American teen, peck-
> ing away in his bedroom, cribbing from yet another source of suspect rigor,
> has some professional expertise in the isolation, purification and toxicology of
> plant proteins.
>   This is not the case. But because the legend of ricin on the internet is so
> often repeated by news sources viewed as authoritative—politicians believe it, a
> large assortment of experts view it as true, terrorist-hunters go by it and, pre-
> sumably, terrorists and criminals themselves accept it.[27]

While there may be some truth to Smith's argument, there is also a great deal of evidence to suggest that many online recipes for poisons and explosives are accurate. It is easy to find many examples of incidents involving home-made explosives created using information obtained via the Internet. Over the past decade, incidents have been reported from Australia, the United Kingdom, Finland, France, Canada, South Korea, Japan, and a number of other countries. In the United States alone, a number of serious incidents have been reported from major cities such as Los Angeles and New York. Other incidents have taken place in Tennessee, Vermont, Utah, Michigan, and New Jersey, to name just a few.

One of the most notorious episodes involving explosives manufactured from instructions obtained via the Internet took place in Columbine, Colo-rado, in 1999. Eric Harris and Dylan Klebold, both students at Columbine High School, killed 12 of their classmates and a teacher before committing suicide themselves.[28] Before the attack, Harris and Klebold prepared a num-ber of explosive devices using information obtained from the Internet. It is estimated that Harris and Klebold were able to plant 30–50 bombs in the school. The boys' original plan called for up to 500 deaths, most of which were expected to result from detonating two bombs in the cafeteria. Fortu-nately, these devices and a number of others failed to detonate, greatly reduc-ing the number of casualties.

In cases such as Columbine, much of the information used to produce explosives and create other weapons comes from so-called "underground"

WHAT IS VIRAL MARKETING?

Viral marketing is a technique that exploits social networks in order to promote a product. Essentially, viral marketing relies on the fact that people will share interesting or useful information with friends, colleagues, and relatives. This creates a kind of "epidemic" where the information spreads throughout the population very rapidly. Companies tend to make use of viral marketing by offering free services (e.g., e-mail) or free content, such as funny video clips or interesting stories. Passing on a video clip or story also passes on the company's message. Viral marketing offers a cheap and highly effective form of advertising since it tends to target only those people likely to be interested in the product.

texts. Titles such as *The Anarchist's Cookbook* have been circulating since the 1960s, making the transition from paper to electronic format in the 1980s. Although much of the information in these documents is inaccurate or outdated, many Web sites continue to host them, enabling millions of users to download them each year. The popularity of these texts has inspired the creation of terrorist encyclopedias called *The Mujahideen Handbook* and *The Mujahideen Poisons Handbook*. Authored by Abdel Aziz (most likely a pseudonym), these materials can be downloaded from various Web sites and provide detailed instructions on how to create explosives and poisons.[29]

In order to promote these materials and expand them with further information, Aziz has emulated the way in which modern Internet-based businesses market their goods. Using viral marketing to reach those who might wish to use these materials, Aziz has been able to disseminate the encyclopedias very widely in a short time. Anyone downloading the encyclopedias is asked to repay the favor by submitting more material that can be added to them.

FUNDRAISING

The Internet provides a number of ways for terrorist groups to raise funds. Obviously, one of the simplest ways is to ask people for donations that can be made via electronic payment systems. Some Web sites list information that allows people to make payments directly into the organization's bank accounts.[30]

Another common method involves establishing a charity and then soliciting donations. In his testimony to the House Committee on Financial Services in 2002, Steven Emerson, a writer and terrorism expert, reported that a number of charities were being used to raise funds for terrorist groups. Not only were some of these charities located within the United States, but some were even receiving grants from the U.S. government:

... terrorists do in fact utilize charitable organizations within the United States to accomplish their funding purposes. Furthermore, because charities face far less scrutiny from the IRS ... occasionally, these same charities that engage in terrorist pursuits have succeeded in receiving financial assistance from government-sponsored grant programs ...[31]

Unlike a terrorist Web site, an online presence established as a charity enables groups to request donations from a much broader spectrum of people. Ironically, it might even be possible to collect donations from those who actively oppose terrorism. A number of terrorist groups have developed sophisticated networks of Web sites that are used to gather funds from around the world. For instance, Al Qaeda's "... global fund-raising network is built upon a foundation of charities, nongovernmental organizations, and other financial institutions that use websites and Internet-based chat rooms and forums."[32] Another example is given by *The New Atlantis*[33] and describes a group called Hizb ut-Tahrir, which "... uses websites across Europe and Africa to solicit funds for its operations. Its message: Kill nonbelievers and enemies of Islam wherever you find them."

The Internet can also be used to raise funds in a number of other ways. Some terrorist groups establish profit-making enterprises with the intention of diverting profits to support their activities. Software piracy and other forms of copyright theft are also used to raise funds, whether by charging people to download files or by selling software, music, and movies via Web sites and e-mail campaigns. Other criminal activities involving the Internet can include credit card fraud, auction fraud, and extortion. Many of these issues are discussed in other sections of this book.

RECRUITMENT

There are no accurate figures regarding the number of Web sites serving terrorists and their supporters. However, according to Dr. Gabriel Weimann, a professor of communications at Israel's Haifa University, the number of terrorist Web sites grew from just 12 in 1997 to more than 4,000 in 2004.[34] Weimann[35] is also unequivocal in stating that "... all active terrorist groups have established their presence on the Internet." Many sites are intended for one main purpose: to recruit new members for the organization.

Although most terrorist Web sites openly attempt to recruit people to their causes, some use a variety of more sophisticated and subtle methods. As one might imagine, many of these methods are directed towards young people and others likely to be receptive. As Weimann points out, even visiting a terrorist Web site may invite contact from recruiters. In addition, Weimann also makes the point that terrorist groups have become more proactive in their attempts to win over potential converts. Instead of relying on people being drawn in by the relatively static content of a Web page, recruiters actively seek new members through various means:

In addition to seeking converts by using the full panoply of website technologies (audio, digital video, etc.) to enhance the presentation of their message, terrorist organizations capture information about the users who browse their websites. Users who seem most interested in the organization's cause or well suited to carrying out its work are then contacted. Recruiters may also use more interactive Internet technology to roam online chat rooms and cybercafés, looking for receptive members of the public, particularly young people. Electronic bulletin boards and user nets (issue-specific chat rooms and bulletins) can also serve as vehicles for reaching out to potential recruits.[36]

A report from the Anti-Defamation League[37] supports Weimann's opinion regarding the use of *chat rooms* by terrorists. The report, entitled *Jihad Online: Islamic Terrorists and the Internet*, also describes some of the other techniques used to gather recruits. One Web site, for instance, publishes biographies of fighters killed in countries such as Afghanistan and Bosnia. According to the report, these accounts "... clearly intend to inspire prospective recruits to take up arms."[38]

Another example cited in the report involves a site maintained by the Qassam Brigades and used to recruit suicide bombers. They can be little doubt about the intent of the site, since it deals with questions such as "How can I come to Palestine and commit a suicide act?" Once initial contact has been made, a great deal of effort is made to deal with any doubts the recruit may have:

If a prospective recruit has questions, he or she can chat, online, with a current member of the group, post the question on a bulletin board, or ask for a fatwa (legal ruling) from a Hamas cleric.[39]

The New Atlantis[40] also reports that Al Qaeda uses Web sites and online chat rooms to recruit new fighters from around the world. The journal also quotes comments made by Rita Katz, from the Search for International Terrorist Entities Institute, who states "We know from ... captured Al Qaeda fighters who say they joined up through the Internet ... that this is one of the principal ways they recruit fighters and suicide bombers."

It is worth noting that potential recruits may sometimes come to the attention of terrorist groups through their Internet activities. Weimann[41] describes the case of Ziyad Khalil, a student who became a Muslim activist and operated a Web site supporting Hamas. After coming to the attention of bin Laden, Khalil eventually became Al Qaeda's procurement officer in the United States.

INTELLIGENCE GATHERING

There can be little doubt that the Internet represents an important source of intelligence for terrorist groups. For instance, *The New Atlantis*[42] reports that "Computers confiscated in Afghanistan suggest that the September 11 attacks were largely coordinated via encrypted e-mail, and planned with intelligence gathered online." The journal goes on to quote an Al Qaeda training manual, which states "... it is possible to gather at least 80 percent of all information required about the enemy [by] ... using public sources openly and without resorting to illegal means."[43]

To those who know where to look, a great deal of information that might be considered sensitive is freely available on the Internet. Even relatively simple tools, like search engines, can be used for basic *data mining*. The online diaries *(blogs)* created by some of the soldiers serving in Iraq provide a good example of how data mining can be used to yield important information. By locating and searching these diaries, it is possible to gather valuable intelligence about matters such as troop movements. This is not to suggest that soldiers are deliberately publishing classified information—even the most innocuous diary entry might accidentally provide an enemy with a useful piece of information.

Peer-to-peer networking (P2P) also poses a security risk because soldiers may not realize that they are sharing the entire contents of their hard disks with other people. This makes it possible for someone to download information from their computers with little fear of detection. At least one case has already been reported where classified documents related to military operations in Iraq have been available for download via P2P networks.[44]

DATA MINING

So much information is available via the Internet that it is sometimes difficult to find a specific item needed. Occasionally there may be hidden patterns in a body of data that have been overlooked for one reason or another. Data mining aims to uncover these hidden patterns and help people locate the specific pieces of information they need. No special software, hardware, or skills are needed to carry out simple data mining—in many cases all that are needed are a personal computer and some standard office software. Of course, when data mining is carried out on a commercial scale, then specialized software and suitably trained staff are needed.

Consider the example of the online diaries mentioned earlier and how someone might go about finding the movements of a specific unit. The first step would be to locate Web sites that allow people to publish their diaries. This could be done by using one or more search engines. Next, the search facilities offered by these sites could be used to locate any diaries published by soldiers or with entries containing the word "Iraq." The unit to which a particular soldier belongs could be found by examining the detail of his or her diary entries. Once one or more soldiers belonging to the unit are found, their diaries can be monitored in order to pick up information about troop movements. As an example, just before moving to a new location, a diary entry might mention how much a soldier likes or dislikes his current location. Combining information from several diaries will provide more detail and greater accuracy.

In the examples given here, sensitive information was leaked inadvertently, but there have also been cases where confidential information has been published deliberately. As an example, it has been claimed that some U.S. Web sites have published information such as code names and radio frequencies used by the U.S. Secret Service.[45]

As all of these examples suggest, rather than struggling to find information of value, terrorist groups might sometimes suffer from *information overload* because too much information is available. Weimann offers some examples of the information available to terrorists selecting a target for attack:

> Terrorists ... can learn from the Internet a wide variety of details about targets such as transportation facilities, nuclear power plants, public buildings, airports, and ports, and even about counterterrorism measures.[46]

In some cases, terrorists can find the information they need by misusing legitimate services. Google Maps,[47] for instance, is a perfectly innocent service that allows users to display detailed satellite images of virtually any point in the world. This free service even allows users to overlay maps onto the photographs, making it easier to identify specific features, such as buildings. It is easy to imagine how the service could be abused by using it to help plan an attack against a specific target.

Even *webcams* can be misused by employing them as surveillance devices. A live feed could be used to monitor a potential target, assess the damage caused by an attack, and so on. It is possible to view live feeds from a variety of locations around the world, many of which might make attractive targets for terrorists. Some examples include Times Square in New York, Covent Garden in London, and the Eiffel Tower in Paris.[48]

FURTHER INFORMATION

Reading

Janczewski L. and Colarik A., 2005. *Managerial Guide for Handling Cyber-terrorism and Information Warfare*. Hershey, PA: Idea Group U.S.

Weimann G., 2006. *Terror on the Internet: The New Arena, the New Challenges*. Washington, DC: United States Institute of Peace.

Cronin B. and Crawford H., "1999. Information Warfare: Its Application in Military and Civilian Contexts." *The Information Society 15*, pp. 257–63. Available online at: http://www.indiana.edu/~tisj/readers/full-text/15-4%20cronin.pdf.

Online

The United States Institute of Peace has a wide range of materials related to cyberterror, including an annotated list of web resources: http://www.usip.org/aboutus/resources/terrorism.html.

InfoSysSec provides links to a wide variety of resources related to information warfare: http://www.infosyssec.com/infosyssec/infowar1.htm.

Cyberattacks

Experts tend to agree that any offensive use of technology by terrorists is likely to focus on attacks against the physical and information infrastructure. In general, the *physical infrastructure* means the equipment, software, and services needed to provide public services, such as controlling power stations, running hospitals, and so on. This term also refers to the equipment needed to run an information system, such as a company network, the Internet, an e-mail system, or an e-commerce system. The *information infrastructure* means the data used by all of these systems. As an example, destroying or shutting down the computers used to manage a company's e-commerce system (physical infrastructure) would cause a great deal of damage, but destroying all of the company's customer records and other data files (information infrastructure) would cause considerably more.

Many potential targets are simply too difficult to attack in a way that is likely to cause a great deal of damage. In general, it is difficult to attack the physical parts of an information system, especially if the system is very large. For instance, a physical attack against a bank's computer systems would be unlikely to cause significant damage, since these kinds of systems tend to be distributed over a large geographical area, use several layers of physical protection, and may even have one or more backup sites. However, there are many targets that are particularly vulnerable to *cyberattacks,* that is, attacks mounted via technology, such as the Internet. In general, cyberattacks on civilian targets tend to be directed against the information infrastructure—data and services—and aim to cause financial harm of one sort or another. Cyberattacks against military targets and government agencies are usually made with the intention of depriving these agencies of their *information assets* and important services. As an example, a loss of communications or real-time intelligence during a military operation might easily result in human casualties.

Some experts believe that the danger of terrorists launching a series of cyberattacks against government services is negligible. Denning, for example, has been quoted as saying "I don't lie awake at night worrying about cyberattacks ruining my life. Not only does [cyberterrorism] not rank alongside chemical, biological, or nuclear weapons, but it is not anywhere near as serious as other potential physical threats like car bombs or suicide bombers."[1]

Such a view seems somewhat shortsighted, since there is evidence to suggest that the threat is a genuine one. For instance, Dan Verton, a writer and computer security expert, has written extensively on cyberterrorism and has suggested that "... an orchestrated attack exploiting well-known vulnerabilities could be launched with little regard for precise targeting, and could cause significant disruption and financial loss to the 'softest targets,' the bulk of which are in the private sector."[2] In addition, a report produced by Michael Vatis from the Institute for Security Technology Studies at Dartmouth College, says this about a potential cyberattack:

> Such an attack could significantly debilitate U.S. and allied information networks. A catastrophic cyber attack could be launched either externally or internally on United States' information infrastructure networks and could be part of a larger conventional terrorist action.[3]

If much of this seems speculative, then a concrete example may be helpful. In June 2005, the UK's National Infrastructure Security Co-ordination Centre (NISCC)[4] released a briefing claiming that the UK was under cyberattack.[5] The briefing[6] stated:

> Parts of the UK's Critical National Infrastructure (CNI) are being targeted by an ongoing series of email-borne electronic attacks ... Unlike "phishing" attacks and email worms, the attackers are specifically targeting governmental and commercial organisations.[7]

With regard to motive, the briefing says: "The attackers' aim appears to be covert gathering and transmitting of commercially or economically valuable information." Although these kinds of cyberattacks are unlikely to result in human casualties, they are still capable of causing widespread damage. As an example, a cyberattack against CNN, Yahoo, and eBay in 2000 resulted in losses estimated at $1 billion.[8] Although this attack was not orchestrated by terrorists, it demonstrates how easily major companies—and even entire industries—can be damaged or destroyed.

Most cyberattacks involve the use of computer viruses, Trojan horse programs, distributed denial of service attacks, Web site defacements, and intrusion attempts. All of these methods are discussed in more detail in other parts of this book.

While defacing a Web site is unlikely to result in a great deal of damage, other methods are potentially far more dangerous. This can be illustrated by considering the list of cyberattacks given in Table 2.1. In each case, had the attack been orchestrated by a terrorist group, the outcome might have been far more serious.

Table 2.1   Some Examples of Cyberattacks that Demonstrate a Potential for Significant Damage or Casualties[9]

In 1994, a 16-year-old British boy compromised approximately 100 U.S. defense systems.

In 1996, the U.S. General Accounting Office reported some 250,000 attempts to break into Defense Department systems during 1995. It was reported that approximately 65 percent of the attempts were successful.

In 1997, a hacker was able to shut down control tower services at an airport in Massachusetts. There were no accidents or casualties, but services were affected.

In 1997, a group of 35 computer specialists took part in a simulation involving a cyberattack against the United States. The specialists were able to shut down large segments of the U.S. power grid. They also silenced the command and control system of the Pacific Command in Honolulu.

In 1998, a 12-year-old boy was able to gain control of a dam in Arizona and was in a position to release a flood that could have endangered up to one million people.[a]

During the first Gulf War, it was alleged that Dutch hackers were able to obtain information about U.S. troop movements from U.S. Defense Department computers. The hackers attempted to sell the information to the Iraqis, who turned it down because they thought it was a hoax.

In 1999, it was alleged that hackers took control of a British military satellite and demanded money to relinquish control.[b]

In 2000, a former employee gained access to a waste management control system and released millions of gallons of raw sewage into an Australian town. Although the incident resulted in ecological damage, there were no human casualties. It took the employee 46 attempts to access the system, meaning that the first 45 attempts went undetected.

In Japan, it has been reported that groups have been able to compromise the computerized control systems for commuter trains, paralyzing major cities for hours.

Gazprom is the world's largest natural gas producer and the largest supplier to Western Europe. Aided by an insider, hackers were able to gain control of the central switchboard that controls gas flows in pipelines.

During the Kosovo conflict, it was reported that a Serb hacking group had deleted data on a U.S. Navy computer.

It has been claimed that Iraqi hackers were able to disrupt troop deployments during the first Gulf War.

[a]A subsequent investigation into this incident concluded that it had been vastly exaggerated and that the young person had never been in a position to cause any harm.

[b]The British military denied the incident ever took place and security experts agree that hackers would be unlikely to be able to take control of a satellite.

It is debatable whether some of these incidents can be considered acts of cyberterrorism. As mentioned earlier, most definitions require an attack to result in mass destruction or human casualties. Although some of these incidents may not have caused any deaths directly, the *potential* for human casualties should be clear.

Most critical computer systems are protected from attack or intrusion by a wide variety of mechanisms. The ultimate security measure, however, is to physically remove the system from danger. As an example, if there is a risk that someone may gain access to a system via the Internet, then the system can be disconnected from any equipment that allows contact with the outside world, e.g., modems, network cables, and Wifi connections. Disconnecting a system from a network is sometimes called *air gapping* and is a highly effective measure because it virtually eliminates the possibility of an outsider gaining access to the system. However, systems still remain vulnerable to insiders, such as disgruntled employees or those sympathetic to terrorist ideals. Perhaps a greater danger arises from the risk of a terrorist obtaining a position that involves working with a critical system. As an example, in March 2000, Japan's Metropolitan Police Department discovered that a software system bought to track police vehicles had been developed by the Aum Shinryko cult—the cult responsible for poison gas attacks on the Tokyo subway system in 1995. It was also found that the cult had received classified tracking data on more than 100 vehicles. Further investigation found that the cult had developed software for at least 80 Japanese firms and 10 government agencies.[10] They had been able to do this by subcontracting their services through other companies.

ASSESSING THE THREAT

When most people think of cyberterrorism, they picture scenes of drama and mass destruction as depicted by movies like *Hackers* and *Goldeneye,* TV shows like *24,* and even computer games like *Counter-Strike* and Tom Clancy's *Rainbow Six.* Although they recognize these works as fiction, they cannot help wondering if there might be a grain of truth to some of the scenarios presented to them. Could cyberterrorists detonate a nuclear weapon, cause planes to fall out of the sky, make nuclear power plants go into meltdown, or put trains on a collision course?

Some of the examples given in this chapter show that it might be possible for terrorists to launch a serious cyberattack against the United States and her allies. However, it is also clear that terrorists would need to remove a number of obstacles in order to stand any chance of success. Some systems are considered so secure that it would take a huge investment of resources to mount an attack. In simple cost-benefit terms, this makes these systems unattractive as targets and serves to reduce the risk to them. Some experts are convinced that their systems are nothing less than invulnerable. For instance, it is considered impossible for terrorists to take control of a plane remotely.[11] The risk of cyberterrorists detonating a nuclear weapon by remote control is also considered negligible because "... nuclear weapons systems are protected by 'air-gapping': they are not connected to the Internet or to any open computer network and thus they cannot be accessed by intruders, terrorists, or hackers."[12]

Many experts agree that the biggest threat lies in an attack that combines a physical assault, such as a bombing, with an accompanying cyberattack. A typical scenario described by experts involves terrorists detonating a number of bombs in a crowded city center. Immediately after the bombs detonate, a series of cyberattacks is launched against public utilities and services. In this kind of situation, terrorists target communications, public transport, traffic control, and power systems. This effectively paralyzes the city. The number of casualties increases dramatically since emergency services are unable to reach those needing help. Additional casualties are caused by traffic accidents, people being trampled, and so on. Without communications, police and other agencies are unable to mount an organized response and the terrorists are able to escape or mount further attacks. Power blackouts and a lack of news means the public begins to panic; public order begins to break down and looting takes place.

As this fictional example demonstrates, although the cyberattacks described here do not result in many direct casualties, they act to increase the harm caused by the explosions. In this kind of two-stage attack, the second part might be described as a *force multiplier*, since it enables the terrorist group to cause far more damage than might be expected from just a few individuals.

The kind of attack described here requires a huge investment of resources and might take several years to prepare. Until a given group is able to assemble the resources and expertise needed, they are likely to focus on simpler and easier attacks against the information infrastructure. It is easier and safer to steal or destroy information than to attack hardware or buildings. For this reason, as mentioned earlier, most cyberattacks tend to involve the use of computer viruses, Trojan horse programs, distributed denial of service attacks, Web site defacements, and intrusion attempts. This means that a basic strategy aimed at preventing cyberterrorism needs to focus on several broad areas: making information systems less vulnerable to the most common forms of cyberattack, making it harder for terrorists to infiltrate positions that allow access to key systems, and attempting to detect and counter any attempt to compromise the security of key systems.

Although these objectives may seem quite simplistic, they require a number of complex issues to be dealt with. For instance, attempting to prevent terrorists from accessing a key system means much more than simply installing a *firewall*—it may involve major changes to the way that a company does business, recruits staff, and designs products. Unfortunately, a full and detailed examination of these issues is beyond the scope of this book. However, other sections of the book look at a number of related issues that are likely to be of interest.

SAFETY AND PREVENTION

The advice given here is drawn from a variety of different sources, including Reid (2005), Bocij et al. (2005), Mitnick and Simon (2002), About. com, Sun Microsystems, the Computer Crime Research Center, the Federal Emergency Management Agency, CSO magazine and others.

BUSINESS USERS

At present, most cyberattacks result in relatively little damage. Providing organizations have taken sensible precautions—such as creating backup copies of all important data—losses can be minimized and the company can get back to normal quickly.

It is worth remembering that the advice offered here is only relevant for small to medium-sized companies (often called SMEs). Larger organizations will usually have a whole department dedicated to security and safety issues. It is also important to understand that this book can offer only the briefest advice; it would probably take more than a score of books to offer comprehensive guidance on all of the issues raised here. The points made in this section should be thought of as a starting point for improving information security. A great deal of further reading and research will be needed to develop the ideas given before they can be put into practice.

A *threat assessment* should be carried out in order to identify which systems and resources are most important to the organization and which are most vulnerable to attack. Immediate action should be taken to protect those assets most at risk.

It is essential to understand that improving security against attacks carried out via the Internet or other forms of technology involves looking at the organization as a whole. By way of illustration, it was mentioned earlier that terrorists could try to gain employment with an organization in order to access key systems. Reducing the chances of this happening will involve reevaluating and improving recruitment policies. For instance, fake degrees and other qualifications are widely available via the Internet. Terrorists can easily use such documents in order to gain employment so that they can access important systems or buildings, such as university laboratories.[13] A quick and easy way of preventing this involves changing the procedures used to recruit staff. At present, many organizations verify a job applicant's qualifications and references only when some kind of problem is suspected. By verifying the qualifications of *all* new employees, this particular security threat can be virtually eliminated.

As well as hardware and software, a wide variety of other assets needs to be protected. Of particular importance are information resources and key personnel. In terms of personnel, companies often fail to realize that they may be placing a great deal of reliance upon a handful of key employees. In addition, a great deal of important information is never codified by writing it down or storing it in a database. When writing software or developing a Web site, a programmer or Web designer might use variables or methods that are not recorded in any documentation. When the software or Web site needs to be updated, the original developer will be needed to make any changes. If the developer is not available, it will be necessary to recruit someone and allow them time to become familiar with the system. Obviously, this can be time consuming and expensive, and it means that it will not be possible to make urgent changes quickly.

Research has shown that most security incidents originate from within the organization. For instance, a report from Symantec that deals with Internet security states: "Cases of internal misuse and abuse accounted for more than 50% of incident response engagements [in 2002]."[14] Many incidents will involve *social engineering* as a way of obtaining important passwords and other information needed to support an attack of some kind. Social engineering exploits human psychology in order to trick people into revealing confidential information. Someone posing as a technician, for instance, might call a legitimate computer user with a plausible excuse that allows him to ask for her log-in details. The risk posed by social engineering can be reduced by providing employees with training and by implementing formal procedures for dealing with information requests. In the case of the fake technician, for instance, employees could be instructed to call the help desk back, so that the identity of the technician can be verified.

The previous point helps to underline the importance of establishing formal procedures that can used to protect company assets. At a basic level, the creation of an *acceptable use policy* (AUP) can provide a great deal of protection against threats to important systems, information, and people. An acceptable use policy sets out how company systems are to be used and makes it clear what behaviors are forbidden. The AUP also sets out the penalties for misuse of company facilities. By providing people with clear guidance about how they must use company systems, it becomes difficult for anyone caught misusing them to claim ignorance. Since employees are aware of the consequences of misusing systems, the AUP also acts as a strong deterrent. Publicizing cases that have resulted in prosecution or other action will also help to deter outsiders.

A more comprehensive approach towards security is often based around the development of a *formal security policy*. This is a formal document that sets out all of a company's security arrangements and often contains detailed procedures for dealing with particular situations, such as backing up data. The AUP often forms part of the more detailed and wide-ranging security policy. Information on developing an acceptable use policy or a formal security policy is easily available via the Internet. The *IT Security Cookbook*,[15] for example, provides detailed guidance on a wide range of security issues, including how to develop a formal security policy.

According to research, most of the attacks experienced by companies involve viruses, Trojans, worms, and other malicious programs. For instance, a study of 201 companies by the United Kingdom's National Hi-Tech Crime Unit in 2004 found that 77 percent had experienced virus attacks in 2003. This is in keeping with a study from Symantec, which found that 78 percent of respondents had faced attacks involving worms and other malicious software.[16] These figures make it clear that companies must invest in security software such as firewalls, virus scanners, and intrusion detection packages.

It is also important to keep operating systems and other critical software up to date. Security vulnerabilities found in software tend to be exploited very quickly by hackers, virus writers, and others. In order to reduce risk, software updates and *patches* should be installed as soon as they become available.

ANTICIPATING TROUBLE

What happens if a machine breaks down, or a supervisor calls in sick? Most managers know what to do in everyday situations. If a supervisor calls in sick, someone else in the same department can take on some extra responsibility for a few days. If a machine breaks down, there will be someone to call who will repair it quickly.

But what happens when an unexpected problem arises that no one in the company has dealt with before? A lot of time can be wasted while managers gather information and try to make decisions. The decisions they make will be hurried, and there will be plenty of opportunities for mistakes to happen. If a wrong decision is made, even a trivial one, the situation may become worse. For some companies, the cost of a wrong decision or a delay in dealing with a problem can be measured in millions of dollars per hour.

Disaster recovery planning asks "what if?" and tries to come up with ways of dealing with an organization's worst-case scenarios. A bank, for instance, might look at the effects of a terrorist attack on its computer systems. The resources needed to deal with an emergency may already be in place, simplifying the planning process and reducing expense. In the case of banks, most will have *backup facilities* that duplicate important systems. These will have been created to deal with a wide range of disasters, such as earthquakes or floods. In the event of a disaster, the backup site can be activated immediately, allowing the bank to continue working normally with minimal disruption. Of course, all organizations must also look at how they can protect their staff and the public from harm; disaster recovery planning is not just about protecting profits.

No matter what precautions are taken, the possibility of a successful attack against company systems can never be eliminated altogether. Most security professional recognize this and try to plan how the company can resume normal operation as quickly as possible following a serious disruption to its activities. This kind of planning is often called *disaster recovery planning* or business continuity planning. Developing action plans is more than just a sensible precaution; the planning process can often identify points of vulnerability and help to improve overall security.

INDIVIDUALS AND FAMILIES

Home users are fortunate in that only a relatively small number of precautions are needed to safeguard their computer systems.

As mentioned earlier, most cyberattacks are based around the use of computer viruses, Trojan horse programs, distributed denial of service attacks, Web site defacements, and intrusion attempts. Many of these methods rely on compromising the computers owned by ordinary users, so ordinary members of the public become unwitting accomplices to terrorism. *Computer viruses* and worms provide a good example of how innocent computer users can be made to contribute to an attack against a company or government agency. Most activities on the Internet expose users to the possibility of infection by a computer virus. Whenever someone receives an e-mail, visits an interactive Web site, or downloads software, there is a risk of virus infection. Obviously, some activities are riskier than others: Downloading pirate software or using file-sharing programs are more likely to result in infection than simply reading news headlines. A single infected computer can easily cause thousands of other systems to become infected within a matter of hours. By planting viruses and worms on just a few systems, terrorists and others can rely on ordinary computer users to help distribute their programs for them.

Business machines are also susceptible to infection when employees take work home from the workplace, unknowingly infect documents or

HOW FAST CAN VIRUSES AND WORMS SPREAD?

In 2003, the Slammer worm was launched via the Internet and was able to spread around the world in less than 30 minutes. A study of the incident found that within three minutes of launch it was carrying out 55 million scans per second and within ten it had infected 90 percent of the 75,000 vulnerable servers it had discovered.[17]

The Mydoom e-mail virus appeared on January 26, 2004 and within three days was responsible for 1 in 12 of all e-mail messages. One anti-virus company suggested that the problem was more serious when it estimated that the virus was responsible for up to 30 percent of all e-mail traffic.[18]

spreadsheets, and then return them to the office computer. Misusing the office computer, for example by downloading pirate software, can also result in virus infection.

By reducing the risk of virus infection, home users can make their systems faster and more stable. Just a few simple measures can also make it harder for their systems to be exploited by terrorists, hackers, and others.

- Install and use antivirus software. Keep the software up to date and scan the computer regularly.
- Install and use a firewall package. Keep the software up to date.
- Keep operating systems and other programs up to date by installing security updates and patches when they become available.
- Look out for unusual activity, such as a lot of modem or network activity at a time when the Internet is not being used.
- Make regular backups of important data in case the machine becomes infected.

Additional information on dealing with viruses, Trojans, and other malicious software is given in later chapters of this book.

FURTHER INFORMATION

Reading

Verton, 2003. *Black Ice: The Invisible Threat of Cyber-Terrorism.* Emeryville, CA: McGraw-Hill/Osborne.

Mitnick K. & Simon W., 2002. *The Art of Deception.* Indianapolis: Wiley Publishing Inc.

Online

The National Institute of Standards and Technology (NIST) has a Computer Security Resource Center that publishes a number of useful publications related to security: http://csrc.nist.gov/.

The Information Warfare Site (IWS) publishes a wide variety of documents dealing with security issues, including a great deal of material on protecting critical infrastructure: http://www.iwar.org.uk.

The CERT Coordination Center provides a variety of resources covering all aspects of computer security. In addition to news on current threats, recent statistics, and the results of various surveys, the site also provides a wide range of articles, reports, and training materials: http://www.cert.org.

Part 2

Malicious Software

Viruses, Trojans, and Worms

Programs designed to steal, alter, or destroy information are common on the Internet and are known by a baffling variety of names, for example, viruses, spyware, Trojans, worms, adware, and key loggers. In general, malicious software of any kind is known as *malware,* which is a contraction of "malicious" and "software." A program is considered malicious if it causes disruption of any kind, such as preventing the intended use of a computer or network. A program is also considered malicious if it steals, changes, conceals, or destroys information stored on a computer or network system.

Different types of malware tend to be created for different purposes: Viruses usually destroy data; key loggers steal passwords; and Trojans provide a way of controlling the victim's computer. However, as programs become more sophisticated, the distinctions between different kinds of malware have become blurred. For most computer users, there is little difference between a virus and a worm because both can have virtually the same effect on their systems.

This section takes a detailed look at the different kinds of malware currently in circulation. As well as describing how these programs spread and what they do, the material also looks at their impact on organizations and home users. Throughout this section, two important questions are addressed: Who are the people that create malware, and what motivates them?

VIRUSES, TROJANS, AND WORMS

As will be shown, viruses, Trojans, and worms are closely related. This means that much of the material in this section applies to all three types of software.

The term "computer virus" was coined by Fred Cohen in a 1984 academic paper entitled *Computer Viruses: Theories and Experiments*. However, naturally occurring computer viruses, usually arising as a result of programming errors, were reported as early as 1974. In addition, papers describing mathematical models of the theory of epidemics were published in the early 1950s and can be said to have laid the theoretical foundations for modern computer viruses.

More information about Fred Cohen, including the full text of his article, *Computer Viruses: Theories and Experiments*, can be found at his Web site: www.all.net.

In essence, a computer virus is a small program that is capable of copying itself from one computer to another. Each "infected" computer acts to spread the virus to other computers. The way in which a virus spreads is very much like the outbreak of a disease, where just a few carriers have the potential to infect the entire community.

Most viruses are programmed to carry out a series of actions at a specific time. These actions can be triggered in a variety of ways; some viruses become active on special dates (these viruses are sometimes called *logic bombs* or *time bombs*), while others respond to events like trying to send an e-mail message or run a word-processing program. The action a virus takes is usually referred to as the *payload*. The use of military-style terms when discussing malware signifies the common belief that computer users and security experts are involved in a war against those who create and distribute viruses. We will return to this theme a little later on.

In general, viruses tend to be created for two basic purposes. Most viruses are created to cause damage to infected computer systems, usually by damaging or destroying important files. A small number of viruses are created as practical jokes or to make some kind of statement. These programs usually display messages or carry out some other kind of prank, like pretending to delete files from the infected computer. In fact, one of the first major virus incidents to come to the attention of the public involved a simple practical joke. The virus, called CAC, appeared in late 1987 and only infected the Commodore Amiga home computer. At the time, IBM-compatible machines had yet to become popular in the home and the Amiga was arguably the best-selling home computer. The virus waited until it had been activated three times and then displayed a simple message: "Something wonderful has happened ... your Amiga is alive!" The publicity given to CAC meant that new viruses quickly appeared that were aimed at other computer brands, including the Atari ST and IBM-compatibles.

Although some people believe that viruses like CAC are harmless, this is not really the case. All viruses damage or change data in some way. As an example, when a virus first infects a machine, it stores a copy of itself on the computer's hard disk or somewhere else, sometimes overwriting important data. A badly written virus may also cause the computer to become unstable, corrupting important files or causing users to lose their data when the machine crashes.

It is widely believed that the first IBM-PC virus appeared in 1985.[1] The virus, called *Brain,* was written by two brothers, Basit and Amjad Farooq, as a way of keeping track of the software they sold. Annoyed that their work was being stolen by software pirates, the virus was designed to infect any computer running an unregistered version of the software. When activated, the virus made users contact the brothers for help in removing it. Although the virus spread very quickly, it received relatively little attention from the media and caused very little panic. This was probably because the virus was not intended to cause damage and was targeted at a small, specific group of users. In addition, viruses were fairly new, and the public was not familiar with the damage they could cause.

It was not until the late 1980s that the public started to become uneasy with regard to the rapidly growing number of viruses. In 1987, two relatively harmless programs affected thousands of machines across the United States. The IBM Christmas Card virus was created to display a friendly greeting to anyone who used the program. Unknown to users, the program secretly sent copies of itself to people in the user's e-mail directory. When the virus found its way onto IBM's network, it sent out millions of copies of the card and paralyzed the network for days. The MacMag virus was released in November 1987, supposedly as a way of spreading a message about world peace. The virus quickly spread throughout Canada, Australia, and the United States, infecting approximately 350,000 Macintosh computers. The virus became active on May 2, 1988, when each copy displayed a simple message on the user's screen before deleting itself. Although the author of the virus, Richard Brandow, said that his intent was to spread a peaceful message, the media and the public saw things differently; instead of displaying a message on the screen, Brandow could have easily deleted all of the data on 350,000 systems. Just a few months later, concern grew further when a copy of the virus found its way onto the media used to distribute a commercial software package, Freehand by Aldus Corporation. Although completely accidental, this incident showed that viruses could even infect software bought off-the-shelf.

More information about the history of computer viruses, including MacMag and the IBM Christmas Card viruses, can be found at the Computer Knowledge site: www.cknow.com/categories/Virus-Tutorial.

VIRUS OR WORM—WHAT IS THE DIFFERENCE?

For most people, there is little difference between a worm and a virus. After all, both tend to be destructive and both try to spread to other systems. Worms tend to be seen as an offshoot of the computer virus, and the main difference between these types of software involves the way in which they spread from one computer to another. Viruses need some kind of human intervention to help them infect other systems. Without such intervention, the spread of the virus halts, and it eventually dies out. As an example, if a virus has been embedded in a program file, it will not become active (and therefore cannot copy itself) until the user runs the program. Worms, on the other hand, are able to spread without any help from computer users. Worms make use of the very same technology that allows us to surf the Internet, send e-mail, share files, and chat with one another. If a computer is connected to a network and is not adequately protected, it is immediately vulnerable to attack from worms and other malicious software.

Since worms do not need help from human beings, they are able to spread more quickly than viruses and can sometimes infect thousands of systems within a matter of minutes. As an example, imagine that a worm embedded in an e-mail message sends copies of itself to everyone in the user's address book. Each copy of the worm then sends out further copies to everyone in the address book held on the newly infected machine. After this process has been repeated a few times, millions of copies of the worm will be active. Since creating and sending even hundreds of e-mail messages often takes just a few seconds, thousands—even millions—of machines could become infected within minutes.

If people were not already concerned about viruses and worms, two more incidents in 1988 and 1989 helped to make them so. In November 1988, Robert Morris, a postgraduate student at Cornell, released a worm onto the Internet.[2] Morris took care to ensure that the worm appeared to originate from MIT, presumably to avoid any repercussions from his actions. The worm began to spread faster than anticipated because of a programming error and soon began to affect systems around the country, including those at military installations, universities, and medical facilities. It is difficult to assess the damage caused by the worm around the world, but estimates vary from $10 million to $100 million. In addition, the estimated cost of dealing with individual incidents ranges from $200 to more than $53,000.[3] Morris was eventually prosecuted for his reckless behavior and sentenced to three years of probation, 400 hours of community service, and a fine of more than $10,000. Despite this incident, and despite trying to make it seem that the worm originated from the university, Morris is now an assistant professor at MIT.

The second incident has become known as the Aids Virus Trojan, even though a virus was not involved. In December 1989, around 27,000 disks were sent out from London to addresses around the world. Since the disks were supposed to contain important information about the AIDS virus, many people installed the software immediately. However, during installation, extra files were copied onto the system that monitored how many times the computer booted up. When a certain number was reached, the hard disk was encrypted so that users could no longer access their data. In order to restore their files, users were instructed to send a payment of $189 or $378 to an address in Panama belonging to a company called PC Cyborg.[4] The distribution of disks in Europe was intended as a trial run for a more ambitious target—had the scheme been successful, some 200,000 disks were to be sent out across the United States.

The case of the Internet Worm made many companies and other organizations start to worry about the risks posed by viruses, worms, and other malicious programs. Concerns also grew about the Internet and how it could be used to distribute a virus or worm. The Aids Virus Trojan incident showed that malicious software was not only capable of destroying data; it could also be used to blackmail companies by holding data hostage. These incidents, together with a few similar ones, led to new laws meant to deal with computer crime.

TYPES OF COMPUTER VIRUSES

There are many different types of computer viruses and it is not possible to describe all of them here. However, the way in which certain viruses work has an impact on how they spread from system to system. For example, some viruses are particularly suited to distribution via the Internet. With this in mind, it is worth taking a brief look at some of the major types of virus in circulation.

A *boot sector virus* is able to infect all kinds of disks, including hard disks. The *boot sector* of the disks contains various instructions that will be carried out every time the computer is switched on or reset. Since these instructions are processed before any other programs run, the virus is loaded first. Boot sector viruses were particularly problematic when floppy disks were used more commonly than they are today. This is because the boot sector of a floppy disk is automatically read when the disk is inserted into the drive. Each time the disk is used on another machine, the virus has a chance to infect it. To make matters worse, an infected system will go on to place a copy of the virus onto every floppy disk used with it.

Parasitic viruses (sometimes called *binary file infectors*) embed themselves in program files. Each time the program runs, so does the virus. Usually the virus will have been created so that it does not interfere with the operation of the program, allowing it to remain undetected for longer. Instead, the virus loads a copy of itself into the computer's memory so that it can remain active even if the program ends. While active, the virus monitors the system, looking for other files to infect or carrying out other actions secretly.

Macro viruses take advantage of the built-in programming languages now found in many software packages. The virus is stored within a data file, such as a word-processing document, and is activated whenever the file is loaded. In just a few years, macro viruses have become very common and are now seen more often than any other kind.

Worms are viruses that can spread without needing human intervention. Most worms rely on networks, such as the Internet, to help them locate and infect vulnerable computers.

Trojans disguise themselves as legitimate programs in order to gain access to a system. Trojans rely on users infecting their own machines when they run what appears to be a useful program.

As mentioned earlier, there are many other types of virus in circulation. Some further examples include:

- *Stealth viruses,* named after the military technology, use a number of different techniques to hide themselves from users and virus scanners.
- *Polymorphic viruses* are able to change their structure in order to avoid detection.
- An *armored virus* tries to prolong its life by making itself difficult to take apart, so that it takes longer to find a way of dealing with it.
- *Multipartite viruses* use a combination of methods to infect files—if they are unable to infect the system using one method they simply use another.

WHAT'S IN A NAME?

The Trojans that infect our computers draw their name from the story of the Trojan War. When Paris stole Helen and ran away to Troy, Menelaus and Odysseus led the Greek army in a war against the great city. The fighting went on for many years, but the Greek army was unable to gain entrance to the city. Finally, Odysseus ordered a large wooden horse to be built. The horse was hollow so that soldiers could be hidden inside. Odysseus and some warriors hid inside the horse while the rest of the Greek fleet sailed away. In thinking that the war was over and that they had been victorious, the Trojans brought the horse into the city as a trophy. That night, when most of Troy was asleep, the Greeks left the horse and slaughtered the Trojans.

HOW MANY VIRUSES ARE THERE?

There are many estimates of the number of viruses in circulation today. Some of the differences between these estimates are so great that a little further explanation is needed before looking at any figures.

Many viruses have a number of variations, for instance NetSky number of different forms identified as NetSkyA, NetSkyB, NetSk on. Clearly, how these variations are counted will affect estimates number of viruses in circulation.

Another consideration involves the fact that certain viruses tend to resurface from time to time. A new outbreak might occur or someone might create a new variant of a particular virus. This creates difficulty in deciding which viruses are active and which have effectively died out.

Finally, some people distinguish between computer viruses created to cause destruction and those created for other purposes. For instance, some viruses are created as experiments and are never intended to be released outside of computer laboratory. These viruses seldom spread very far because they have not been designed to survive "in the wild." Should a virus be counted if it poses no real threat because it is unlikely to be able to spread far?

In 1989 it was believed that fewer than 50 viruses existed.[5] By the end of 2004, it was estimated that there were more than 100,000 viruses in existence.[6]

The number of viruses is now so large that a virus is set to trigger for every day of the year. In fact, one company, Symantec, publishes a calendar that shows that 25 or more viruses are set to trigger on certain days.[7]

As the figures just given suggest, the number of viruses discovered each month has also changed dramatically over the years. In the 1990s, it was estimated that a minimum of 50 viruses were being discovered each month. At the end of 2002, Sophos reported that it has detected 7,000 new viruses, worms, and Trojans over the year—an average of more than 500 viruses each month. In 2004, Sophos announced that it had detected 959 viruses in May alone. Another antivirus company, Trend Micro, reported that it had detected 1,700 viruses, worms, Trojans, and other malware in April and 1,050 in May.[8]

NEW AND EMERGING VIRUSES

Viruses are not restricted to computers alone. Over the past few years, viruses have appeared for a number of other devices.

- Some of Creative's Zen Neeon MP3 players were shipped with a copy of a Windows worm, W32.Wullik.B.[9]
- Marcos Velasco has published several viruses capable of infecting cell phones equipped with Bluetooth technology.[10] Such viruses could potentially infect other Bluetooth devices.
- WinCE4.Dust, the first virus capable of infecting Pocket PCs, was discovered in late 2004.[11]
- In 2005, a virus capable of infecting "smart" mobile phones was discovered. Mabir.A infects phones using the Symbian operating system and is capable of spreading itself via multimedia messaging services and text messages.[12]

THE DAMAGE CAUSED BY VIRUSES

It is difficult to estimate the losses that result from a virus infection because many organizations are reluctant to supply information that may show them in a poor light. Despite this, it is possible to gain some idea of the potential losses faced by businesses and home users by looking at the figures published by several well-known organizations.

Business users stand to lose most from virus infections because of the number of systems they operate. Thousands of employees working with thousands of computers multiply the chance of a virus infection and the cost of repairing any damage caused. Each hour lost due to a virus infection results in losses that may run into millions of dollars, especially for companies reliant on the Internet for sales.

One way of measuring the harm caused by viruses is by considering the average cost of dealing with an incident. According to Microsoft,[13] around 6 percent of all business computers experienced data loss in 1998. Of these, viruses accounted for 7 percent of all incidents. The average cost of each incident was around $2,500. This figure relates to the cost of removing the virus and replacing any data lost. As viruses have become more sophisticated, and companies have started to face more attacks, the cost of dealing with an incident has soared. ICSA Labs, an information security organization, publishes an annual report that looks at the impact of viruses on business. The report is based on a survey of 300 respondents who collectively own and manage almost a million computers. According to the company's 2003 report, the average cost of a virus incident was $99,000.[14]

A second way of measuring the impact of viruses involves looking at how many incidents take place each month for a given number of systems. Typically, figures are given as the number of incidents recorded each month per 1,000 systems. The ICSA report states that the monthly rate of virus infection per 1,000 computers grew from just 10 in 1996 to 108 in 2003.[15]

Another common way of measuring the harm caused by viruses is by measuring how long the company is deprived of its computers, especially the servers used to distribute e-mail, host Web pages, manage transactions, and so on. The cost of *downtime* is important because it can have a significant effect on overall profitability. Ultimately, a company's survival may depend on how quickly it is able to restore its systems. A specialist data recovery company, American Data Recovery,[16] has collected and published a number of important statistics related to data loss. These figures suggest that almost every company (93 percent) deprived of its data center for 10 days or more due to a disaster, such as a virus attack, might be likely to file for bankruptcy within a year of the incident. In addition, half (50 percent) of companies deprived of data management for 10 days or more might be expected to file for bankruptcy immediately.

The suggestion that just one major incident might cause a company to collapse seems more reasonable when the monetary cost of downtime is considered.

According to figures from the *2001 Cost of Downtime Survey*[17] (which are also published on the American Data Recovery site), around half of respondents (46 percent) reported that each hour of downtime cost up to $50,000. However, almost a fifth of respondents (18 percent) valued each hour of downtime at between $251,000 and $1 million, while a smaller group (8 percent) stated that each hour of downtime would cost their companies $1 million or more.

The survey also asked respondents to estimate at what point the company's survival might be at risk. None of the respondents felt that their companies could survive longer than 72 hours. Significant groups of respondents felt that their companies could be at risk after fairly short intervals: eight hours (8 percent), four hours (9 percent), one hour (3 percent), and less than one hour (4 percent).

Before moving on to look at the effects of computer viruses on home users, it is worth taking a moment to look at how much damage some of the world's most notorious viruses have caused over the past few years. Table 3.1 shows the estimated losses associated with specific viruses between 1999 and 2004. Note that some of the viruses listed occasionally reappear and cause fresh outbreaks. The LoveLetter virus (also called the Love Bug), for instance, continues to resurface from time to time, even though it has been easy to detect and remove since 2000.

Although most home users are unlikely to suffer serious financial losses, people who work from home may sometimes find their livelihoods jeopardized. Losing a list of customers or sales records can easily cause a small business to

Table 3.1   Examples of Estimated Losses Due to Computer Viruses from 1999 to 2004

Year	*Virus*	*Estimated Loss ($ billions)*
1999	Melissa	1.10
2000	LoveLetter	8.80
2001	Code Red	2.60
2001	Nimda	0.64
2001	SirCam	1.15
2002	Klez	9.00
2003	Blaster	0.40
2003	Slammer	1.20
2003	SoBig.f	1.00
2004	MyDoom	4.75
2004	Sasser	3.50
2004	NetSky	2.70
2004	Bagle	1.50

Sources: Lemos (2003), Leyden (2002), Computer Economics Inc. (2003), Klein (2004).

collapse. People who enjoy flexible working can also cause problems for themselves and others. Office workers who bring a report home to finish over the weekend may not only lose the report but might also lose all of the data on the family PC. A person who is particularly unlucky may even bring a virus back to work on Monday morning, accidentally causing even more damage.

For some people, it is the data stored on their computers that is most valuable to them. Many people keep a great deal of personal or sensitive information on their systems: family photographs, home accounts, letters, e-mails, credit card information, or school or college work. Losing a collection of sentimental photographs or a thesis can be extremely painful, but many people fail to take even the simplest precautions, such as installing antivirus software.

A survey of 329 computer users carried out by the National Cyber Security Alliance[18] found that around two-thirds of users (67 percent) did not have up-to-date antivirus software and that one in seven (15 percent) had no antivirus software at all on their computer. In addition, around two-thirds of respondents (63 percent) said they had the victim of a virus infection in the past and almost one in five users (19 percent) reported that they had at least one virus infection on their home computer at the time of the survey.

Some additional figures have been published by ConsumerReports.org,[19] a part of the Consumers Union of the United States. The organization carried out a survey of 8,000 users in order to assess the effectiveness of security software. More than half of the respondents (58 percent) had found a virus on their home computer within the last two years and almost a fifth had found a virus on four or more occasions.

Of those who found a virus on their computer, almost a fifth (17 percent) said that their systems had suffered damage because of the infection. Almost a third of those infected (32 percent) said that important files were lost permanently, and almost as many said that dealing with the infection took two weeks or more. In terms of financial damage, significant numbers of users reported paying $100 dollars or more for repairs (22 percent), having to replace components (9 percent), or even having to replace the whole system (6 percent).

CAN VIRUSES DAMAGE HARDWARE?

It is widely believed that viruses are incapable of causing permanent damage to computer hardware. This belief, however, is incorrect, since viruses can cause damage to computer components in a number of different ways. Both Magistr and Kriz, for instance, are capable of effectively destroying a computer by overwriting the *BIOS*, the special software needed to control the keyboard, display screen, disk drives, serial communications, and a number of other functions.[20] Without a functioning BIOS, a computer is unable to start up. To repair the machine, it may be necessary to replace the computer's main circuit board *(motherboard)*, which is a time-consuming and expensive operation.

How Viruses Spread

Computer viruses are often compared to their biological counterparts, and the way in which they spread tends to be discussed in terms of epidemiology.[21] Like an outbreak of influenza or SARS, a computer-virus epidemic has a life cycle that moves through various stages.

The Virus Threat Center hosted by TechRepublic offers an interesting description of the life cycle of a virus outbreak.[22] Once a virus appears, it moves through four stages: emerging, epidemic, exiting, and eradicated. In the *emerging* stage, the virus is identified as a potential threat. In the *epidemic* stage, the virus begins to spread more widely, and there may be a sharp increase in the number of machines infected. Alternatively, there may be a small but sustained growth in the number of machines infected over a long period of time. In the *exiting* stage, the rate of infections begins to decline as antivirus companies update their programs and users are able to remove the virus from their machines. In the final stage, the virus no longer poses a significant threat and is considered to have been *eradicated*. Note that few viruses are ever truly eradicated, and there may be new outbreaks from time to time.

Some of the major causes of virus infections have remained constant for more than two decades. In addition, virus writers still rely on a small number of basic principles to distribute their handiwork. The next sections look at how viruses are spread, moving from a fairly simple means, used in the 1980s, to the technically sophisticated methods employed today.

The writers of early viruses were limited in their choice of distribution methods. Since few computers were equipped with hard disks, viruses needed to be hidden on floppy disks or, occasionally, on the audio cassettes that some home computers used for storage. Instead of the Internet, text-only *bulletin board systems* (BBS) were used by a relatively small number of users. BBS were the forerunners of today's *message boards*, allowing people to keep in touch with each other, share knowledge, and swap software (both legally and illegally). Many BBS hosted file libraries containing software updates, drivers, utility programs, and collections of shareware and freeware. As well as being able to download files, users could also upload files they wanted to share with others. This created a perfect opportunity to distribute a virus as part of a program that users might find desirable.

As time went on, computers began to be equipped with large hard disks, CD or DVD drives, and faster modems. In addition, the Internet started to become a part of everyday life, moving outside of universities, offices, and schools and into the home. At work, many computers were connected to company networks so that users could share files and work collaboratively. All of these changes have provided new ways to distribute viruses on an unprecedented scale.

The next sections look at some of the most common ways in which viruses spread.

Macro Viruses

As software applications have become more sophisticated, they have started to include powerful programming languages that can be used to automate routine tasks. At the simplest level, users can create *macros* to handle repetitive actions, such as automatically entering the date or a signature block into a letter. However, it is also possible to create more complex applications, such as stock-control systems or accounting applications. This versatility has made it possible to create new viruses that can be distributed as part of a word-processing document, spreadsheet, or database file. Any program that includes a programming or scripting language is a potential target for a virus.

Businesses, government agencies, universities, and other large organizations are most at risk from macro viruses for two main reasons. First, in these environments people are more likely to share documents with others. For instance, several people might work on a sales report or a school project. Secondly, many of these organizations rely heavily on their network systems to maintain productivity and support communications. If a macro virus is able to infect files held centrally, the infection might be passed on to everyone who accesses them. As an example, many organizations store standard letters, forms, company manuals, and other files in a central location. If a virus infects one of these files, it will have the potential to infect almost every machine connected to the network.

Most programming or scripting tools provide the ability to create a special macro that runs as soon as a document or data file is opened. This type of macro is usually called an *autoexec macro*. When macro viruses first appeared, they were able to spread very quickly because most software packages were configured so that autoexec macros ran automatically. As soon as the user opened what appeared to be an interesting document, spreadsheet, or other file, his machine would become infected and immediately set about trying to infect other systems. The simple act of preventing macros from running without the user's permission reduced virus infections dramatically. Today, all major software applications have a default configuration that prevents autoexec macros from running without the user's consent.

Many macro viruses are designed to spread by e-mail, usually disguising themselves as an attachment to an important or amusing message. When a computer is first infected by one of these viruses, the virus scans the machine for e-mail addresses. Most versions of Microsoft Windows have a built-in address book that is used to store contact information for a range of other applications. Other packages, such as e-mail software, also have address books that can be accessed by macro viruses. The virus sends a message to every contact in the address book, together with a copy of itself disguised as a word-processing document, electronic greeting card, amusing video clip, picture, or sound file. A little social engineering is used to encourage the recipient to open the message (and infect his own machine). The subject line of the message will be designed to appeal to the recipient's curiosity. Messages may have subjects like "You have GOT to see this" or "Important message from USERNAME," where the virus automatically substitutes USERNAME for the infected user's name. Making the message appear to have come from a friend or colleague increases the chances of it being opened. If the virus successfully infects a new machine, the process begins again with a new address book and a new set of potential targets.

These kinds of *e-mail viruses* were initially considered crude and unlikely to pose any serious threat. The writers of these viruses were often called *script kiddies,* a derogatory term used to describe people with limited programming skills. However, the chaos caused by e-mail viruses such as Melissa and LoveBug showed that they were capable of causing significant damage. In addition, virus writers were quick to improve their programs, making them more destructive and more difficult to detect. As an example, it was possible to detect some early macro viruses by looking for unusual e-mail or Internet activity, since this might indicate that the virus was sending e-mail. New versions of these viruses were designed to send e-mail only when the user sent or received messages. By hiding the activity of the virus in this way, virus writers were able to eliminate a simple way of detecting infection.

HAVE E-MAIL WILL TRAVEL

A conventional view of computer viruses held that they could not be transmitted by e-mail. This was (and remains) essentially true: An e-mail message is nothing more than a block of text, so a virus cannot be transmitted as part of the message. However, a virus can be transmitted as a *file attachment.* Opening an infected file attachment activates the virus and allows it to infect the computer. It is possible to store a virus within almost any kind of file, including word-processing documents, spreadsheets, databases, screensavers, and any kind of executable file.

Virus writers are attracted to macro viruses for a number of reasons. First, they are quick and easy to create. It is known, for instance, that many new viruses are based on code taken from existing ones. Although parts of the code may change as each new generation of virus appears, it will usually be possible to identify the progenitor of any given "strain."

Second, e-mail provides a very secure and effective distribution mechanism. Thousands of messages can be transmitted within a matter of seconds, and *anonymous e-mail* accounts make it difficult to trace the creator of a virus.

Third, it has already been mentioned that macro viruses are able to spread very quickly in certain environments, such as large companies. This makes them capable of causing a great deal of damage within a very short space of time. A typical virus spreads in a haphazard way, making it unlikely to infect most or all of the computers in a particular location. However, macro viruses infect the data files that whole groups of people will use every day. As an example, consider the production schedule a typical manufacturing company might use. Sales people will need to access the schedule to see if a potential order can be produced to meet the customer's requirements. Production staff will need to use the schedule to make sure enough staff are available, that there is sufficient production capacity to meet outstanding orders, and so on. Logistics will need the schedule so that supplies of raw materials can be obtained. They will also need to know when the work is likely to be completed so that delivery to the customer can be arranged. Finally, accounting staff will need the schedule so that they can manage the company's cash flow, paying for raw materials when necessary, preparing invoices, and so on. This example shows how a macro virus infecting a single data file can quickly spread throughout an organization. If the company is closely linked to its customers and suppliers, the situation becomes even more serious. Some companies share production information with suppliers to ensure that adequate raw materials are always available. Companies also share production information with regular customers to help them plan their orders. If the infected production plan is shared with customers and suppliers, it should be easy to see how a whole group of companies might become infected in a very short time.

All of the factors discussed here help to explain why macro and e-mail viruses are now the most common form of virus infection.

SWAPPING FILES

A common way of distributing viruses is based upon the fact that many people enjoy swapping files with others, legally or otherwise.

In terms of legal file swapping, it is possible that many users inadvertently pass on computer viruses to their friends, relatives, and colleagues when they share photographs, family videos, and other files.

Another risk involves people who use shareware and freeware software.[23] In the past, numerous shareware and freeware libraries allowed users to obtain collections of software for little more than a small fee intended to cover expenses and generate a relatively small profit. Users chose software from a printed catalogue, ordered by mail and received the programs on floppy disks. If a virus writer was able to plant a virus in the library's collection, hundreds of customers might order the infected program. Many of these users would then go on to infect other computers when they shared the software with others. The Internet has replaced mail-order libraries with huge online software collections that can be accessed free of charge. These collections still remain attractive to virus writers because they offer an easy way of infecting thousands of machines over a short space of time. Although many organizations check the files they offer to the public very carefully, others are not quite as thorough.

WHAT IS SHAREWARE AND FREEWARE?

Shareware is often described as being supplied on a "try before you buy" basis. The software can be used free of charge for a limited period of time, usually no more than 30 days. After the evaluation period, users must buy the software or remove it from their systems. In order to encourage people to pay for the software, some programs have limited functionality or will cease to function after a specified period of time.

As the name suggests, freeware can be copied, distributed, and used free of charge. Although there may be some restrictions on how the program is used, the author does not require payment for his work.

Those who traffic in illegal software face a much higher level of risk. Virus writers have been quick to recognize that planting a virus on a disk containing a new or popular commercial program, such as a game, can almost guarantee widespread distribution. People can also be encouraged to share their software with friends, colleagues, and relatives by making it easier for them to copy disks. This is often achieved by *"cracking"* the software to remove any copy-protection routines designed to prevent piracy.

Additional risks are faced by those who frequent Web sites that supply serial numbers or special programs designed to defeat copy-protection routines. These programs, called *cracks,* allow users to modify a restricted or trial version of the program so that it functions the same as a legitimate copy. However, crack files sometimes contain viruses or Trojans that are activated when the program runs.

P2P SOFTWARE

The past few years has seen a great deal of interest in *peer-to-peer* (P2P) applications. Peer-to-peer file sharing allows computer users to connect their systems together directly so that they can communicate with each other and share files. Although a central server is required to connect users together initially, once a private connection has been made it is no longer needed. Many of the latest P2P systems use decentralized networks, meaning that a central server is not needed at all. As with sharing files by other means, users of P2P services run the risk of virus infection when they work with downloaded files.

One of the attractions of P2P networks is that they provide access to millions of files while maintaining a high level of security. Modern packages provide sophisticated security features such as encryption and anonymous communications. However, all P2P networks rely on users making their files available to each other. Thousands of users, each sharing a few hundred files, can create a software library containing millions of programs, pictures, songs, and games. Many networks encourage users to make their files available to others by offering various incentives, such as increased download speeds or access to a larger variety of files. Unfortunately, when users make their files accessible to each other, they can also make their systems vulnerable to intrusion, making it easier for a virus to be introduced into the computer.

ACCIDENTAL INFECTION

Research has shown that employees are responsible for a large proportion of the virus infections experienced by organizations. Up to 60 percent of virus infections may result from such actions as downloading files, using illegal software on company computers, and viewing inappropriate Web sites.[24] Infections also occur when employees carry work between home and the office.

The availability of low-cost flash drives (sometimes called pen drives) has made things more difficult because of the large amount of storage they offer to users. In the past, users were only able to carry a few files at a time on a floppy disk. This meant that only a few files would be vulnerable to a virus infection. Today, even a modest flash drive has a capacity hundreds of times greater than a floppy disk. This allows employees to carry huge amounts of data with them, raising a variety of problems for the company. As an example, imagine a scenario where an employee works on a report at home. When he returns to work, he copies the latest version of the report from a flash drive onto the company's network system. However, since a virus has infected the computer he uses at home, the report is also infected. Anyone who works on the report runs the risk of infecting his or her computer. To make matters worse, when the report was copied onto the network system, it replaced the older version of the document. This means that the only uninfected copy of the report has been destroyed. If it is not possible to remove the virus from the document, the whole report may be lost.

WHO WRITES VIRUSES?

The stereotypical image of a virus writer is of a teenager who spends most of his time alone in his room. Socially inept and unable to form any meaningful relationships, he writes viruses as an act of revenge against society. But is this an accurate image?

Behind any stereotype there is always a grain of truth. In the case of virus writers, various studies have concluded that a "typical" offender is likely to be the young male described a moment ago. For instance, Wired.com, the online companion to the highly influential *Wired* magazine, states that "... statistics ... indicate that a virus writer is apt to be a male between the ages of 16 to 23 who mostly wears black clothing and has between three-to-five pierced body parts."[25] A similar view is shared by Jan Hruska, a well-known antivirus expert and the chief executive of Sophos, one of the world's largest antivirus software producers. According to Hruska, a typical virus writer is a male, aged 14 to 34, obsessed with computers and said to be lacking a girlfriend.[26]

While most people agree that the majority of viruses are created by young people, some disagree with the image of a virus writer as "... a dysfunctional, pasty-faced teenager with no girlfriend and no life, who taps out malicious code to a backbeat of trance music."[27] Sarah Gordon, an expert in the psychology of virus writers, has been quoted as saying, "Most virus coders are well-adjusted youths who have normal relationships with their family and friends and intend no real harm with the viruses they write."[28]

Over time, other groups have become more active as virus writers. In the 1990s, Gordon[29] noticed that many virus writers tended to "age out," that is, they reached an age and level of maturity where they began to lose interest in creating viruses. Typically, this happened when they entered a profession at around the age of 22. This loss of interest might occur for a number of reasons, including the fear of being caught or simply because entering a career results in less free time. However, some people did not "age out," and others started to write viruses at a later age. The motives behind creating a virus also started to change at the turn of the century, attracting a different kind of virus writer.

As a result of these changes, the average age of today's virus writer is 25 to 28.[30] These older virus writers tend to work in the computing industry as engineers or system administrators. There also been an increase in the number of female virus writers. Although most female virus writers are relatively young, there have been cases involving women aged in their forties and fifties.[31] At present, the majority of viruses are still written by young people,[32] but this is likely to change as viruses become used to support criminal activities, such as extortion.

WHY PEOPLE WRITE VIRUSES

This section outlines some of the main reasons people create viruses.

CURIOSITY

Some viruses are said to be created out of curiosity or as an experiment to test the author's knowledge and skills. As an example, when Brazilian software developer Marcos Velasco came across the Cabir virus, he noticed that its ability to spread was limited. He corrected the problem and then published the source code on his Web site to illustrate his solution.[33] The availability of source code opens up the possibility that someone may modify the virus and release one or more variants. The source code may also help to teach virus writers new techniques that can be used in their own programs. Velasco claims that creating and publishing viruses is nothing more than a hobby and has stated: "I don't publish viruses to cause a panic, I only publish to spread knowledge."[34]

EDUCATIONAL

Some virus writers see themselves as performing a public service. They claim that their viruses are intended to highlight security problems in systems operated by companies and other organizations. By doing this, they are helping these organizations to protect themselves against those with less benevolent motives.[35]

Some consider developing a small, powerful virus a useful educational experience. Only through practical experience can one develop the skill and discipline needed to write compact code that does not compromise functionality.

Interestingly, a similar view has been taken in higher education. In 2003, the University of Calgary announced plans to launch a course in writing viruses. This decision was defended by suggesting that programmers need a thorough understanding of viruses before they can write effective antivirus software. The new course was launched in the fall of 2005, together with "Spam and Spyware," an additional course with assignments that involve "… implementing spamming and spyware techniques, and their countermeasures, under controlled conditions."[36]

SOME OTHER REASONS FOR WRITING VIRUSES

- Proof of concept. Some viruses are written to illustrate an idea or technique. For example, it has been suggested that the Cabir and Velasco viruses were created to demonstrate how a virus could spread using Bluetooth (wireless) technology.
- Free speech. Some virus writers believe that viruses are an expression of free speech. Distributing the virus can be thought of in the same way as publishing a newspaper or book.
- Gang warfare. Virus writers sometimes organize themselves into groups. Sometimes, one group will release a virus as a way of taunting another.

ENJOYMENT

There can be little doubt that some people enjoy making mischief. Writing a virus can be compared to acts of vandalism, such as painting graffiti on a wall or damaging a car.[37] Using these examples, creating a virus to display a message on a screen is comparable to painting graffiti, while deleting files from a user's hard disk is a little like scratching or denting a car. Some of the reasons people spray paint on walls or puncture someone's tires can help to explain why others create and distribute viruses. Virus writers and vandals may share any number of motives for their behavior, including boredom, misplaced anger, or an urge to rebel against authority.

The idea that some people enjoy creating viruses has been supported by various studies carried out over the years. In particular, interviews carried out with virus writers[38] tend to show many of them as self-centered and immature. This is often demonstrated by the indifferent attitude they adopt towards the damage caused by their creations.[39]

SOME UNUSUAL VIRUSES

- The Amus worm uses the speech-synthesis features in Windows XP to taunt users.
- One version of MyDoom contains a request for work in the antivirus industry.
- Walk the Plank and Dust Bunny are both Trojans that are distributed via P2P networks and are targeted at those who use pirate software. When activated, "Bad Pirate!" is shown in large type, followed by other messages.
- Yusufali-A monitors the Web sites visited by users. If the text in the title bar of the browser window contains sex-related terms, such as "xxx," the window is minimized and a verse from the Koran is shown instead. If users persist with their behavior, they are made to log off or shut down the computer.[40]

STATUS AND SOCIAL BENEFITS

Graffiti artists usually attempt to create a reputation for themselves by attempting the most ambitious exploits possible. They often adopt nicknames, called "tags," which are used to sign their handiwork. If a gang of graffiti artists clashes with another, a "battle" may take place to settle the disagreement. Each gang attempts to achieve dominance over the other by demonstrating superior skills, or by creating the most pictures.

All of this is very similar to the subculture shared by virus writers. Just like graffiti artists, virus writers also adopt nicknames and belong to groups.[41] Often, a virus writer will sign his work by embedding his nickname or some other text into the virus. Disagreements between groups—called *crews*—tend to be settled through competition. Winning such a competition might involve creating the virus that infects the most systems, or simply creating the largest number of new viruses within a given period.

The more daring and ambitious a graffiti artist, the more well known his work becomes and the more his standing rises within the crew. In the same way, a virus writer's status increases if he is able to produce a particularly sophisticated or virulent program. Creating such a program also meets the author's fundamental need for attention,[42] especially if the virus becomes a topic of discussion in the media, on message boards, and on Web pages.

Writing viruses can also help to improve social status in the offline world. Some virus writers use their skills to impress their peers at school or in the local neighborhood. Showing their advanced technical skills may be the only way to gain a higher social standing, especially if they are unable to compete in other areas of social life, such as sports. The problem here is that writing viruses is considered "cool,"[43] even if doing so is immoral and harmful to others.

HERO OR ZERO?

The Netsky and Sasser viruses are thought to have caused losses of more than $6 billion worldwide. Both viruses were written by a German teenager called Sven Jaschan. Following his arrest, Jaschan claimed that he had never intended to make the viruses destructive but was persuaded to change his mind by his classmates, who also helped him to distribute the viruses.[44] In a magazine interview, Jaschan is reported to have said: "It was just great how Netsky began to spread, and I was the hero of my class." While awaiting trial, Jaschan became something of a minor celebrity and even gained his own fan club called the Sasser Support Team.[45]

Since he was arrested just short of his eighteenth birthday, Jaschan received only a suspended sentence for his actions. He was also offered employment with Securepoint, a computer security company.

The notion that virus writers are somehow special is partly due to the widespread belief that creating a virus requires a great deal of skill.[46] While this may be true of some viruses, many others are created by people with limited technical knowledge.[47] Since the late 1980s, it has been possible to find *virus construction kits* on various Web sites. Examples of well-known programs are Virus Creation Laboratory, Instant Virus Production Kit, Nuke Randomic Life Generator, Trojan Horse Construction Kit, and VBS Worm Generator. Some of these programs allow someone to create a virus by simply choosing options from various menus. In some cases, the process of creating a virus has been simplified so much that it takes just a few minutes to produce a fully working program.

More sophisticated viruses can be created using various utilities that are also widely available via the Internet. Most of these can be thought of as add-ons that give a virus new features. One of the earliest and best-known tools was Dark Avenger's Virus Mutation Engine (sometimes called DAME), which first appeared in 1992. This was a code library that could be used to turn any virus into a polymorphic virus, giving it the ability to disguise itself and avoid detection by some antivirus software.

It was mentioned earlier that some virus writers publish source code on their Web sites. In addition, many Web sites also host message boards, file libraries, and collections of documents related to virus programming. In some cases, all that is needed to produce a fully working virus is to download some source code, make any changes desired, and then compile the code into a program.

It should be clear that all of the resources mentioned in this section bring creating a virus within the capability of most regular computer users. This means that the reputation of many virus writers is undeserved.

POLITICAL REASONS

Many groups have been quick to realize that creating a virus provides an inexpensive but efficient way of spreading a political message. Viruses can also be used as weapons of war, targeting an enemy's information in order to cause widespread damage and confusion. Although there are no documented cases where one government has deliberately attacked another in this way, there have been many instances where political groups have attempted to use viruses as weapons. Two recent examples involve the Iraq conflict in 2003. First, at least four viruses appeared during the conflict that attempted to exploit interest in the progress of the war. One of these viruses, Prune, used subject lines intended to attract the interest of people with friends or relatives in the military who wanted information about the war. When activated, the virus attempted to erase operating system files.[48]

Second, in 2002, a virus writer based in Malaysia threatened to release an "über-worm" called Scezda if the United States invaded Iraq. The programmer, Melhacker, was taken seriously because he was thought to have been involved in several virus outbreaks in the past. Although Scezda was never released, Melhacker has been credited as the author of many other viruses including W32.Kamil, W32.Cbomb, W32.BleBla.J.Worm, VBS.Melhack@mm, VBS.Melhack.B, and VBS.Melhack.C@mm. Some of Melhacker's viruses are a clear reflection of his Al Qaeda sympathies. For instance, the Nedal virus is named after Bin Laden (Laden spelled backwards), while the VBS.OsamaLaden@mm worm displays a message regarding the September 11 attacks before attempting to delete important system files.[49]

Despite the destruction they cause, virus writers are sometimes seen as heroes in their own communities. Some examples include:

- In the Philippines, Onel de Guzman, the author of the LoveBug virus, was regarded as a hero and publicly thanked by the president. Although he was eventually arrested, the case was later dropped.[50]
- In Taiwan, Chen Ing Hau, the author of the Chernobyl virus, was paraded in public before being detained by the authorities.[51] Although he admitted creating the virus, no charges could be brought against him because no complaint had been made by a Taiwanese citizen. According to the VMyths[52] Web site, his only punishment appears to have been a college demerit for creating a destructive virus. As a result of creating the virus, at least 20 Taiwanese firms competed to hire him, and he eventually accepted a position with Wahoo International Enterprise.
- In Holland, Jan de Wit, the author of the Anna Kournikova worm, was applauded by his local mayor and was even invited to apply for a job managing the town's computer systems.[53] He received a sentence of 150 hours community service.[54]

SOME EXAMPLES OF VIRUSES
CREATED FOR POLITICAL REASONS

In the early 1990s, the Fu Manchu (also known as Jerusalem) altered documents by replacing the names of political leaders with expletives. Margaret Thatcher, Ronald Reagan, and P. W. Botha were some of the leaders targeted. In addition, if a user entered certain expletives into a document, the virus erased them from the screen. Even resetting the computer had little effect and resulted in the virus displaying, "The world will hear from me again!"

The Quaters worm was released in 2003 and replaced files with the text ""Infected by the WIN32.SORT-IT-OUT-BLAIR Virus!" As well as attempting to launch a *denial of service* attack against 10 Downing Street, the worm also displayed a message directed at UK Prime Minister Tony Blair:

> Dear Tony Blair,
> Why are you spending all our taxes on illegal immigrants!?!
> How about you stop worrying about other countries and worry about ours???
> Stop spending money on immigrants and spend it on things like OAP's who fought to keep this country free but are now getting treated worst than illegal immigrants!
> How about spend a little money on the NHS or the education system!?!
> Think about it Mr Blair. Your career depends on it. We've had enough.[55]

The Maslan-C worm was discovered in 2004. The worm was spread via e-mail and encouraged users to infect their own systems with a file attachment called "Playgirls2.exe." Once activated, the virus attempted to launch a series of denial of service attacks against Web sites owned by Chechen rebel separatists.

Injustice appeared in 2001 and was used to spread this message: "Do not worry. This is a harmless virus. It will not do anything to your system. The intension is to help Palestinian people live in PEASE in their own land." After displaying the message, the virus opened a number of Internet Explorer windows and used them to display various pro-Palestinian Web sites.[56]

Zafi-B was released in 2004 and was notable because of the speed with which it spread and its ability to display messages in a number of languages.[57] Part of the reason the worm was able to spread so quickly was because it replaced any program containing the words "firewall" or "virus" with a copy of itself. It also disabled several Windows utilities, such as Task Manager, so that they could not be used to get rid of the worm. When activated, the worm displayed a message in Hungarian that translates to: "We demand that the government accommodates the homeless, tightens up the penal code and VOTES FOR THE DEATH PENALTY to cut down the increasing crime. Jun. 2004, PÉcs (SNAF Team)."

It is worth remembering that some countries may regard virus writers as heroes if they are perceived to be acting out of patriotism. In the Philippines, for instance, it was argued that the LoveBug virus showed that even a relatively poor country, with limited military strength and limited technology, could become a force to be reckoned with through the ingenuity of its people. Guzman's actions were seized upon by some of those holding anti-American views as a warning to the United States: Despite having the most powerful military forces in the world, it was still vulnerable to attacks against its economy and information infrastructure. Guzman's image was also helped by the nature of the virus he created. In the Philippines, Internet access is considered very expensive and is out of reach for many students. Since the LoveBug virus was intended to steal Internet passwords, Guzman was seen as a Robin Hood of the Information Age, stealing Internet access from the rich Internet companies to give to the poor.[58]

FINANCIAL GAIN

Many virus writers have learned how to exploit their skills for financial gain. For many years, they have earned money in two main ways: through paid employment and through extortion. While some people have offered their expertise to antivirus software developers in exchange for some very generous salaries, others have used the threat of a malicious virus to extort payments from vulnerable companies.

Extortion attempts tend to take several common forms. The first involves threatening to attack a company's systems unless a payment is received. Sometimes, the company is subjected to a brief attack before any demand for money is made in order to demonstrate that the threat is a serious one.

Another method involves threatening to attack a company's customers or suppliers. This can be done by creating a virus or Trojan designed to steal passwords, credit card numbers, and other sensitive information. SoBig is a well-known example of a virus used to gather banking and credit card information.[59] The demand for money can then be accompanied by a threat to make the stolen information public. Banks and other financial institutions are particularly vulnerable to this approach, since a reduction in public confidence can translate into huge financial losses. Virus writers can also use any information stolen from customers to transfer money from bank accounts or to charge goods and services to customers. By limiting thefts to accounts or credit cards operated by a particular company, the company will face financial losses and a damaged reputation. Some sources suggest that virus writers have successfully extorted millions of dollars from banks, but that incidents are seldom made public because the victims are afraid of public embarrassment.[60]

Some new ways of making money from viruses have started to emerge over the past few years. Criminals, working alone or as part of an organized gang, have started to hire virus writers to create customized viruses and Trojans.

These programs have then been used for various criminal purposes, such as extortion.

Another way of using viruses and Trojans involves creating networks of zombie computers that can be used to send commercial spam or launch distributed denial of service attacks. Some Trojans are designed to take full or partial control of a computer when they receive instructions from the author. The Trojan remains inactive most of the time, only connecting to the Internet every now and then to check for new instructions. When activated by the author, the Trojan begins to generate e-mail or fake Web traffic directed towards one or more specific targets. This type of Trojan is often called a *bot* or a *zombie*. Since the Trojan can be placed on a computer weeks or months before it is needed, it is possible to create entire fleets (sometimes called *botnets*) made up of thousands of computers. A single instruction can result in millions of e-mail messages or huge amounts of traffic being directed against a single company. This type of attack is usually called a *distributed denial of service attack* (DDoS) because it uses computers distributed around the Internet to flood the target system with so much fake traffic that it becomes unable to function properly.

Rather than enabling criminals to create their own zombies, virus writers have taken to hiring out their own fleets. Occasionally, they will also create small fleets to order but will retain overall control in order to guarantee repeat business. An article from *TechNewsWorld* explains how little it can cost to attack the Web site of a major corporation:

> High-profile Web sites may be knocked offline for as much as US$10,000, while smaller sites would cost closer to $1,000. Such dedicated DOS [denial of service] activity is used by extortion rings, which have been known to demand $50,000 to $100,000 to avoid a site takedown and can cost even more in lost productivity or sales.[61]

Zombies can also be used to send *spam* and are capable of posting millions of messages within a matter of minutes. As an example, *USA Today*[62] reported a case where a computer owned by a grandmother of three was

INDUSTRIAL ESPIONAGE

As an example, in 2005 several major firms—including TV, mobile phone, car import, and utility companies—were accused of using Trojans to spy on their competitors.[63] According to Israeli police, the software used was extremely effective in gathering commercially sensitive information. Over a period of time, the Trojan was able to collect and transmit approximately 10,000 documents taken from 30 to 40 companies.[64]

found to be infected by a zombie that was posting as many as 70,000 messages a day. Clearly, hiring zombies provides an inexpensive and secure way for spammers to distribute unsolicited e-mail.

REVENGE

Some people release viruses as an act of revenge against someone they feel has wronged them. Sometimes, the target might be an employer or anyone else perceived to hold a position of authority. Occasionally, virus writers will fight amongst themselves, each using his most sophisticated viruses as weapons. Even schoolchildren have been known to use viruses against classmates considered enemies.

Although there is a never-ending competition between virus writers and those who develop antivirus software, the contest seldom becomes a battle of personalities. Occasionally, however, a quarrel can become personal, and a virus writer may begin to target specific people in the antivirus industry.

A good example concerns a long-running dispute between a virus writer named Gigabyte and Graham Cluley, a well-known figure in the antivirus industry. According to the media, Gigabyte was a 19-year-old female student who lived in Belgium, near Brussels. She had started programming at 6 and was writing viruses by 14.[65] Cluley, an antivirus expert working for Sophos, was known for making disparaging comments about virus writers, such as suggesting that most are young males who are unable to find girlfriends. These comments antagonized Gigabyte, who set out to prove that female virus writers were just as skilled as males at creating destructive viruses.

As the feud continued, Gigabyte released several viruses targeted directly at Cluley. One virus made people take part in a quiz about Cluley, whom she nicknamed "Clueless." Another involved a game where users were forced to knock Cluley's head off.[66] The media has labeled Gigabyte as "obsessive" because of her determination to win her dispute with Cluley. However, it can be argued that Cluley made the situation worse by provoking Gigabyte to an extent. In one case, for example, he suggested in the media that Gigabyte's actions were due to her infatuation with him. While none of this excuses the act of creating a computer virus, it does raise the question of whether or not Gigabyte's viruses would ever have existed had Cluley behaved differently. If not, then Cluley himself could be said to share responsibility for the damage caused by those viruses. Certainly, it could be argued that goading Gigabyte publicly was somewhat irresponsible, especially for someone regarded as a spokesperson for the antivirus industry.

DETECTING VIRUSES

In general, *virus scanners* provide the only accurate and reliable way of detecting viruses. This section describes how virus scanners work and how their efficiency can be measured.

Viruses and virus activity can be detected in several different ways. Most viruses have one or more unique features that can be used to identify it. There may be a message or other text embedded in the program file, or the virus might change a system file in a very specific way. The set of characteristics that is unique to a specific virus is called the *signature*. Early virus scanners worked by searching for the signatures of known viruses. As new viruses appeared, their signatures were added to the database used by the virus scanner and users were sent software updates.

The introduction of polymorphic and stealth viruses meant that searching for signatures was no longer sufficient to protect against infection. Modern antivirus programs use *heuristics* to detect virus activity. This kind of analysis uses a set of rules that finds a virus through its behavior, rather than simply relying on a signature. Certain behaviors are common to most viruses, so the virus scanner monitors the computer for any suspicious actions. As an example, a typical virus will try to make a copy of itself on the user's hard disk, usually in one of a small number of locations. If an attempt is made to store data in one of these locations, this may indicate the presence of a virus. This type of monitoring has a number of advantages for users. First, this approach is relatively fast, so it does not affect the speed of the computer significantly. Second, since scanning is so quick, the virus scanner can be active all of the time, allowing files to be scanned as they are accessed. This provides a higher level of protection and reduces the need to scan the whole system frequently. Finally, this method makes it possible to protect the computer against new viruses because the software looks for suspicious behavior, not just signatures.

There are many other ways of detecting virus activity, some simple and some complex. As an example, *checksums* are an easy way of determining if a file has been altered. A checksum is created by performing a calculation on the size of a file. If a file is altered in any way, the change can be detected easily because repeating the calculation will produce a different checksum.

While not entirely foolproof, modern virus scanners tend to be very accurate when it comes to locating and identifying a virus. Tests of virus scanners usually involve infecting a test machine with a selection of different viruses. Some tests even include viruses not usually found "in the wild" as a way of checking a virus scanner's ability to detect new or unknown viruses. The *detection rate* is a measure of how well the virus scanner is able to find viruses. A perfect score of 100 percent suggests that the virus scanner offers complete protection against all the known and unknown viruses. In reality, however, few programs achieve a perfect score. In addition, even if a given program achieves 100 percent, this does not guarantee that it will detect every single one of the 100,000 or so viruses in existence today, nor does it guarantee that it will always be able to detect new types of virus.

DEALING WITH VIRUSES

Once a virus has been detected, it can be dealt with in one of three ways: disinfection, deletion, or quarantine. *Disinfection* attempts to remove the virus from the system and repair any files it has changed. If it is not possible to disinfect a file, it may be necessary to *erase* it. Sometimes, a user may be reluctant to delete a file when attempts to disinfect it fail. In this case, the file can be placed in *quarantine* by moving it to a new location where the virus will not be able to reinfect the computer. Each time the virus scanner is updated, a check is made to see if it has now become possible to disinfect the file. If so, the file is disinfected and moved out of quarantine.

DELETING VERSUS ERASING

It is important to distinguish between erasing and deleting a file. *Deleting* a file removes its entry in the disk's directory structure. This does not destroy the file itself, only the information needed to locate the file's data on the disk. The contents of the file remain intact until another file overwrites it. This is a little like removing an address from a phone book. Even though the address is no longer listed, the building itself still exists. It is worth remembering that files that have been deleted can often be recovered. Deleting a virus may not destroy it or make it become inactive.

Erasing a file removes its entry in the disk's directory structure and overwrites its contents with new data. An erased file can be almost impossible to recover. For this reason, virus killers erase viruses.

Removing a virus is best left to an appropriate virus scanner. This is because the panicked attempts by users to destroy the virus sometimes result in more damage than the infection might have caused. If the virus scanner installed on the computer is unable to deal with the virus, then an online service can be used instead. Some examples of online services are given later on. If even an online virus scanner fails to remove the virus, specialist help will be needed.

THE IMPORTANCE OF BACKUPS

It must be stressed that keeping backups of important data is an essential precaution against viruses and other malware. If attempts to remove a virus are unsuccessful, it may be necessary to format the computer's hard disk. In this event, all of the programs and data held on the hard disk will be lost unless a backup has been made. It is worth remembering that it is unwise to copy data from an infected computer onto a "clean" one, as this may copy the virus too.

Until recently, it was recommended that users only make backups of important data. This was because storage devices and media were relatively expensive, so substantial savings could be made by minimizing the amount of data stored. Since programs and operating systems could be replaced using the original installation media, it was not necessary to make backups of them. In the event of a virus infection, it would be inconvenient and time-consuming to reinstall all of this software, but nothing of importance would be lost.

Nowadays, the cost of storage has fallen so low that it has become common to use portable hard disks to hold backups, instead of floppy disks, magnetic tape cartridges, and even rewritable DVDs. It has also become feasible to store all of the data held on a computer system, including the operating system, programs, and other files. *Disk imaging programs* make an exact copy of a computer's hard disk, creating a snapshot of the entire system at a specific date and time. These programs have become incredibly sophisticated within a very short time. Some of the features offered by the most advanced programs include:

- The ability to compress the disk image so that it is quicker and easier to work with
- The ability to encrypt the image so that the data it contains remains secure
- Disk images can be written to CD or DVD along with special installation software. This makes it easier to restore data because the disk is entirely self-contained and no other software is required.
- The ability to create *incremental backups*. This means that only the data that has changed since the last backup is copied into the disk image. This lowers the time needed to create backups, allows users to keep several versions of their files, and reduces the amount of storage space needed.
- Disk images can be created (and sometimes restored) from within Windows, without the need to restart the computer.

There are two main advantages associated with using a disk imaging program. First, since the whole hard disk is imaged, there is no need to identify specific files or folders to back up. Second, the disk image allows the computer to be restored to full working order within minutes. This is because there is no need to format the hard disk, reinstall an operating system and then reinstall programs.

Two examples of well-known disk imaging programs are:

Acronis True Image: http://www.acronis.com

Norton Ghost: http://www.symantec.com

If disk imaging software is inappropriate for some reason, there are many conventional backup programs that can be used to implement a *backup regime*. Some examples of popular commercial programs include:

Moon Software Backup Magic: http://www.moonsoftware.com

ABC Backup Software ABC Backup: http://www.abcbackup.com

Novastor NovaBACKUP: http://www.novastor.com

Genie-Soft Corp. Genie Backup Manager: http://www.genie-soft.com

Uniblue WinBackup: http://www.liutilities.com/products/winbackup

It is worth remembering that Windows includes a free backup tool, although some people feel it is somewhat limited in comparison to other programs. In addition, many compression programs—such as WinZip and WinRAR—provide tools for making backups of data. It is also possible to obtain backup software free of charge. Some examples of freeware programs include:

Cobian Backup: http://www.educ.umu.se/~cobian

Handy Backup: http://www.handybackup.com

SyncBack: http://www.2brightsparks.com

MyBackup: http://www.dioneldelacruz.com

Allway Sync: http://www.allwaysync.com

Back2zip: http://free-backup.info

SOME GUIDELINES FOR MAKING BACKUPS

- Every backup must be tested after it has been made. This is especially important in the case of incremental backups, since an error in one backup file will mean that all of the files created subsequently will be useless. As an example, if the very first backup file is corrupt, it may be impossible to restore any data at all.
- Backups should not be stored on the computer's main hard disk. This is because a hard disk failure will result in the loss of any data stored on it, together with the backup file meant to protect that data.
- If possible, more than one backup copy should be kept. For home users, this might mean keeping one copy of a backup file on a flash drive and another on a floppy disk. For business users, at least one copy of the backup should be taken offsite at the end of each day. This way, a fire or other disaster will not mean that every backup will be destroyed.
- Ideally, several versions of backup files should be kept. This provides a great deal of additional protection for data. As an example, imagine that a company makes daily backups and finds that a virus has been present on its systems for several days. Although the virus infected the company's systems on Wednesday, it was not discovered until Friday. Any backups made on Wednesday, Thursday, or Friday will contain a copy of the virus. However, if the company restores the backup made on Tuesday, the virus will be destroyed and only a relatively small amount of data will be lost.

Figure 3.1   The Grandfather, Father, Son Backup Routine

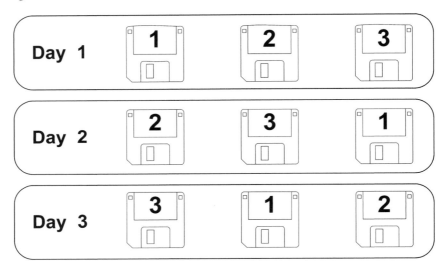

One of the best known and most effective ways of making multiple back-ups is called the *grandfather, father, son method*. This method is used widely because it is easy to use and is very flexible. Three sets of media are needed to implement this method, and each is labeled with a number. Alternatively, the media can be labeled "grandfather," "father," and "son." Any media can be used, including floppy disks, CD-ROM, flash drives, and so on. Each day, a new backup is made and stored on the disk or other device containing the oldest backup file. After the backup has been made, the disk will contain the latest version of the data. In other words, the oldest version of the data (the "grandfather") will be replaced by the newest (the "son"). The process is repeated each day so that three versions of the data are held at any one time. Figure 3.1 illustrates the cycle of grandfather, father, son.

The basic backup procedure described here can be modified to make it suitable for a wide range of individuals and companies. For instance, companies may wish to keep more versions of the data, while individuals may want longer intervals between backups.

CHOOSING ANTIVIRUS SOFTWARE

Selecting antivirus software need not be particularly difficult. In no particular order, some of the criteria that should be considered include the following:

- Cost: As well as the initial purchase price, it is important to consider any ongoing costs. Some companies, for instance, charge an additional fee for regular updates to signature files.

- Speed and impact on resources: Some packages require a significant amount of memory and processor time. This has an impact on the performance of the system, especially when carrying out intensive tasks, such as working with large database files. In addition, full system scans may take a great deal of time, preventing the computer from being used for other tasks.
- Accuracy: Programs should have a high detection rate, preferably across a number of comparisons carried out by different organizations. In addition, programs should not report an excessive number of *false positives*. False positives are "false alarms" caused when a virus scanner mistakenly identifies a legitimate program as a virus. In a business environment, each false positive represents lost working time and an unnecessary drain on resources for technical support. In other environments, false positives cause needless worry and can even lead to unnecessary expense when users hire specialist help to remove a nonexistent virus.
- Internet features: Many programs now offer the ability to scan incoming and outgoing e-mail. Some programs also offer basic firewall functionality, identity theft protection, and other features useful to Internet users.
- Ease of use: Programs should be intuitive so that users at all levels of experience can use them effectively.
- Real-time protection: Virtually all modern antivirus programs constantly monitor the computer, scanning files as they are used. As an example, whenever a file is downloaded via the Internet, it is scanned just before it is written to disk. This process is carried out so quickly that users seldom notice any delay.

Although there are numerous commercial virus scanners available, it is also possible to obtain programs free of charge. Sometimes, these programs are offered in several different versions, where the free version has a limited set of features and is intended to encourage users to pay for a more functional version. In some cases, fully working programs are offered free of charge for noncommercial purposes. This means that home users, for instance, can use the program without restraint, but companies, schools, government departments, and other users must pay for the software.

Some well-known programs that can be used free of charge include the following:

Grisoft produces AVG, which is free for noncommercial use: http://www.grisoft.com.

AntiVir produces AntiVir PersonalEdition Classic, which is offered as freeware: http://www.free-av.com.

ALWIL Software produces avast! Home Edition, which is free for noncommercial use: http://www.avast.com.

BitDefender produces versions of its BitDefender software for Windows and Linux. Both programs can be used free of charge: http://www.bitdefender.com.

ClamWin is a program produced under the GNU General Public License, meaning that it can be copied, used, and even modified freely: http://www.clamwin.com.

F-Prot produces of versions of its F-Prot Antivirus program for various operating systems, including Linux, BSD, Solaris SPARC/Solaris x86, and DOS. All of these versions can be used free of charge: http://www.f-prot.com.

ONLINE VIRUS SCANNERS

Sometimes, it is not possible to use or install a virus scanner on a given computer. For instance, some antivirus programs cannot be installed if the computer is already infected. Occasionally, a virus scanner may not be able to detect a particular virus, or the user wishes to double-check the results obtained by the virus scanner. In these cases, it is possible to make use of various online virus scanners that are easily accessible via the Internet. In general, using one of these services means navigating to a certain page and then allowing the web browser to download the various files needed to perform the scan. Once the machine has been scanned, any viruses found can be disinfected, erased, or quarantined.

Some examples of online virus scanners that are available free of charge include the following:

BitDefender: http://www.bitdefender.com

McAfee FreeScan: http://us.mcafee.com

Trend Micro Housecall: http://housecall.trendmicro.com

Symantec Security Check: http://www.symantec.com

Panda ActiveScan: http://www.pandasoftware.com/activescan/activescan/ascan_1.asp

SAFETY AND PREVENTION

The risk of virus infection can be minimized by taking a number of simple, inexpensive measures. The following guidelines come from a variety of sources including Bocij, et al. (2005), Stuart (2003), Amazon.com, the British Computer Society, PC World, and Microsoft.

BUSINESS USERS

In addition to the guidelines given for individuals, the following points are relevant to business users.

- Unauthorized access to machines and software should be restricted as much as possible. This refers to both physical access and remote access.
- Install antivirus software on every computer, including laptops, handhelds, and any machines not kept on company premises.
- Keep all antivirus software up to date. This is usually best achieved by installing updates from a central server or by making sure each copy of the software is set to update automatically via the Internet.
- Regular virus scans can be scheduled to take place at times when the company's computers are not being used, for example at lunchtime or at the end of the working day.

- Encourage employees to install antivirus software at home, especially if their home PCs are used to connect to the company network. Sometimes, it can be useful to offer employees discounted software, or to supply them with copies of free software.
- Installing software to scan all incoming and outgoing e-mail can help to reduce virus infections significantly. A policy preventing employees from sending or receiving executable files may also be helpful.
- Educate employees about the risk of virus infection. Ensure that simple guidelines are publicized across the entire company. A good way of doing this is by including information in company handbooks and internal newsletters.
- Encourage employees to back up work regularly and to store several copies of their backups. Copies of work can be stored on the employee's system, the company's network server, and on floppy disks or flash drives. For added security, daily backups can be made of all data stored on the network.
- Introduce policies that can help to minimize the risk of infection. Some companies, for instance, forbid employees from installing any software on the computers they use. Since employees are prevented from installing pirate software of any kind, the risk of virus infection is reduced.

INDIVIDUALS AND FAMILIES

- Install a virus scanner and keep it up to date by downloading updates at least once a week.
- Scan your entire system periodically, preferably once a month or more often.
- Do not rely on a single virus scanner. Carry out additional scans from time to time using a different program or one of the online services described earlier.
- Do not open e-mail attachments that arrive from an unknown source. Many e-mail viruses are harmless until activated, usually by opening an e-mail attachment.
- Check the file names of any e-mail attachments received. Files with extensions like .JPG, .GIF, .PNG, .BMP, and .TXT are usually safe to open. Files with extensions like .EXE, .BAT, and .COM are executable files and are not safe to open. It is also unsafe to open script files (.VBS) and data files capable of storing macros, such as Word documents (.DOC).
- Scan files for viruses before opening any e-mail attachment or using any file downloaded from the Internet.
- Delete messages that are obviously junk mail without opening them.
- For additional protection against some types of virus, install a firewall package.
- Download and install any updates available for your operating system and any applications you use.
- If using floppy disks, keep them write-protected whenever possible, since it is physically impossible for a virus to copy itself to a write-protected disk. Many flash drives also have a write-protect switch that can be used to protect against infection.

- Obtain software only from trusted sources and scan the installation media before using the program.
- Make regular backups of all important files. Test all backups to ensure they have been made properly.
- Try to keep up to date with news on new viruses and hoaxes. This can be done by visiting the Web sites of antivirus companies, such as McAfee, and other relevant organizations.

VIRUS HOAXES

From time to time, most users receive e-mail messages warning them of the latest virus threat. Often, users are asked to forward the message to all of their friends, relatives, and colleagues. However, in virtually every case the warning is entirely unnecessary because there is no genuine threat. No matter how well meaning, every person who sends out a copy of the warning achieves little more than adding to the huge volume of e-mail traffic that slows down mail servers around the world. In addition, their warnings cause panic in the very people they are trying to help because they believe that the virus might damage their computers or destroy valuable information.

Some fake virus warnings are accompanied by instructions that explain how to detect and destroy the virus. Usually, these instructions tell users that they can confirm a virus infection by looking for the presence of certain files. Additional instructions explain how to delete these files in order to remove the virus. However, since the virus infection does not exist, anyone following the instructions only ends up deleting important system files. Since the people most likely to be deceived by this trick are likely to be inexperienced as computer users, repairing the damage can be expensive and time-consuming.

Security experts recommend that virus warnings should never be passed on to others. Reputable companies tend to issue virus warnings via their Web sites and the media.

Any virus warning can be checked by visiting Web sites belonging to antivirus companies, such as Norton, Kaspersky, and McAfee, or other organizations, such as the Computer Emergency Response Team.

Another good source of information is the Virus Myths Web site operated by Rhode Island Soft Systems (www.vmyths.com). This site contains information on a large number of virus hoaxes.

Perhaps the best-known example of a virus hoax concerned the Good Times virus. This took place in 1994 and was the first major hoax. Essentially, an e-mail message appeared around the world, warning people to be alert for any messages containing "Good Times" in the subject line. Opening the message would cause physical damage to the user's computer, so people were told to delete the message without reading it. Variations on this hoax continue to appear today and many computer users continue to send out pointless warnings.

MORE ABOUT TROJANS

As mentioned earlier, a Trojan will usually appear as a game, utility, or some other innocuous file in order to gain access to a computer system. When the user launches the program, it first installs the Trojan before continuing to work in the way the user expects. In this way, the user becomes responsible for infecting his own machine.

Like viruses, Trojans are able to alter files, delete data, and display messages. However, Trojans tend to be designed for two main purposes: gathering information and taking control of an infected system.

Once active, a Trojan will scan the user's hard disk for sensitive information, such as passwords, credit card details, and anything else of value. Once this information has been gathered, the Trojan will wait for an opportunity to *phone home.* Usually, the Trojan waits until the user is online and then sends the information it has collected in an e-mail. By waiting until there is some Internet activity, the Trojan often escapes the user's notice.

Some Trojans install a *key logger* to monitor all activity on the infected computer. A key logger records every key pressed by the user and stores the data in a file on the computer's hard disk. By monitoring a computer over a period of time, the key logger is able to collect a wide variety of information, including all passwords and user names typed by the user, the contents of any outgoing e-mail messages, the contents of word-processing documents, and any information entered into any forms displayed on Web pages. Even a single online transaction may provide enough information to defraud the computer's owner. For instance, if a user makes a purchase from an online store, such as Amazon.com, the key logger will have an opportunity to record his account details and credit card information.

From time to time, the key logger will need to send the information it has collected to its owner. It is at this time that the user may notice an unusual surge in Internet traffic caused when the key logger sends its data by e-mail. Some of the most sophisticated key loggers try reduce the risk of detection by minimizing the amount of data transmitted by e-mail. This is achieved by compressing the data file after deleting any data that has been sent before. It is also possible for a key logger to transmit the data file at regular intervals or when it reaches a certain size. This prevents the program from attempting to send large files that may cause increased Internet traffic for hours at a time. Some programs are even capable of splitting a large data file into several parts so that it can be sent a little at a time.

As mentioned earlier, some Trojans are used to establish control over the computers they infect. Sometimes, only partial control is needed and users may be unaware that a Trojan is sending out e-mail or taking part in a denial of service attack. However, some Trojans allow a third party to take complete control over the infected computer, just as if they were sitting in front of it. The Trojan acts as a remote-control application, allowing its owner access to all of the computer's resources including programs, data files, printers, disk drives, webcams, and network services, such as Internet access. Once control has been taken over the machine, users are virtually powerless to interfere except by switching the power off. The best-known example of this kind of Trojan is Back Orifice, which was produced by a hacking group known as the Cult of the Dead Cow.

DEALING WITH TROJANS

Many virus scanners are also capable of dealing with Trojans and other malicious software. However, the level of protection offered varies from package to package. For this reason, it is a good idea to use a separate Trojan scanner to perform periodic scans of the computer.

As with antivirus software, a number of free Trojan scanners are available. Some well-known programs include:

Emsisoft provides a² (a-squared) free of charge for personal use: http://www.emsisoft.com

SwatIt.org provides the SwatIt Trojan scanner as freeware: http://swatit.org/

Emco Software produces Malware Destroyer as freeware: http://www.emco.is

It is worth remembering that many antispyware programs can also be used to remove Trojans and worms. It also possible to buy commercial Trojan scanners that can be used in conjunction with a virus scanner. Some example⌄ of popular and well-known programs include the following:

MooSoft Development The Cleaner: http://www.moosoft.com/products/ cleaner

Agnitum TauScan: http://www.agnitum.com

Mischel Internet Security TrojanHunter: http://www.misec.net/trojanhunter

ONLINE SERVICES

There are a number of online Trojan scanners that can be used free of charge. Some well-known services include:

WindowsSecurity.com   TrojanScan: http://www.windowsecurity.com/ trojanscan/

Panda ActiveScan: http://www.pandasoftware.com/products/activescan.htm

Some of the online services provided by antivirus companies can also be used to detect Trojans. The details of some of these services were given in an earlier section.

SAFETY AND PREVENTION

Most of the guidelines given earlier for viruses also apply to Trojans. However, there are some additional points worth remembering. The following guidelines are drawn from a variety of sources including Bocij et al. (2005), Anti-Trojan.org, Computer World, and F-Prot.

BUSINESS USERS

- Some Web sites prompt visitors to install a special viewer or other software, implying that the site cannot be viewed properly otherwise. When the visitor agrees to install the software, a Trojan is installed. A similar trick involves sending a disk or CD to employees that appears to contain a presentation, business proposal, or other important document. The Trojan is installed when the user attempts to view the file. This kind of trick can be prevented by stopping users from installing any software at all. This can be accomplished in several ways, for instance by implementing a policy requiring that software may only be installed by a member of the technical support team. Various tools can be used to enforce such a policy by filtering Web content, auditing installed software, and so on.

INDIVIDUALS AND FAMILIES

- Install a firewall and keep it up to date. This will help to detect any programs trying to make unauthorized use of the Internet.
- Alter the security settings in Internet Explorer and Microsoft Outlook (or any other *Web browser* or e-mail software you use) to make sure that any

potentially dangerous behaviors have been disabled. For instance, make sure that Internet Explorer does not download and install ActiveX components automatically.

- Scan all files received through file-sharing services such as ICQ, MSN, Kazaa, and so on.
- Check the processes that are running on your system from time to time. Look for any unusual activity or unidentified processes, since these may indicate the presence of Trojan. Note that some Trojans are capable of hiding their processes from the Windows Task Manager. This means that it may be necessary to download specialized software to find out exactly which programs are running on the system. A wide range of commercial and freeware programs are available for this purpose. Examples of freeware programs include the following:

What's Running: http://www.whatsrunning.net/whatsrunning/main.aspx

myProcMan: http://www.trsecurity.net/myprocman/

ProcX: http://www.ghostsecurity.com/index.php?page = procx

Process Explorer: http://www.sysinternals.com/Utilities/ProcessExplorer.html

FURTHER INFORMATION

Reading

Gordon, S., 1994a. *The Generic Virus Writer* [online]. IBM. Available at: http://www.research.ibm.com/antivirus/SciPapers/Gordon/GenericVirusWriter.html.

Gordon, S., 1994b. *The Generic Virus Writer II* [online]. IBM. Available at: http://www.research.ibm.com/antivirus/SciPapers/Gordon/GVWII.html.

Online

VMyths provides comprehensive information regarding common virus hoaxes and misconceptions: www.vmyths.com.

How Stuff Works provides a simple but comprehensive explanation of computer viruses: http://www.howstuffworks.com/virus.htm.

Symantec's Security Response resource provides up-to-date information about new and emerging threats. A searchable virus encyclopedia is also available: http://securityresponse.symantec.com/.

Virus Bulletin is an independent source of news, information and advice regarding malware: www.virusbtn.com.

4

Spyware and Adware

The explosive growth of malware illustrates just how quickly changes can take place in the computer industry. In terms of malware, we can trace a number of significant changes that have taken place over the course of just a few years.

First, the people who create malware seem to have grown up a little since the 1990s. Where once an introverted teenage boy sat in front of the keyboard, now sits a man in his twenties, an experienced computer professional who is highly educated. More women have also taken to creating viruses and other destructive programs.

Second, the motives behind creating viruses and other malware have started to change too. Virus writers once claimed that their programs were written for fairly innocuous reasons—out of curiosity or to point out security vulnerabilities. Only a small number of virus writers confessed to darker motives, such as a wish to make a political statement or a desire for revenge against a former employer. Today's malware writer is not concerned with impressing a few friends at school or establishing a reputation. Instead, he is focused on just one thing—making big money, fast.

Third, many of the earliest malware writers were somewhat naïve, seemingly oblivious to the world outside of the computer security community. Some undoubtedly pictured themselves as rebels engaged in a battle of wits against the antivirus programmers they saw as representatives of the major corporations and the authorities. But outside of this microcosm, other people had seen the potential to turn malware into a business tool. Organized crime and terrorist groups saw an opportunity to generate millions of dollars through extortion and other activities. Companies also saw new business opportunities, ranging from finding ways to target advertising more efficiently to selling products of dubious value, such as wonder cures.

Fourth, financial interests have changed the type of malware being produced. The number of new viruses seen every month appears to be declining, while the number of spyware programs is increasing dramatically. Stealing financial information and creating networks of zombie computers (botnets) seem to the main priorities of today's malware producers.

Finally, many computer users have been forced to change their working habits in order to protect their computer systems. At the turn of the century, few computers had firewalls installed and none used spyware scanners to detect zombie software or other dangerous programs. Today, all of the security suites sold by companies like Norton, McAfee, and Trend Micro feature powerful firewalls. Most also have features intended to defeat spyware and ensure that sensitive information remains confidential. This increased emphasis on security has had an impact on business users at all levels; managers may be banned from taking work home for fear of spreading viruses, and the actions of office workers may be monitored in case unauthorized Internet use causes a piece of spyware to be installed on company systems.

The growth in malware has also affected home users, especially as people have come to rely on the Internet for e-mail, social activities, and entertainment. High-speed Internet connections allow people to spend more time online, encouraging them to download more software or music, or perhaps to take part in new activities, like visiting chat rooms or playing online games. However, each e-mail, download, or visit to a new Web page brings with it the risk of encountering malware. In turn, this necessitates changes to the way people use the Internet, requiring them to be more cautious when carrying out activities like responding to e-mail or even browsing a Web site. The need for caution also imposes other tasks on users, for example by creating the need for them to learn how to use virus scanners and other security software. Fortunately, there is some consolation in the fact that as people become more security conscious, the creators of malware will need to work harder and take more risks to access our computer systems.

WHAT IS SPYWARE?

Spyware represents a new type of malware that poses a significant threat to business and home users. Unlike those who create other forms of malware, such as viruses, spyware authors are not motivated by curiosity or a desire to establish a reputation. Instead, they are attracted to the possibility of making large amounts of money quickly and easily.

In general, *spyware* describes a category of software designed to capture and record confidential information without a user's knowledge or consent. Key loggers, as discussed in chapter three, are a typical example of spyware. Some Trojans can also be classified as spyware.

Applications for spyware range from monitoring the actions of a spouse to industrial espionage. Although early spyware programs were quite primitive, modern applications have a number of sophisticated features that make them difficult to detect and remove. Like viruses, the most advanced programs are able to disable or delete security software, and some even pose as spyware removal tools.

Spyware can be grouped into a number of categories, including the following:

- Data miners: Programs that collect information about a user, supposedly with his knowledge and/or consent. Spyware developers sometimes justify the use of such software by referring to the use of *clickthrough agreements.*
- Monitoring tools: Software intended to report on a user's activities, including the use of Trojans and key loggers.
- Trackers: Programs that monitor Internet activity, recording information such as the sites visited by a user. Trackers do not necessarily record personally identifiable information.
- Annoyware: A type of adware that attempts to force advertising on users by opening multiple browser windows, pop-ups, and so on.
- *Browser hijackers.* Sometimes called *home-page hijackers,* these programs hijack the user's home page and can also make other changes, such as changing the default search engine or altering system settings.
- *Dialers.* A type of program that alters the settings used to make dial-up connections to the Internet, usually with the aim of calling premium rate numbers at the expense of the user. The numbers called are often linked with services that provide pornography, causing some people to become too embarrassed to make a complaint.

READ THE FINE PRINT

The developers of spyware programs often claim that users have consented to the installation of their software and the collection of personal information. This claim is usually justified by referring to the clickthrough agreements displayed when a new piece of software is installed. When a program is installed, the installation routine normally displays details of the program's software license in a dialog box or pop-up window. Installation halts until the user agrees to the terms of the license by clicking on an "OK" button. Since relatively few people read *license agreements* carefully, clicking the button may signify consent for additional software (the spyware) to be installed, or for personal information to be collected.

There is some debate as to the legality of this method. It can be argued that clickthrough agreements are insufficient to show that informed consent has been obtained. In addition, the terms set out in license agreements may not constitute a legally binding contract for one reason or another. For instance, it would be difficult to apply such a contract to a child who buys a piece of software with his allowance.

Although some people may find the categories described here useful, it is perhaps more helpful to look at spyware in more basic terms. In general, spyware tends to be used for two reasons: for criminal purposes or to support the business activities of companies that might be described as morally challenged.

Criminal uses of spyware typically involve stealing financial information, such as credit card details, from unsuspecting users. The information is then used to carry out a series of fraudulent transactions. Banks and other institutions are sometimes able to detect when stolen credit card information is used because fraudulent transactions tend to follow a fairly predictable pattern. Stolen information needs to be used as quickly as possible, so thieves will usually carry out a whole series of unusual transactions shortly after the information is obtained.

Some people steal financial information without any intention of using it themselves. Instead, they collate lists of credit card numbers, bank account details, PayPal passwords, and other information for sale to others. Often, the buyers are criminal groups involved in other illegal activities, such as organized crime, drugs, counterfeiting, and terrorism. Working on a very large scale, these groups are able to steal or launder millions of dollars at a time.

Occasionally, information that has been stolen from individuals or companies is used for other purposes, such as blackmail. A number of incidents have been reported where criminals have threatened to publish credit card numbers or other sensitive information unless their demands for money were met. As an example, a well-known case involved the theft of 300,000 credit card numbers from CDUniverse.com in December 1999.[1] The hacker, a Russian teenager who used the name Maxim, demanded $100,000 from the company. When his demands were not met, he published 25,000 numbers via the Internet.

Extortion need not involve financial information—any confidential information will do. For instance, in 2005, Myron Tereshchuk was jailed for five years after pleading guilty to "attempted extortion affecting commerce." Tereshchuk had demanded $17 million from MicroPatent LLC in exchange for not revealing proprietary information he had stolen from the company.[2]

ADWARE

Many people consider *adware,* also known as *advertising-supported software,* to be a category of spyware.[3] Many companies produce useful software tools that are distributed free of charge or at low cost. In order to generate revenues, the software displays advertisements on behalf of other companies. However, some companies attempt to target their advertising more effectively by monitoring how people use their computers and the Internet. The software collects information, such as details of any Web sites visited, and reports back to a central server. The information is then analyzed so that appropriate advertisements can be chosen and sent back to the user. Although a lot of companies claim that they do not collect any data that can identify a specific individual, many people frown upon the idea that their activities are being constantly monitored and reported on.

Most concerns about adware are about the collection of *personally iden-tifiable information* (sometimes called PII). This describes information that is tied to a specific individual, allowing detailed information about his or her activities to be collected. This is very different from the collection of anonymous data, such as usage statistics. As an example, many Web sites collect information about their visitors. This may include details of which pages have been visited, which browsers people are using, what search terms were used to locate the site, and so on. All of this data can be collected without needing to know the identities of individual visitors. It may sometimes be necessary to make sure that data is collected only once for each visitor, but even this can be accomplished without needing any personal information. A common approach involves saving a *cookie* containing a unique number to each user's computer. When a user visits the Web site, the number from the cookie is retrieved and checked against a database stored on the site. If the number matches an existing record, there is no need to store any data about the user.

While many software companies are up-front about the information they collect, others are not as honest. Installing a program downloaded from the Internet may also cause a variety of spyware programs to be installed secretly. Computers without security software installed are particularly vulnerable because of their susceptibility to some of the methods used to distribute adware. As an example, in 2004 a simple experiment was carried out by StillSecure, a network security firm. A number of computers were loaded with different operating systems, connected to the Internet, and then left for one week. None of the machines had a virus scanner or other security software installed. Over the course of a week, the six machines used in the experiment were scanned 46,255 times and subsequently attacked 4,892 times by "… a staggering variety of worms, Trojan Horses, viruses, spyware, and other forms of malware."[4] In 2005, another crude experiment was carried out by Symantec, a leading producer of security products. Researchers from the company took a brand new computer without any security software installed, connected it to the Internet, and then browsed a number of Web sites aimed at children. After just one hour, the machine was examined for malware, and it was reported that a total of 359 pieces of adware were found.[5] Although unscientific, this experiment suggests that some adware producers are deliberately targeting young people.

WHY CREATE SPYWARE?

In keeping with most forms of crime, the main motive behind the use of spyware and adware is money. It is estimated that adware generated

$2 billion in 2004 from pop-up advertisements, home page hijacking, and other methods.[6] This amounts to more than a fifth of the amount spent on legitimate forms of Internet advertising over the same period ($9.6 billion).

The revenues generated by adware are remarkable because of the speed with which the market has grown. Before 2004, made-to-order adware was virtually unheard of. The sudden boom in spyware and adware is partly a result of virus writers realizing that their skills represent a valuable commodity. The skills needed to create a successful Trojan or virus can also be used to create adware programs that are difficult to detect and remove.

Greed has also motivated programmers working in other areas to moonlight as adware creators. Those with suitable skills include people working in the antivirus industry, Web programmers, and those with specialist knowledge of operating systems. There have also been reports suggesting that some programmers have left their regular jobs to become self-employed, working as freelancers who specialize in creating spyware and adware. Those who have left the security industry to begin creating malware are sometimes described as having "gone over to the dark side."

THE EXTENT OF THE PROBLEM

Various surveys have concluded that spyware now represents a more serious threat to computer users than viruses and spam. As an example, a survey of 500 IT managers carried out on behalf of Trend Micro in 2005 found that 95 percent of companies frequently find adware in their organization.[7] The majority of respondents also ranked spyware among their top three IT priorities for 2005.

Although estimates vary, up to 300,000 malware programs may exist at present and at least 1,000 new variants of keystroke loggers and Trojans appear every week.[8] The sheer number of programs in circulation may help to explain why so many computer systems are infected by spyware. In industry, a survey of IT managers by Harris Survey reported that 92 percent of participants said that their organizations had been infected with spyware, with an average of 29 percent of their computers infected.[9] Home users have fared little better. According to a survey from Webroot, a security software developer, which looked at data gathered by its online Spy Audit service during the first part of 2005,[10] of the machines studied, 88 percent of all home computers contained some form of unwanted software. Spyware was also found on 87 percent of all business computers. In all, an average of approximately 28 spyware programs were found on each computer scanned.[11] Other surveys have reported similar results, suggesting that the figures given here are relatively accurate. For instance, a survey by America Online and National Cyber Security Alliance[12] estimates that 80 percent of home computers are infected with spyware.

Like viruses, spyware has an impact on the speed and reliability of any infected systems. According to Microsoft, 50 percent of all PC crashes are caused by spyware.[13] In addition, a 2004 press release from Dell, one of the world's largest manufacturers of computer equipment, reported that 20 percent of its technical calls involve spyware. Inevitably, the problems caused by spyware create a drain on resources that few organizations can afford. Just in terms of lost productivity, spyware can cost large organizations millions of dollars each year. As an example, an experiment carried out by Computer Associates[14] measured how long it took a PC to start under various conditions. A computer with no adware present took 115 seconds to start. With one adware program present, the time taken to start up increased to 415 seconds. This figure rose to 880 seconds when two adware programs were present. Using this last value, the company estimates that an employee may lose up to 60 hours per year simply waiting for his or her computer to start.[15] Add to this time lost for other reasons, such as crashes, and a simple adware infection can result in annual losses of thousands of dollars per employee.

CONTRACTING SPYWARE

In general, there are four basic methods used to infect a computer with spyware. These include drive-by downloads, bundling spyware with other programs, making users believe that they are updating their systems, and offering free goods and services.

Just visiting certain Web sites, clicking on pop-up advertisements, or a variety of other actions may instruct a Web browser to download special software. This functionality has a number of legitimate uses and helps to make the Internet easier to work with. Extra software is sometimes needed to view certain types of content or provide additional services for users. Documents stored in Adobe's Portable Document Format (PDF), for instance, can be viewed within a Web browser window if a special plug-in is available, while various versions of Windows download a special component that allows the operating system to be updated automatically at regular intervals. However, the ability to download software on demand is easily abused. If a browser's security settings are incorrect, it can be made to download software automatically, without the user knowing. This is known as a *drive-by download* and is a very common way of distributing spyware.

One way of reducing the risk of drive-by downloads is by altering browser security settings so that permission is needed before any new software can be installed. However, such a precaution is not foolproof and can be circumvented in various ways. The simplest method is by lying to the user about the software, for example by claiming that the program is a plug-in for viewing special content. Another way is by gaining permission to install a legitimate program, then installing one or more spyware programs at the same time.

A second way of distributing spyware is by including it with other programs. A useful program, such as a file-sharing package, may be accompanied by numerous adware and spyware programs. In some cases, removing or uninstalling the spyware will cause the program to stop working, giving users a simple choice: Keep the spyware or lose the program. It is also worth noting that spyware often accompanies pirate software and the small utility programs used to defeat copy protection.

A third method involves displaying a warning message to the user. A typical message will claim that a virus or other piece of malware has been detected on the user's computer. The user can remove the virus by using an online virus scanner or downloading a free antivirus tool. Choosing either option results in a spyware program being installed before a fake report is shown about a virus scan that never really took place. A variation on this technique uses an official-looking message warning users to update their systems in order to protect against a new security threat. These messages often seem authentic because they use the same pictures, logos, fonts, and other elements—usually stolen from the appropriate Web site—as the company they pretend to come from. Seeing a message that appears to come from Microsoft or another well-known company, many users automatically follow the instructions given. Ironically, it is the fear of viruses, spyware, and other malware that causes these users to compromise their computer systems.

Finally, one of the most effective ways of distributing spyware is through offers of free goods and services. A pop-up ad offering a free entry into a raffle, a full virus scan, e-books, or other items is undoubtedly attractive to many users. However, accepting one of these offers effectively gives permission for one or more spyware programs to be installed. A growing trend involves offering users a free spyware removal tool that turns out to be an adware program. Some of these programs are extremely difficult to remove, reinstalling themselves each time an attempt is made to delete them. A small number of adware programs go even further by disabling functions, such as the Windows Task Manager, that might be helpful to someone trying to uninstall malware.

PUSH THE BUTTON

Modern Web browsers are designed to ask the user's permission before installing any software that might compromise the system. However, since it is possible to display custom messages and buttons, users can be tricked into installing spyware onto their computers.

Imagine a dialog box that contains a message saying "PasswordStealer is trying to install itself on your computer. Do you wish to proceed?" In addition, there are two buttons in the dialog box; one marked *Yes*, the other *No*. Clearly, the likelihood of anyone pressing *Yes* is extremely low, but what if the text shown in the dialog box is changed? If the message is altered to "SuperLotto is offering you a free $10 entry. Do you want to enter the draw?" the likelihood of users clicking *Yes* increases significantly.

DEALING WITH SPYWARE AND ADWARE

It is worth remembering that some of the antivirus programs listed in earlier sections can also be used to detect other forms of malware. However, since the level of protection offered varies from package to package, it is a good idea to use a specialized adware scanner to perform periodic scans of the computer.

Some well-known adware removal programs that can be used free of charge include:

Lavasoft produces the Ad-Aware range of software. The standard edition of the software is free for noncommercial use: http://www.lavasoft.de/software/adaware

Spybot Info produces Spybot Search & Destroy. Although the program is provided free of charge, the author requests a voluntary donation: http://spybot.safer-networking.de

Javacool Software produces SpywareBlaster, which is distributed as freeware: http://www.javacoolsoftware.com/

GRC produces OptOut, which is offered as freeware: http://grc.com/optout.htm

Spyware Info produces a range of freeware programs that are useful in removing spyware. These tools include HijackThis, which detects and removes home-page hijackers, and Itty Bitty Process Manager, which provides information on Windows processes: http://www.spywareinfo.com/~merijn/index.html

Emsi Software produces a^2 (a-squared), which can be used free of charge for personal use: http://www.emsisoft.com/en/software/free

Many adware removal tools are available in several different versions. Commercial versions of Ad-Aware, for example, are available for home users and business users.

ONLINE SPYWARE SCANNERS

A number of free online services can be used to detect and remove spyware. Some examples of well-known services include:

Ewido Networks: http://www.ewido.net/en/

Trend Micro Housecall: http://housecall.trendmicro.com/

Computer Associates PestScan: http://www.pestpatrol.com/pestscan/index.htm

Some of the online services provided by antivirus companies can also be used to detect other types of malware. The details of some of these services were given in an earlier section.

SAFETY AND PREVENTION

Most of the guidelines given in previous chapters also apply to spyware. However, there are some additional points that are worth remembering. The following guidelines are drawn from a variety of sources including Bocij et al. (2005), vnu net, About Inc., US-CERT, Yahoo!, Fortune, and PC World.

BUSINESS USERS

- A great deal of spyware and adware is distributed via e-mail. Filtering incoming e-mail can reduce infections significantly.
- Spyware may sometimes be installed on company systems by employees or contractors. This makes it important to monitor access to systems and carry out regular scans for Trojans, key loggers, and other spyware.
- Companies that own and support a large number of computer programs may find it difficult to check all of the software licenses they must abide by. EULAlyzer is a free program that analyzes license agreements for phrases that may indicate potential problems. The software is available via: http://www.downloadsquad. com/2005/09/16/software-that-reads-eulas-so-you-dont-have-to/.

INDIVIDUALS AND FAMILIES

- Check and alter browser security settings as necessary in order to reduce vulnerability to spyware.
- Consider adopting a browser that is considered secure. Programs such as Mozilla, Firefox, and Opera are available free of charge and are considered very safe against spyware.
- Before downloading any software, including browser add-ons, check the source of the program. This can be done by searching Google or another search engine for the name of the program or the name of the producer.
- Read the software license before installing any program. In particular, be alert for clauses that allow additional software to be installed or for information to be collected from your computer.
- Take measures against unsolicited e-mail, since spyware is often distributed this way.
- Check pop-up messages and warnings carefully. Be suspicious of messages that ask for permission to download ActiveX controls or other software. If in doubt, choose *No* or *Cancel*.
- Do not follow links embedded in e-mail messages or pop-up windows. These may lead to fake Web sites or cause other unexpected problems.
- Obtain and use one or more specialized spyware scanners regularly. No current spyware detection software has a perfect detection record so it is a good idea to use two or more programs in combination.

FURTHER INFORMATION

Reading

Tittel, E., 2005. *PC Magazine Fighting Spyware, Viruses, and Malware*. Hoboken, NJ: Hungry Minds Inc.

Moshchuk, A., Bragin, T., Gribble, S., and Levy, H., 2005. *A Crawler-based Study of Spyware on the Web* [online]. University of Washington. Available online at: http://www.cs.washington.edu/homes/gribble/papers/spycrawler.pdf.

Australian Government Department of Communications, Information Technology and the Arts, 2005. *Spyware Discussion Paper May–June 2005* [online]. Australian Government Department of Communications, Information Technology and the Arts. Available online at: http://www.dcita.gov.au/__data/assets/pdf_file/25973/Spyware_discussion_paper.pdf.

Online

Intranet Journal offers concise but thorough information on spyware: http://www.intranetjournal.com/spyware/.

PC World's Info Center provides links to news stories, articles, and tutorials related to spyware and adware: http://www.pcworld.com/resource/browse/0,cat,1713,00.asp.

Spyware Info provides a regular newsletter, a message board, and other resources: http://www.spywareinfo.com/.

Core Competence publishes a list of resources related to spyware and adware: http://hhi.corecom.com/spyware.htm.

Part 3
Identity Theft and Fraud

Identity Theft

A man enters a bank in New York and asks to set up a multimillion-dollar account. He is in his early thirties, is overweight, and has dark, curly hair. His skin is somewhat dark, suggesting a Middle Eastern origin, but his accent is American. Asked for his name, the man introduces himself as Steven Spielberg. Another day, another bank, and the man asks to set up another account. This time he is Oprah Winfrey. Impossible? Ridiculous? Not on the Internet. The man's name was Abraham Abdallah and he was responsible for impersonating more than 200 celebrities before his arrest in 2001.[1]

What Is Identity Theft?

Identity theft (also called identity fraud) involves impersonating someone, often by using his or her personal information, such as a Social Security number, address, and credit card details. Usually, identity theft is carried out with the aim of obtaining money, goods, or services at the expense of the victim.

It is worth remembering that the Internet did not create identity theft: It has existed in one form or another for centuries. For instance, a report by Caslon Analytics[2] provides many examples of identity theft throughout history. The report also points out that even the Old and New Testaments of the Bible refer to identity theft with warnings of false prophets.

A number of attempts have been made to classify different forms of identity theft. While some of these typologies are undoubtedly helpful to law enforcement and others, they are sometimes a little too cumbersome when discussing online identity theft. As an example, Emily Finch[3] proposes a typology of online identity theft that takes into account factors such as duration and immersion. *Duration* refers to how long the impersonation continues, while *immersion* refers to "... the depth with which the impostor delves into the victim's life and to the range and extent of the personal details that are misappropriated." Although these are powerful ideas in many different contexts, such as the academic study of identity theft, they might be seen as somewhat neglectful of the practicalities of computer crime. In terms of immersion, for instance, while one person could take months to gather detailed information about a victim, another might gather the same (or more) information in a matter of minutes. In addition, the ability to automate tasks such as gathering information can enable a computer-literate thief to steal from hundreds of people every hour. If each victim is impersonated for only a few seconds, and if detailed private information is gathered by impersonal spyware programs, the significance of duration and immersion becomes questionable.

The U.S Department of Justice has created a simple typology of identity theft that can easily be applied to the Internet.[4] According to this typology, there are two basic motives behind identity theft: financial gain and concealment. Concealment refers to hiding a person's true identity or covering up a crime. Identity theft can also be described in terms of high commitment and low commitment. High-commitment identity theft involves a great deal of planning and may require a large investment of resources, such as money, time, and expertise. Low-commitment identity theft is opportunistic in nature and is usually carried out with little planning. Combining these factors produces four types of identity theft: financial gain–high commitment, financial gain–low commitment, concealment–high commitment, and concealment–low commitment. Each of these categories can be applied to the Internet without difficulty. An example of concealment–high commitment identity theft might involve a terrorist establishing a false identity in order to avoid capture after an attack.

Another way of classifying identity theft is by looking at the offenders themselves. One classification describes four kinds of offender: the circumstantial identity theft offender; the semi-pro; the professional and co-op identity theft offender; and the survivalist.[5] The circumstantial offender is opportunistic and may only ever offend once. The semi-pro has gained experience at committing identity theft and has learned that he is unlikely to be caught. Having learned from his experiences, his methods are more sophisticated than those of the circumstantial offender. The professional offender sees the use of identity theft for material gain as a career. Alone or as part of a criminal group, he may have developed an expertise in obtaining and using certain kinds of information, allowing him to act on a larger scale than other offenders. The final type of offender, the survivalist, assumes another identity for reasons other than financial gain. He may wish to avoid arrest following a crime, or he may be an illegal immigrant attempting to obtain accommodation. Again, this classification is easily applied to the Internet, and it is fairly simple to locate examples of each type. For instance, the following provides a good example of circumstantial identity theft. In 2001, a female graduate student from Iowa State University repeatedly accessed the e-mail accounts belonging to a male friend.[6] She was able to impersonate the friend to turn down a $200,000-a-year job he had been offered. The incident only came to light when the employer contacted the friend to express disappointment that he had refused the offer. It was later found that the student had been able to access the accounts by using her personal knowledge of the friend to guess his password.

One of the latest typologies to be proposed places offenders into high-frequency and low-frequency categories.[7] Low-frequency offenders include crisis responders and opportunity takers. Crisis responders use identity theft as a way of dealing with a perceived crisis. As an example, having ruined his own credit, a man might use a male relative's details to secure a loan. As the name suggests, opportunity takers take advantage of opportunities to profit from criminal acts. As an example, a man might find a wallet on the street and use the credit cards it contains to purchase goods. High-frequency offenders include opportunity seekers and stereotypical criminals. Opportunity seekers not only search for criminal opportunities—they sometimes manufacture them too. Stereotypical criminals are the most prolific offenders and often come from troubled backgrounds. This group may carry out all types of identity theft but have a propensity towards activities involving organized crime and drug-related crime, including drug use and distribution.

IDENTITY THEFT AND THE INTERNET

In the offline world, the information needed to assume another person's identity can be gathered in a wide variety of ways. Common methods include *dumpster diving* (searching through a person's trash), stealing mail, buying counterfeit documents that carry the victim's name, bribing employees to supply information from company or government databases, stealing documents from cars or houses, and even pick-pocketing wallets. Some of these methods can also be used to support Internet-based fraud. As an example, *shoulder surfing* involves looking over someone's shoulder as they enter a password or other confidential information. Although this is typically used to learn the PINs of ATM users, it is also one of the most common ways of stealing network passwords in an office environment. Having stolen a password, it becomes easy for one employee to impersonate another in e-mail messages, perhaps to damage his reputation or play a prank. However, it may also become possible to place orders, access (or even change) company records, and so on. Since many companies allow employees to access their systems from home, these kinds of actions can often be carried out from Internet cafes or similar places, greatly reducing the chances of being caught.

As mentioned elsewhere, technology often acts as an enabler for deviant or criminal acts. Technology sometimes allows people to do things that were once difficult or impossible. At other times, it allows people to act on a large scale, usually by automating repetitive or complex tasks. Although shoulder surfing allows criminals to gather a small number of PINs or passwords, the Internet enables the collection of thousands of passwords in a short space of time. Using the Internet also helps to shield identity thieves from capture since they can operate their schemes from virtually anywhere in the world. This means, for instance, that Americans should not worry only about other Americans impersonating them—they are equally vulnerable to criminals operating in Europe, Australasia, the Far East, and elsewhere.

Identity thieves tend to rely on a small number of simple techniques to gather the information they need. These include phishing, pharming, and e-mail fraud.

PHISHING

Those interested in computing have a tendency to replace "f" with "ph," so *phishing* is the high-tech version of the word "fishing." Phishing involves directing potential victims to a fake Web site using various techniques. A typical phishing scam involves sending out millions of e-mail messages that appear to come from a genuine organization, such as a bank. The message directs victims to visit their online banking services and log in so that a potential problem can be dealt with. A handy link is provided within the message so that victims can go directly to the Web site with as little trouble as possible. However, despite appearing legitimate, the link leads to the fake Web site created by the con man. Once at the site, victims are asked to log in to their accounts so that their identities can be verified. After entering their details, victims are shown a message reassuring them that the problem has been solved.

Despite a number of variations, virtually all phishing scams follow the basic approach described here. Some common variations worth noting include:

- The e-mail messages used to lure victims to fake Web sites can take a number of different forms. Some warn people that criminals have attempted to carry out fraudulent or unauthorized transactions on a large number of bank or credit card accounts. They are then asked to visit their accounts to make sure they have not been affected. Other messages appear to be receipts for large payments made on the victim's behalf. This can be a very effective approach since the panic felt by victims is likely to overcome any suspicions they may have.
- The fake Web sites used to collect information can vary a great deal in terms of their sophistication. Some of the crudest Web sites consist of just a single page. Attempting to follow any links given on the page will result in an error, making it easy to see through the deception. However, some sites use custom error pages that make it look like a technical fault is preventing users

from seeing other pages. The most advanced sites appear almost identical to those being impersonated, even going as far as duplicating all of the content. Only the login page is different: After entering their account details, victims are shown a message telling them that their accounts cannot be accessed because of a technical fault. When they visit the genuine Web site later on, the technical problem will seem to have disappeared and everything will look normal. Alternatively, the victim may be told that they must wait a while before accessing their accounts because various records need to be updated.

A QUESTION OF SCALE

One of the reasons phishing scams tend to be profitable is because they operate on a huge scale. A typical scam will involve millions of e-mail messages being sent out each day. Even if only a few people in every million respond to the bogus message, this may represent tens of thousands of dollars that can be stolen every day.

It is also worth noting that large organizations are more vulnerable to phishing scams than smaller companies are. Citibank, for instance, has more than 200 million accounts in over 100 countries.[8] The sheer number of accounts held by the company makes it an attractive target for con men. This is because the odds of a phishing e-mail reaching a Citibank customer are high when compared to the odds of reaching a customer from any other bank. For this reason, Citibank has been targeted a number of times in recent years. As an example, 492 attacks against Citibank were recorded in just one month in 2004.[9]

A variation of phishing involves targeting a single company or domain. This approach, called *spear phishing,* has arisen in response to the ever-increasing effectiveness of e-mail filters used by individuals, companies, and ISPs. Such *filters* prevent a large proportion of phishing e-mails from ever reaching their destinations, drastically reducing the number of potential victims that can be reached. This development has made it necessary for con men to find ways of targeting their messages more effectively. Spear phishing draws upon social engineering methods, taking advantage of the fact that people are more likely to respond to a message that appears to come from someone they know. In a business environment, this means creating a message that seems to have come from inside the company, perhaps from a colleague or a manager. People are also more likely to respond to messages sent to them personally, especially if the message addresses them by name. Such messages can be made to look more convincing if they include additional information, such as the intended victim's job title.

In an attempt to highlight the risk posed by spear phishing attacks, more than 500 cadets at West Point were sent an e-mail from Colonel Robert Melville, informing them of a problem with their grade report and instructing them to click on a link to verify that the grades were correct. More than 80 percent of the students followed the link as instructed, despite the fact that none of them had ever heard of Colonel Robert Melville ... because he did not exist.[10]

At first glance, creating personalized messages like those described here seems complex and time consuming. However, the process is no more difficult than performing a mail merge with a word-processing package and is well within the capability of anyone with a reasonable level of education. The information needed to create a series of messages is often freely available from Web sites, printed directories, and other sources. As an example, many companies publish staff directories on their intranets. If a network has not been secured properly, gaining access to a company directory can take just a matter of seconds. Even if the network is secure against intrusion from the outside, it may be possible to bribe an employee or gain access to information in other ways.

Once enough information has been obtained, it can be stored within a database so that it can be used with specialized e-mail software, called a *bulk e-mailer*.[11] The software generates personalized messages by inserting information from the database into a ready-made template—a little like filling in a form. The speed of bulk e-mail software is only limited by hardware and the speed of the Internet connection being used. Even a typical personal computer is capable of generating hundreds of messages simultaneously.

As with other forms of Internet crime, there are a number of variations on spear phishing. Of particular importance are variants that target ordinary Internet users with personalized messages similar to those sent to companies. Attempts to target Internet users are largely possible because of the availability of software that can be used to harvest e-mail addresses and other data from sources such as Web sites, message boards, and *newsgroups*.

Some idea of the scale of spear phishing attacks can be given by the fact that more than 35 million spear phishing e-mail messages were sent to U.S. companies in the first half of 2005. In addition, the number of messages sent grew at a rate of 1000 percent in over just six months.[12]

PHARMING

Pharming involves redirecting the victim's web browser to a fake Web site. Browsers can be redirected to other sites using malware or by "poisoning" local domain name servers. Various kinds of malware including Trojans and browser add-ons, such as toolbars, can be made to intercept any Web addresses entered by the user so that the browser can be directed elsewhere. Users often remain unaware that they have been sent to a different Web site, because the address they typed can be made to remain visible in the browser's address bar. It is also possible to display the name of the site above the menu bar, together with additional information in the status bar at the bottom of the browser window.

Using malware to redirect web browsers is inefficient, since the majority of the users affected are unlikely to be part of the group being targeted for fraud. As mentioned earlier, the chances of finding customers with accounts held at a specific bank are relatively low. It may be necessary to infect hundreds of machines before a single customer is found. Even then, the customer must use Internet banking for there to be any chance of obtaining a password or other confidential information. This raises two major problems for criminals using this approach to pharming. First, the more time and effort needed to send potential victims to a fake Web site, the lower the potential profit. Second, the need to infiltrate a large number of computers and place malware on them increases the risk of detection. One way of dealing with these problems is by taking advantage of the way in which the World Wide Web works, in particular how Web browsers locate specific Web sites and pages.

A *domain name server* converts human-friendly web addresses into a computer-friendly numeric format. A *domain name*, or web address, called a *URL* (Uniform Resource Locator), provides an easy way for people refer to Web sites. Greenwood Publishing Group, for example, has a Web site located at www.greenwood.com, an address that is easy to remember or to type into a web browser. When a URL is typed into a browser, the address needs to be converted into a numeric format called an *IP (Internet Protocol) address* before the site can be located. For instance, Greenwood's URL (www.greenwood. com) becomes 65.215.112.149 when converted into an IP address.

By altering the information on a domain name server, it is possible to direct Web browsers to one or more fake Web sites. As an example, someone might alter Greenwood's IP address from 65.215.112.149 to 165.193.130.83. This would cause anyone who enters www.greenwood.com into a browser to be directed to a competitor's Web site instead (in this case, a rival publisher). Users would not notice anything out of the ordinary, since the redirection would happen seamlessly and everything would appear normal. The act of altering information on a domain name server is usually referred to as *poisoning*.

Poisoning a domain name server is an effective way of targeting specific groups and avoids the scattergun effect that results from circulating malware. For instance, altering the address of the login page used by an online banking service targets only those customers who use online banking, leaving everyone else unaffected. The risk of detection is also lowered, since the need to distribute malware on a large scale is removed altogether. This prevents

Internet users from being selected indiscriminately, helping to reduce the suspicion that arises when people receive messages demanding that they verify the details of accounts they do not have. In addition, no malware means that nothing is altered on victims' computers, leaving no evidence for people—or security software—to find.

In order to begin redirecting people to a pharming Web site only one record on one domain server needs to be altered. This can be achieved in a number of different ways, some of which need little or no technical knowledge. Since there are many domain name servers located around the world, the effects of altering the information on just one are likely to be limited in one or more ways. As an example, any changes may be limited to a relatively small number of users, Web addresses, or geographical areas.

The difference between phishing and pharming can be explained by referring to push and pull, ideas used by Web designers when deciding how to attract visitors to the sites they create. Pushing traffic to a Web site means locating prospective visitors and directing them to the site. Pulling traffic means making the Web site attractive to the target audience so that people choose to visit by themselves. In general, pulling traffic to a Web site is best because less effort is needed to attract visitors once the site has been created.

Phishing relies on contacting potential victims and luring them to a specially prepared Web site. The criminal needs to be highly proactive, seeking out victims and *pushing* them to the Web site. On the other hand, pharming is more passive, relying on the victim finding his own way to the fake Web site. The victim is *pulled* to the Web site because he wishes to use a service, such as online banking. The notion of push and pull can help to highlight some of the characteristics of different kinds of Internet fraud. In general, methods that push the victim require more time and effort, are indiscriminate, involve more risk, and are ultimately less profitable for the criminal. Methods that pull the victim tend to be relatively simple to set up, target specific groups of people, require little ongoing effort, are harder to detect, and expose criminals to less risk.

THE EXTENT OF THE PROBLEM

Annual losses due to phishing and other forms of identity theft are difficult to estimate. The accuracy of estimates may be affected by a number of factors. Organizations may play down losses because it may harm public confidence. They may also wish to withhold information for competitive reasons. Individual Internet users may also fail to report incidents because of the embarrassment sometimes associated with becoming a victim of fraud. Practical difficulties may also have an impact on the accuracy of estimates. For example, large organizations may find it difficult and time consuming to collect accurate information from their domestic and foreign branches.

Despite what some may believe, the victims of phishing scams are not simply gullible. In 2004, a survey of 1,000 Internet users by MailFrontier Inc. found that 28 percent failed to recognize typical phishing e-mails.[13]

It is also important to distinguish between losses resulting from all types of identity theft and those arising from computer-related crime. In addition, care should be taken to distinguish between global losses and losses arising in the United States.

In terms of global losses due to identity theft, some estimates suggest that annual losses may exceed $100 billion each year,[14] while others give a figure of $221 billion.[15]

Several estimates have also been given for annual losses due to identity theft in the United States. The Privacy Rights Clearinghouse[16] has published a summary of recent studies carried out by organizations that include the Better Business Bureau, the Federal Trade Commission, Gartner, and others. According to the figures given on the site, in the United States the total losses sustained in 2004 ranged from $47.6 billion to $52.6 billion.

At this writing, there are no reliable estimates of global annual losses arising from identity theft carried out via the Internet. However, various estimates exist for losses in individual countries, including the United States. With regard to phishing, a 2004 survey from Gartner suggested that annual losses from phishing in the United States alone amounted to more than $2 billion.[17] A similar survey by TRUSTe, a nonprofit organization devoted to Internet privacy issues, estimated losses at just $500 million for the same period.[18] The organization reported that phishing scams cost Internet users approximately $115 each. The difference between these estimates is difficult to explain and indicates confusion within the computer security industry.

A different way of assessing the extent of phishing, pharming, and other Internet-related crimes is by looking at how many phishing sites exist. Between December 2004 and December 2005, the number of new phishing sites recorded by the Anti-Phishing Working Group[19] grew from 1,707 to 7,197, an increase of more than 400 percent. Such figures illustrate a tremendous rate of growth in Internet-related fraud and have been taken by some to indicate the presence of organized crime groups.

Another way of gauging the extent of phishing is by looking at the number of victims who have been defrauded. Official figures suggest that by 2004 more than 57 million Internet users in the United States had received some sort of e-mail related to a phishing scam.[20] According to research from Gartner, 11 million computer users in the United States were deceived by phishing e-mails over the period April 2004–April 2005.[21]

One of the reasons that so many people have been tricked is because Internet identity theft makes use of social engineering techniques. Research has shown that a large percentage of computer users are willing to divulge sensitive information, such as passwords, for little or no reward. Faced with a request made from authority, or asked for help by someone, many people will respond favorably.

As an example, a survey of office workers in the United Kingdom was carried out for the InfoSecurity Europe 2004 conference. The survey found that a total of 71 percent were willing to reveal their passwords in exchange for a chocolate bar.[22] A large group (37 percent) of the workers was willing to reveal their passwords immediately, without needing any reward. A further 34 percent were made to reveal their passwords through the use of social engineering methods. For instance, the survey found that passwords could be placed in various categories. Popular categories included family names (15 percent), such as the name of a partner or child, the names of pets (8 percent), and the names of football teams (11 percent). This information meant that a few harmless questions about an individual's family life might give a 34 percent chance of identifying a password. Such odds could be improved further by also trying some of the most commonly used passwords, some of which include admin, password, God, love, money, and qwerty.

Social engineering tends to rely on a relatively small number of basic techniques. In general, these techniques rely on our innate fears and desires, including our fear of punishment, the need to be liked by others, the desire to be seen as helpful, and our tendency to respond to authority. Many of the methods used offline can also be used online, especially where direct, one-to-one communication can take place. As an example, a 2004 study by Gartner found that 1.78 million Americans had willingly provided credit card numbers, bank account PINs, and other information in response to fake e-mails.[23] The study also suggested that up to a million more people may also have been tricked without realizing it.

IDENTIFYING PHISHING E-MAILS

Phishing e-mails can be recognized by looking for common characteristics. The information and advice provided here is drawn from a number of sources, including Visa, the Anti-Phishing Working Group, Microsoft, Computerworld, and others.

Messages should be considered suspicious under certain circumstances:

- The message contains spelling and grammatical errors. This is because many phishing e-mails are written by people for whom English is a second language. Messages may also contain foreign slang or inappropriate words and phrases. For example, a message distributed across the United States might mention a "tap" instead of a "faucet."
- It is not clear who sent the message or where it came from.
- The message does not address you by name and contains no evidence of any relationship between you and the sender. A genuine message sent by a bank,

for example, would provide a reference number or part of your account number.

- The message asks for confidential information, such as a password. No reputable organization asks for this kind of information by e-mail.
- The message contains a link that you are asked to follow so that you can access your account. It is sometimes possible to detect a phishing attempt by checking if the link will take you to the correct location. This can be done by moving the mouse pointer above the link so that its destination can be displayed in the status bar at the bottom of the browser window. Note, however, that this method is not foolproof and will only detect the crudest phishing attempts. It is possible to create links that appear genuine and will stand up to a casual inspection of the kind described here. With this in mind, you should never use a link contained in an e-mail message to access an account or check confidential information.
- The message tries to force you into taking some kind of action. A typical ploy is threatening to suspend your account unless you verify certain details or log in within a time limit.

SAFETY AND PREVENTION

The following advice is drawn from a number of sources including Microsoft, the National Consumers League, the United States Computer Emergency Response Team (US-CERT), the American Bankers' Association, the Federal Trade Commission, and others.

BUSINESS USERS

- Ensure that company Web sites follow industry guidelines and standards concerning fraud. For instance, most financial organizations publish anti-fraud information for the public. Web sites also display contact information prominently so that customers can report problems.
- Stay up to date with phishing scams that may affect your organization. Regular "sweeps" of the Internet, newsgroups, and message boards should be carried out so that emerging threats can be identified early.
- Ensure that all incoming e-mail is scanned to remove phishing messages before they reach employees. This protects employees and reduces the chance of company information being leaked. It can also help to reduce virus and spyware infections.

INDIVIDUALS AND FAMILIES

- Whenever submitting confidential information, such as a credit card number, you should always make sure that you are using a secure site. This can be done by checking that the address shown by the browser signifies a *secure Web server*—secure addresses begin with https:// instead of http://. Secure Web sites can also be identified by the graphic of a small padlock that appears towards the bottom-right of the browser window. Figure 5.1 shows how the Firefox browser informs users that they are visiting a secure site, in this case PayPal.

Figure 5.1   The Padlock Denotes a Secure Web Site

- Consider installing antiphishing software. The functionality of Internet Explorer can be extended by adding specialized toolbars. Many toolbars can be downloaded free of charge, and several can be used to provide protection against phishing attempts. As an example, EarthLink provides a free toolbar with various features including a ScamBlocker tool, which can be obtained from www.earthlink.net/software/free/toolbar.
- If using Internet Explorer, consider moving to an alternative browser. Browsers such as Firefox are considered extremely secure and are available free of charge. A number of security add-ons are available that can be used to offer additional protection against phishing. Firefox is available from www.mozilla.com.
- Whichever browser you use, ensure that it is kept up to date and that the latest security fixes are installed.
- Remember to check online accounts and statements regularly. This may help to identify and deal with any attempt to defraud you.

If you are concerned because you have given out confidential information, the Anti-Phishing Working Group provides useful advice and information at: http://anti-phishing.org/consumer_recs2.htm.

- Report suspected fraud or other financial crimes related to the Internet via the Internet Crime Complaint Center (IC3), an organization operated by the FBI and the National White Collar Crime Center: www.ic3.gov.

FURTHER INFORMATION

Reading

The Honeynet Project & Research Alliance, 2005. *Know your Enemy: Phishing* [online]. The Honeynet Project & Research Alliance. Available at: http://www. honeynet.org/papers/phishing/.

Ollman, G., 2004. *The Phishing Guide: Understanding & Preventing Phishing Attacks* [online]. Next Generation Security Software Ltd. Available at: http://www. ngssoftware.com/papers/NISR-WP-Phishing.pdf.

Online

The Anti-Phishing Working Group provides news, information, and advice related to phishing. Phishing attempts can also be reported online: www.antiphishing.org.

Scamdex is a searchable database of e-mail scams: www.scamdex.com.

NoticeBored provides an annotated list of resources related to e-mail security: http://www.noticebored.com/html/email.html.

E-Mail Fraud

Fraud carried out via e-mail takes many different forms and has become so common that many people receive several fake e-mails every day. My own e-mail account receives a minimum of 10 such messages every day; on some occasions, I have received 30 or more messages in a single day.

Most of the frauds carried out by e-mail can also be worked via a Web site. Some can even be carried out by telephone, especially schemes that involve fake lotteries and raffles.

An exhaustive list of frauds that are carried out by e-mail is beyond the scope of this book. However, by describing some of the most common frauds, it is hoped that readers will be able to identify a broad range of cons, including any new variations that appear from time to time. Other sections provide additional guidance, such as how to identify suspicious e-mail messages.

ADVANCE FEE FRAUDS

In this type of fraud, victims are made to believe that they will achieve some kind of benefit by sending money to a con man. Typically, victims are told that they have won a prize in a national or international lottery. In order to receive the prize, the victim must pay a small fee to cover handling and shipping charges. Often, the victim is asked to send the fee to the lottery company's headquarters in Europe. Since the prize must travel from Europe, victims are also told that delivery may take several weeks. Convincing people that a long delivery time is necessary enables the con man to collect as many payments as possible before people start to become suspicious and contact the authorities. Of course, the prize is nonexistent, and after a matter of weeks, the con man will move to another location to begin the scheme all over again.

The same basic method tends to be used with a variety of incentives. However, no matter what the incentive, it is always chosen for its ability to convince victims to part with their money. Cash, jewelry, holidays, cars, and other expensive goods regularly feature in these lotteries

Occasionally, the message sent to the victim will claim that he has won a mystery prize from a lengthy list of items that appear to be very valuable. However, some of the items listed will be nothing more than inexpensive trinkets. For instance, a gold bracelet listed between a holiday cruise and a large screen TV may turn out to be made from a cheap, thin chain and worth only a dollar or so. Since the cost of claiming the bracelet will be many times more than its value, the con man will be perfectly happy to ship the prize. The aim of supplying a cheap prize is to cause confusion and make it difficult to prosecute the con man. After all, victims received a mystery prize from the list, as promised.

Other forms of advance fee fraud include scams based around foreign lotteries, money laundering, and charitable contributions.

FOREIGN LOTTERIES

This type of fraud operates in much same way as already described. Victims are contacted by e-mail and told that they have won a major cash prize in a recent lottery. In order to receive the prize, a processing fee is required, which may amount to hundreds, or even thousands, of dollars. Often, victims are persuaded to give their bank details to the con man in the expectation that the prize money will be wired into their accounts. Instead, the information is used to empty the victim's account or to charge fraudulent transactions to the victim.

In some cases, the people who operate these schemes will take great pains to avoid suspicion so that they can continue tricking people for as long as possible. They may rent offices in downtown office buildings, install multiple phone lines, hire secretaries to answer calls, and set up legitimate-looking Web sites. A suspicious person who chooses to investigate the company is likely to find it based in offices at prestigious location, with real staff and with credentials and references that seem completely authentic.

NIGERIAN 419 FRAUD

This fraud is often carried out by organized groups operating from Nigeria or elsewhere in West Africa. Occasionally, such groups will have accomplices located in Europe or in the United States. The *419 fraud* is based around an exciting scenario that draws victims into what they believe is a real-life adventure story.

The 419 fraud is named after the relevant section of the Nigerian Criminal Code.

An individual or a company receives an urgent e-mail message from an official of a foreign government. A huge sum of money needs to be transferred from abroad into the United States. In exchange for helping with the transfer, a commission amounting to millions of dollars will be paid. If action is not taken quickly, the money will be lost forever.

When the victim agrees to help, he becomes part of a complex plan to bring the money out of Africa. However, as the scheme progresses, various problems begin to surface. Bribes need to paid, special licenses or taxes are needed, and other operating expenses arise. For one reason or another, the government official does not have enough money to make any necessary payments, so the victim is asked to finance these parts of the venture.

From this point, the fraud can move in different directions. If the victim has been persuaded to supply the details of his bank account so that money can be sent or received electronically, the gang may decide to empty the account and end the deception. Alternatively, the gang may choose to stretch things out for as long as possible, continually inventing new expenses for the victim to pay. A third option involves convincing the victim to travel to Nigeria in order to carry out various tasks in person. When the victim arrives, the gang may use threats to force him to give access to his money. As well as threats of violence, they may also threaten to turn the victim over to the authorities for his part in the attempt to smuggle millions of dollars out of the country.

It has also been suggested that some victims have been held for ransom, sometimes for hundreds of thousands of dollars. For instance, in 2001, Josef Raca was tricked into traveling from Britain to South Africa supposedly to meet a group of Nigerian executives.[1] Upon arrival, he was kidnapped and ransomed for £20,000 (approximately $35,000). He was eventually freed by the kidnappers, who were arrested by the police when they attempted to collect the ransom. Even as early as 1997, a report from the U.S. Department of State[2] commented:

Since September 1995, at least eight Americans have been held against their will by these criminals in Lagos that have come to the attention of the U.S. Embassy. In 1996 the U.S. Embassy helped repatriate ten Americans who came to Lagos looking for their "pot of gold."[3]

Detailed information on 419 fraud can be found at: http://www.crimes-of-persuasion.com/Crimes/Business/nigerian.htm.

The involvement of organized gangs in this type of fraud brings with it a threat of violence that must be taken seriously. As an example, the U.S. Secret Service has stated:[4] "In June of 1995, an American was murdered in Lagos, Nigeria, while pursuing a 4–1–9 scam, and numerous other foreign nationals have been reported as missing." In addition, a 1997 report from the U.S. Department of Justice[5] said that 15 foreign executives, including one American, had been murdered in advance fee frauds over the preceding three years. A more recent case was reported in the international media at the end of 2004. George Makronalli, a Greek citizen, was kidnapped in South Africa and held for a ransom of $160,000. The ransom was not paid, and Makronalli's body was found by police a day later. Both arms and legs had been broken and he had been set on fire, probably while still alive.[6]

A variation on the type of advance fee fraud described here can involve contact being made by someone claiming to be a relative of a government minister, a wealthy businessperson, a lawyer, a doctor, or even an Arab sheik. Another variation involves the supposed source of the money, which may be a large lottery win, a forgotten bank account, money left by a relative who died during 9/11, money collected by overcharging the government for goods and services, and so on. The money may also be held in different forms, including bonds, shares, commodities (e.g., oil), gold, diamonds, and land. This is because asking the victim to collect bonds or deeds or to sign a contract makes it easier to persuade him to travel to Nigeria.

This kind of fraud is often successful because of the groundwork carried out by the perpetrators. For instance, members of the gang may meet with the victim a number of times, both in the United States and in Nigeria, to reassure him and gauge his mood. In addition, many of the claims made by the gang will be supported with large numbers of documents bearing authentic-looking official seals and signatures. Although many of these documents will be high-quality forgeries, many may be genuine, having been obtained through bribery or deception. Bribes may also provide access to a junior official or other person who can verify the authenticity of licenses, legal papers, and other official documents. A call to an accommodating official, bank manager, or lawyer may be all that is

---

RECOVERY FRAUD

In a fairly recent development called *recovery fraud,* some criminals have attempted to trick their former victims for a second time by posing as Nigerian police officers investigating the first swindle. Victims are told that it may be possible for their money to be recovered if they are willing to pay a fee.

needed to dispel a victim's doubts and make him willing to part with his money.

THE EXTENT OF THE PROBLEM

As mentioned earlier, it is difficult to estimate annual losses around the world resulting from some forms of crime because of the reluctance of some victims to come forward. In addition, very few estimates are available for advance fee fraud, and many of those published are more than a decade old. Furthermore, conflicting estimates are sometimes published, increasing confusion. All of this means that the following figures should be treated with caution, since they are unlikely to provide a completely accurate and valid view of the situation.

In terms of global losses, the U.S. Secret Service estimated total losses[7] over the period 1989–1999 to be in the region of $5 billion.[8] This is a difficult figure to verify, since relatively little data is available for analysis. However, figures from around the world suggest that advance fee fraud is a serious problem that is growing at an alarming rate.

With regard to the United States, a number of conflicting figures have been published. Some examples include the following:

- The FBI reported that victims of advance fee fraud suffered an average loss of $5,575 in 2001[9] and $3,864 in 2002.[10] The FBI's 2002 figures also showed that the number of complaints received had tripled since 2001, as had total losses, growing from $17 million to $54 million.
- An estimate that has been quoted widely in the media claims that losses in the United States amount to $1 million every day.[11] However, it seems that the original source of this figure is unknown.
- In 2005, the average loss from 419 fraud was estimated at $6,937 by the National Consumers League. Other advance fee frauds resulted in an average loss of $1,426.[12] However, an estimate from the FBI places the average loss from 419 fraud in 2005 at $3,000.[13]

It is also difficult to obtain realistic estimates for other countries. However, the available information suggests that average losses are similar to those experienced in the United States. Some examples of losses experienced by other countries include:

- In Canada, Phone Busters received 167 complaints over the period from January 2004 to September 2004. Victims lost a total of approximately $4.2 million.[14]
- A 2004 estimate suggests that annual losses in South Africa are in the region of R100 million[15] (approximately $16.5 million).
- In the United Kingdom, the National Criminal Intelligence Service (NCIS) reported that 150 people were defrauded for a total of £8.4 million, an average loss of £56,675,[16] or almost $100,000. Total losses each year could be in the region of £150 million, or approximately $262 million.[17]

BLACK MONEY

A type of advance fee fraud associated with 419 schemes involves a new twist on money laundering. A large sum of money has been contaminated in some way and needs to be cleaned using special chemicals. Victims are offered a share of the money in exchange for financing the purchase of the chemicals that may cost thousands of dollars. Of course, the contaminated money does not exist, nor do the special cleaning chemicals.

In order to make the fraud more convincing, victims are sometimes given a special demonstration. A briefcase containing wads of black paper is shown to the victim, who is told that each piece of paper is really a bank note. One of the pieces of paper is sprayed with a special chemical and is transformed into a crisp bank note within just a few seconds. In reality, the black paper has been replaced by a real bank note, thanks to a simple sleight of hand trick. Convinced that the black money really exists, victims part with sums of $50,000 or more.[18]

THE MOTIVE BEHIND 419 FRAUD

Although the primary motivation behind any kind of fraud is normally a desire for money, 419 schemes appear to have become an important part of Nigeria's economy and are perhaps responsible for supporting millions of its people. This should not be taken to suggest that the Nigerian government supports or condones fraud, merely that the sums of money involved in 419 frauds are so large that they are capable of affecting a nation's entire financial system. For instance, it has been claimed that advance fee fraud generates $5 billion per year in foreign currency for Nigeria.[19] This represents a significant sum when compared to Nigeria's annual exports, which total approximately $34 billion.[20] The importance of this money is increased further because foreign currency is vital for international trade, especially with the United States and Europe.

The idea that 419 fraud may help to support a part of Nigeria's population is not new. The 419 Coalition's Web site[21] was launched in 1996 to provide people with information about advance fee fraud. Since its launch, the site has received more than a million visits by those seeking advice. Of interest on the site is a discussion of a 1997 report from a Nigerian newspaper that implies that up to 85 percent of the population may be benefiting from advance fee fraud directly or indirectly. The discussion disputes this figure, suggesting instead that perhaps only 1–3 percent of the population may be knowingly and directly benefiting from 419 fraud. However, the author acknowledges that even such a small proportion of the population could amount to several million people.[22] It is also acknowledged that 419 fraud is regarded by some as one of Nigeria's largest industries, possibly its third largest after petroleum and petroleum products.

SCAM BAITING

Scam baiting (sometimes known as *reverse scamming*) has developed in response to the huge increase in 419 scams over the past few years. Essentially, scam baiting involves trying to turn the tables on those who operate 419 frauds. The main aim of scam baiting is to cause the gangs behind 419 fraud to waste as much time, effort, and money as possible. Although this is motivated partly by a desire for revenge, it also serves to prevent the gangs from going after other victims.

Scam baiting has also developed a competitive element where scam baiters try to outdo each other in terms of humiliating the gangs. The winners of these informal contests are those who are able to trick the most money from their chosen gang, or who are able to trick gang members into the most ridiculous situations.

In order to gain the admiration of their peers, scam baiters must provide evidence of the deceptions they carry out. In many cases, this will involve publishing photographs, video clips, receipts, and other materials on a Web site. This humiliates the gang further, especially since most sites ensure that gang members are clearly identified and publicly ridiculed.

SCAM BAITING

A number of Web sites carry humorous accounts of successful scam baiting. Please be aware that some sites may contain material that some readers find offensive.

Scamorama (http://www.scamorama.com)
Happy Scrappy (http://www.happyscrappy.com/cp/scam.html)
Mugu.info (http://mugu.info)
PopSubCulture (http://www.popsubculture.com/pop/bio_project/nigeria-fraud.html)
419 Eater (http://www.419eater.com)
Ebola Monkey Man (http://www.ebolamonkeyman.com)

OTHER E-MAIL FRAUDS

Many of the frauds that make use of Web sites and the postal system are easily adapted so that they can be carried out via e-mail. As mentioned earlier, this makes it impractical to describe more than a handful of common swindles.

CHARITY AND DISASTER RELIEF FRAUDS

Whenever a major disaster takes place, it is only a matter of hours before criminals try to take advantage. Online frauds related to disaster relief have appeared after major incidents around the world, including 9/11 and Hurricane Katrina.

Typically, millions of e-mails are sent out asking for donations. Following the link given in the e-mail message takes Internet users to a Web site that appears to belong to a genuine charity. The site asks people to make a donation by credit card, but anyone who does risks becoming a victim of identity theft.

Although criminals carry out many frauds, terrorist groups have been linked with some of the largest and most organized. Organized crime groups from around the world have also been linked with major frauds related to charitable donations.

CHAIN E-MAIL AND PETITIONS

Many different *chain e-mails* are circulating the Internet at any given time. Some of these e-mails rely on fear to convince people to distribute the message to friends and relatives. Many include stories of how death and misfortune befell those who failed to pass the message on. Other messages promise good luck, financial rewards, or even improved health if the message is forwarded to 10, 15, or 20 contacts.

The AOL Death Threat chain e-mail[23] is a fairly typical example of using fear to distribute a message, and a number of variations on this basic theme have appeared since the mid- to late 1990s. It is worth noting that many people are taken in by such messages and that many suffer genuine distress. Presumably, a major factor is the source of the message; if it comes from a close friend or relative, it is likely to be taken more seriously.

Forwarded Message:
Subj: Re: (don't open in front of parents) (sorry guys)
Date: 98–04–25 00:29:48 EDT
<< Five people actually got killed by not sending this piece of mail. The creator of this mail has a program that will track down everyone who sent this mail and whoever that didn't send it will DIE DIE DIE DIE DIE DIE DIE DIE DIE DIE because this program can actually track down your address.
Send this to 15 people within the next fifteen minutes or you will die die die die die, what do you have to lose? Your life? >>

Perhaps the most common types of chain e-mail involve hoaxes such as the *dying child hoax*, in which people are told of a terminally ill child whose dying wish is to spread a message telling people to live life to the fullest. As an added incentive, people are told that the American Cancer Society will donate three cents to the child's care and recovery plan for every copy of the message sent. Obviously, the child does not exist and neither does the American Cancer Society's offer. In any case, such an offer would be impossible to live up to because there would be no way of monitoring how many e-mail messages were sent and no way for the American Cancer Society to control costs. Although some of the details—like the child's name—change from time to time, messages of this kind regularly appear around the world.

Other common hoaxes are related to computer security issues, such as viruses, hacking, and identity theft. New *virus hoaxes* appear almost daily and can spread very quickly if even a fairly small number of people become panicked. Many virus hoaxes begin as jokes that people start to take seriously, or result from simple misunderstandings. As an example, when people received an e-mail message about the sulfnbk.exe virus, they were told that receipt of the message meant that their computers had been infected accidentally. The only solution was to delete a file from their computers manually and instructions were given on how to do so. However, there was no virus and the file to be deleted was a legitimate part of Windows. It has been speculated[24] that the message originated from a well-meaning computer user who incorrectly attributed problems with his computer system to a virus disguised as a Windows file. The warning message sent out was a genuine, but misguided, attempt to help others.

The methods used to distribute chain e-mail are also used to encourage participation in online protests. Scare stories, such as alleged plans to tax e-mail messages, are used to start e-mail writing campaigns or online petitions. E-mail writing campaigns can generate huge amounts of Internet traffic directed towards a specific person or organization, while online petitions can record tens of thousands of electronic "signatures." Given that many of the causes promoted are fake, this represents a major abuse of the goodwill, time, and effort of many Internet users. In addition, it contributes to the ever-growing problem of spam.

Online petitions have become so popular over the last few years that special sites have appeared that allow the creation of a petition within minutes. Sites such as Petition Spot, iPetitions, Gopetition[25] and others provide a range of free services allowing users to host, promote, and manage their petitions.

Some of the ways in which online petitions have started to be used raise a number of interesting ethical issues, especially with regard to whether the public is being deceived and, if so, whether this is acceptable in the pursuit of political or commercial goals. For instance, Internet petitions are beginning to be used to challenge the character and credentials of candidates for public office. In 2004, various online methods, including at least one petition,[26] were used to question Senator John Kerry's record during the Vietnam War and on other, related issues. Companies have also started to use online petitions in their advertising campaigns. For example, Carlsberg—the official beer of the Irish World Cup soccer squad—used an online petition in 2002 to generate "... brand awareness and hype both online and offline for the Irish World Cup campaign."[27] The campaign was considered highly successful; at one point, a person was signing the petition every 27 seconds.

SAFETY AND PREVENTION

Experts in computer security tend to offer a single, simple rule regarding online fraud: If it looks too good to be true, it probably is. As might be expected, there is even a Web site based around this rule at: www.lookstoogoodtobetrue.com.

BUSINESS USERS

E-mail fraud of the kind described in this chapter is unlikely to affect business users.

INDIVIDUALS AND FAMILIES

The rule offered by security experts encourages a healthy level of skepticism that might become extremely useful on receiving the news of a huge win in a foreign lottery, or when offered millions of dollars in exchange for helping someone smuggle a fortune out of Nigeria. Asking awkward questions may well save thousands of dollars. For instance, the author of a Nigerian phishing scam might be hard-pressed to offer convincing answers to questions like these: Who recommended me to you? If you received a personal recommendation, why don't you know my name? What makes you think I might want to become involved in an international money laundering scheme that might see me go to prison for a very long time?

Some further advice may be taken from Stanley Weyman's (1855–1928) *A Gentleman of France,* where a character is advised to "… trust no one, suspect everyone, fear all things." While this may seem a little paranoid, it may sometimes be good advice in relation to the Internet.

FURTHER INFORMATION

Reading

Arata, M., 2004. *Preventing Identity Theft For Dummies.* Hoboken, NJ: Hungry Minds Inc.

Online

TechRepublic maintains a large database of articles, white papers and other documents related to e-mail fraud. Note that free membership may be required to access some items: http://whitepapers.techrepublic.com.com/SECURITY/Intrusion+-+Tampering/Spam+-+E-mail+Fraud+-+Phishing/.

The U.S. Department of Justice provides a basic guide to Internet fraud: http://www.internetfraud.usdoj.gov.

419 Eater is devoted to scam baiting and offers numerous links to accounts of scam baiting: www.419eater.com.

Auctions and Other Forms of Fraud

There are a bewildering number of ways in which criminals use the Internet to defraud others. At one level, a seller might misrepresent an item in an online auction in order to cheat a buyer out of a few extra dollars. At another, a carefully managed stock fraud can damage an entire industry, resulting in losses that can be measured in billions of dollars.

Online fraud also ruins the lives of some victims. Fake adoption agencies and dating agencies can cause emotional harm that damages relationships or leads to problems such as depression. Stock fraud can wipe out people's life savings, leaving their future plans, such as retirement, in chaos. Ultimately, some frauds, such as selling counterfeit medicines, even have the potential to kill.

There are many ways to avoid fraud that are simple, effective, and completely free. Changing to a new browser or using an electronic payment service when buying goods are just two examples of inexpensive measures available to almost all Internet users. It was also mentioned in an earlier chapter that experts in computer security advise people to keep a simple rule in mind: If it looks too good to be true, it probably is. Although some people may feel that such a rule patronizes Internet users, this is not the intention behind it. The rule is meant to remind users to be suspicious of offers that seem overly generous. It is also meant to encourage people to ask questions both of themselves and of the people they are dealing with.

AUCTION FRAUD

Since the birth of eBay in 1995, online auctions have become one of the most popular activities on the Internet. Although many other companies run online auctions, eBay is arguably the best known and most successful of all. The company's own figures for 2005[1] show that it is active in 33 countries and has 168 million registered users, 79 million of which are in the United States. In addition, there are approximately 336,000 eBay stores hosted on sites around the world, with 193,000 located on the U.S. site.

EBay's importance to the Internet is such that many people rely on it as a primary source of income. There are more than 724,000 professional sellers in the United States, and it is estimated that an additional 1.5 million people supplement their incomes via auction sales. The company has had a similar impact in many other countries and has been especially successful in the European Union. In the United Kingdom, for example, eBay's site accounts for 10 percent of all the time users spend on the Internet, and around 50,000 people earn a living from online auctions. As companies like eBay have grown, attempts to defraud buyers and sellers have also increased. In 1997, the Federal Trade Commission recorded 107 complaints regarding auction fraud.[2] By 1999, this had grown to 10,700 complaints, and to 85,000 by 2005.[3] In 1997, customers lost an average of $293 to auction fraud. By 2005, the average loss had grown to $1,155.

Organizations such as the FBI and the National Consumers League report that the most common complaints received about Internet fraud concern online auctions. For instance, in 2001, the FBI reported that 64 percent of complaints received by the Internet Fraud Complaint Center involved online auctions.[4] However, other figures suggest a more serious situation. For instance, a report from eMarketer covering the same period suggested that auction fraud accounted for 87 percent of all online crime. The National Consumers League[5] published a similar figure a few years later, reporting that online auctions accounted for 89 percent of the complaints they received in 2003.

Most auction fraud can be divided into three categories: nonexistent goods, misrepresentation, and shill bidding.

Perhaps the most common type of auction fraud occurs when people pay for goods that are never received. Until quite recently, it was relatively simple to commit this kind of fraud because it was easy to obtain facilities, such as bank accounts and mailing addresses (such as a PO Box), with little risk of being subjected to stringent checks by banks and other organizations. Following 9/11 and other events around the world, a renewed focus on security has made it difficult for some groups to carry out auction fraud. For instance, a number of countries have introduced new rules dealing with money transfers and the opening of bank accounts in order to combat terrorism and organized crime. However, it appears that these rules have also had the secondary effect of discouraging minor domestic fraud. Presumably, this is the result of making it difficult for people in the United States, the European Union, and other countries to cover their electronic tracks.

The growth of electronic payment services, such as PayPal and WorldPay, has also had an impact on this type of fraud. As these services have matured, they have developed into a convenient and secure way of sending money around the world. PayPal, for example, offers a range of services intended to protect buyers against fraud, including PayPal Buyer Protection, a scheme that covers certain eBay purchases.

Online *escrow* services have also developed into an effective way of avoiding auction fraud. Services such as Escrow.com act as an intermediary in a transaction between a buyer and a seller. The escrow service holds the buyer's payment until the buyer reports that the goods have been received. The payment is then sent to the seller and the transaction is complete. Escrow services provide protection for both parties involved in the transaction: Buyers receive their goods and have time to check them before authorizing payment, while sellers are assured of receiving payment and are protected from credit card and payment fraud.

However, escrow services are not without their problems and are not completely immune to fraud. A number of incidents have been reported where criminals have established fake escrow services and then advertised goods for sale via online auctions. As an example, online newsletter *AuctionBytes*[6] reported a story where a criminal copied information about cars advertised for sale and listed them for auction on eBay Motors. When an interested buyer took part in an auction, the criminal posed as the owner of the car and negotiated a sale. After agreeing the sale, the buyer was directed to send payment via an online escrow service called Escrowoncall.net. It was eventually found that the escrow service was fake and had been created by the criminal as part of the fraud.

Since 2005, a variation on this kind of fraud has become common. Operating from locations that include Hong Kong, Singapore, and Germany, sellers offer a wide range of goods at bargain prices. However, for various reasons, some of which may be true, the sellers claim that they are unable to accept payment via PayPal or check. Instead, buyers are advised to pay by money transfer, sometimes directly into a given seller's bank account. The buyer is persuaded to use a service such as Western Union by the promise that the goods will be dispatched more quickly. As might be expected, the buyer never receives the goods and has little chance of recovering his money.

The second category of auction fraud involves misrepresenting goods. At the most basic level, a seller may exaggerate in his description of an item, perhaps making it newer or in better condition than it really is. In more serious cases, organized groups may advertise counterfeit goods, or sell products that are faulty or dangerous. Sometimes, sellers will describe their items in a way that is technically accurate but still misleading. This provides a way for the seller to argue against giving a refund. By taking advantage of the fact that many people dislike confrontation, the seller can be confident that a large proportion of his customers will not take the matter further, allowing him to keep their money.

The third category of common auction frauds involves using an accomplice to manipulate prices. A *shill* is a person who bids at an auction in order

> **URBAN LEGENDS ABOUT ONLINE AUCTIONS**
>
> Over the years, many of the stories associated with the advertisements found in the back of old comic books and elsewhere have made the transition to the Internet. Some of the most common tales of misrepresented goods include:
>
> - People buying a cigarette lighter with a fancy case actually receive a book of matches. A related story tells of a windproof cigarette lighter that is guaranteed to work in all weather and turns out to be a blowtorch.
> - A novelty nutcracker turns out to be a house brick.
> - A lifetime supply of toothpicks is a pocketknife for whittling wood.
> - A universal hands-free kit for any cell phone is an elastic band.

to raise the price of the item. Sometimes, a seller will create several fake auction accounts so that he can control how much items sell for by placing his own bids. Organized gangs also manipulate auctions in this way to ensure that they achieve the highest prices for their goods. Artificially inflating prices can also help to convince genuine buyers that the item they are interested in is more valuable than first thought.

SAFETY AND PREVENTION

The information and advice provided here is drawn from a number of sources, including Bocij (2004), Yaukey (2002), eBay, FraudWatch International, the FBI, and others.

BUSINESS USERS

Auction fraud of the kind described in this chapter is unlikely to affect business users.

INDIVIDUALS AND FAMILIES

- Be suspicious of low-priced, high-value items, such as jewelry and electronics. If several items are being sold, this may indicate an attempt at fraud.
- Check the feedback given to buyers and sellers. Although it is possible to fake feedback, it is relatively rare and easy to spot. Sellers with zero feedback should be checked carefully, perhaps by asking for a telephone number that can be called.
- Some payment methods offer built-in protection against fraud. PayPal and many credit card companies operate schemes that will refund money lost to auction fraud. Where possible, take advantage of such schemes since they are normally free to use.
- Be cautious if asked to send your payment by wire transfer, especially if the seller is located in Nigeria or other countries known for auction fraud.

- Be suspicious of auctions that begin and end on a weekend. This is because they may have been timed to coincide with the period when customer support is normally limited, making it difficult to cancel a check, stop a credit card payment, or contact the auction company.
- Be cautious of sellers who use free e-mail addresses or who are trading from outside the country.
- Consider using an escrow services for high-value items. Only use a service recommended by as trusted source, such as eBay.
- There are many ways to check if sellers are trustworthy or not. For example, a number of Web sites publish blacklists of people and companies known to carry out auction fraud. Other organizations, such as a local Better Business Bureau, may also have an up-to-date knowledge of companies engaged in online auction fraud. A search engine can sometimes provide a great deal of information on a seller, such as whether any complaints have been posted to message boards, newsgroups, or Web sites.

Commercial Business Intelligence has published a report that describes auction fraud in depth. Although a little dated, the report contains some interesting figures and offers advice on avoiding auction fraud. The report can be downloaded from http://www.cbintel.com/AuctionFraudReport.pdf.

OTHER ONLINE FRAUDS

The list of frauds that can be carried out via e-mail is almost endless. For this reason, it is only possible to cover a handful of the most common (and serious) schemes. In addition, the scope of the discussion is limited to how the Internet, and especially e-mail, are used to facilitate fraudulent acts.

It is worth noting that most of the frauds discussed here exploit the misfortune and sadness of others. In effect, the criminals behind these types of e-mail fraud have chosen to victimize some of the most vulnerable people in society, adding another burden to those already suffering with illness, loneliness, or poverty.

It is also important to note that many legitimate companies coexist with the villainous organizations described here. Not every online pharmacy, dating agency, or employment agency is operated by thieves. Since the material presented here focuses on the most dishonest firms, it is easy to forget that reputable companies are just as common.

MEDICINES AND CURES

Perhaps one of the cruelest e-mail frauds is based on offering false hope to those suffering from illnesses, such as diabetes or cancer. Some companies offer miracle cures for diseases that are normally seen as incurable. Diabetes, for example, is treatable through measures such as dietary control, medications, and insulin injections. However, even with recent medical advances, it is not yet possible to cure diabetes. Despite this, some people—and companies—claim that their products will lead to a complete cure for just a few dollars a day.

Perhaps understanding that claims about having a cure are simply too outrageous for anyone but the most desperate to believe, some people take a somewhat different approach. Instead of using the word "cure," for example, their messages may talk about reversing an illness or controlling the root causes of the illness. In the case of diabetes, potential customers might be told that the product being promoted will allow them to normalize or control their blood sugar. The idea of a possible cure is put across more subtly, perhaps by including testimonials from satisfied customers that mention how some have been able to reduce—or even stop—other, prescribed medications or insulin injections. In order to make the product even more attractive, other health benefits may be attributed to it. As an example, common conditions that accompany diabetes include hypertension (high blood pressure), high cholesterol levels, and obesity.[7] This means that the description of a diabetes remedy may mention secondary benefits that include reducing blood pressure, lowering cholesterol, and promoting weight loss.

Making scientific claims about a product provides another way of promoting a miracle cure. Specific approaches include citing obscure medical studies, quoting dubious statistics, using complex scientific terms, including graphs and diagrams, publishing testimonials from medics or scientists, and claiming links with respected organizations.

The products dispatched to customers are also worth some discussion. Some customers may be sent medications that are nothing more than placebos, neither helping nor harming them. Others may be sent medications based on herbal or traditional remedies. While most herbal remedies can be considered harmless, others may have potentially dangerous interactions with other drugs. St. John's Wort, for example, is used in many herbal remedies but may interact with a variety of medicines, including antidepressants, anticoagulants, and oral contraceptives.[8]

None of this should be taken to suggest that herbal remedies and alternative treatments must be considered worthless. The questionable products mentioned here mimic the way in which some legitimate products are marketed, sometimes making it difficult to tell them apart. For instance, where a reputable company might use a genuine scientific study to support its claims, a dishonest company might simply invent any figures needed, leaving it to the customer to determine the truth and which company to trust.

Advertisements for *online pharmacies* present another problem for those suffering from illness. Although there are many legitimate companies operating via the Internet, it can be tempting to respond to an e-mail advertisement that offers essential medications at low cost. Once again, the people most vulnerable to exploitation are those who live in poverty and those without adequate medical cover.

Many people try to reduce the cost of their medications by importing them from Canada or further afield. This is because medicines bought from Canadian online pharmacies are an average of 24 percent cheaper than those from American online pharmacies.[9] As an example, *CBC News*[10] reported in early 2006 that the price of 180 Tamoxifen tablets, a medicine used to treat breast cancer, was $380.97 in the United States, compared with $102.90 from a Canadian online pharmacy. Such a saving supports the view that some people might be able to save over $1,000 a year on each medication needed.[11] In turn, this explains why the annual trade in imported medicines is estimated at more than $1 billion annually.[12]

However, while medicines bought from reputable online pharmacies are perfectly safe, those bought from other sources may turn out to be fake or of poor quality. Counterfeit medicines, for example, tend to be made as cheaply as possible, meaning that they may have no active ingredients or could be contaminated with other substances.

Disreputable online suppliers may also be willing to provide medicines without a prescription, or might recommend alternative products that do not need to be prescribed. Often, such alternative products will be based on herbal remedies. Allowing customers to buy medicines without a prescription runs the risk that they might harm themselves by experimenting with dosages, trying other medicines, and so on. Recommending alternative products may also be unsafe since the new drug may interact with other medicines or have unexpected side effects.

ADOPTION FRAUD

People seeking to adopt a child are vulnerable to exploitation in several ways.

One of the most common frauds is similar in operation to the 419 scams discussed earlier. The fraud begins with the criminal gathering information about people interested in adopting a child. E-mail addresses and other details are often found by searching appropriate newsgroups, message boards, and Web sites. Potential victims are sent an e-mail message supposedly from a parent wishing to place a young child in a new home. A sense of urgency is created by claiming that the child must be adopted quickly because the parent is seriously ill or the family is living in poverty. Sometimes, the parent claims that the child is a survivor of some kind of disaster, such as an earthquake or famine. As victims become drawn into the deception, they may be sent pictures of the child or personal messages allegedly written by the child. Eventually, the adoptive parents start to receive requests for money. Small sums are needed to buy food, medicines, and other essential items. Larger sums are usually justified by claiming that they will help to speed up the adoption process, for example by paying various fees.

Some adoption agents and surrogate mothers carry out similar frauds. In general, each scheme begins by searching the Internet for potential victims. Once one or more victims have been identified, initial contact is made by e-mail.

Bogus adoption agents may offer victims special rates or claim that they are able to accelerate the adoption process. Occasionally, they may claim to have found a child who is a perfect match to the adoptive parents. In order to make his claims more convincing, the agent may even supply the adoptive parents with photographs and other fake documents, such as a birth certificate. Each step of the adoption process will involve a variety of fees that must be paid before any progress is possible. The fraud ends when it is no longer possible to put off a meeting between the adoptive parents and other people, such as the child. However, even at such a relatively early stage of the process, the criminal may have received tens of thousands of dollars, especially if an introduction fee has been charged for finding a suitable child.

A typical example of this kind of fraud is described in a blog owned by Laura Christianson[13] called Exploring Adoption. In one entry, she describes the case of a woman who used the Internet to advertise her services to couples wanting to adopt a child. The woman claimed that she could put couples in touch with birth mothers wanting to have their babies adopted in exchange for a $200 fee. Over a period of more than two years, the woman received money from hundreds of couples across the United States, including people located in California, New York, Utah, Texas, and Florida. None of the couples received the promised introduction.

Birth mothers may also attempt to defraud adoptive parents by offering a child to them in exchange for a fee. Usually the birth mother will have no intention of giving the baby to the adoptive parents, and the same child may be offered to a number of different couples. Since the agreement made with the adoptive parents is likely to be illegal, couples may be reluctant to report the deception. In some cases, the birth mother and the child may only exist within the Internet, having been created through carefully worded e-mail messages, fake photographs, and other methods.

A number of factors, including new regulations and the increased sophistication of Internet users, mean that adoption fraud is becoming more difficult to carry out. For example, stronger regulation in the United States and elsewhere makes it fairly easy to identify fake adoption agents and agencies by checking business licenses and other credentials. Internet users are also more alert to suspicious behavior, such as a birth mother being reluctant to deal with other people, like an attorney or adoption agent.

MAIL-ORDER BRIDES

Although the material that follows concentrates on dating agencies, much of it is also relevant to other services including lonely-hearts groups and Internet dating sites.

Throughout the United States and Europe, men seeking companionship sometimes look abroad to countries such as Thailand, the Russian Federation, Colombia, and the Philippines. In many cases, specialized dating agencies are used to find potential partners and arrange initial introductions via e-mail and other methods. Some agencies also help to organize foreign trips for individuals or groups so that clients can meet promising companions in person. If a couple decides to marry, the agency may also be able to help with visa applications, travel, and other arrangements.

LONELY-HEARTS COLUMNS

Sometimes potential victims are chosen because they have posted an advertisement on a dating Web site or have created a profile on a message board dealing with dating. In these cases, the same basic approach is used: An unexpected e-mail arrives from a woman who claims to have seen the profile or advertisement. Touched by what she read, she decided to contact him by e-mail so that could learn more about him.

The risk of Internet dating fraud is recognized in information issued by the U.S. Department of State Bureau of Consular Affairs to citizens planning to travel to the Russian Federation:

The U.S. Embassy receives reports almost every day of fraud committed against U.S. citizens by Internet correspondents professing love and romantic interest. Typically, the Russian correspondent asks the U.S. citizen to send money or credit card information for living expenses, travel expenses, or "visa costs." The anonymity of the Internet means that the U.S. citizen cannot be sure of the real name, age, marital status, nationality, or even gender of the correspondent. Several citizens' report losing thousands of dollars through such scams.[14]

The potential for fraud exists throughout the client's involvement with the agency. From the very start, a joining fee may only provide access to a handful of records describing women who are genuinely seeking partners. This is because the agency's database may consist of thousands of outdated or fake records. In some cases, records may even be created to match a client's requirements so that the agency can charge additional fees. Once an introduction has been made, the client may be sent photographs or videos via e-mail. There is, of course, no guarantee that any such photographs are of the person the client is in contact with. In fact, the client may come to learn that he was never in contact with a woman at all; his e-mail and instant messaging conversations were held with a man, or a group of men.

Even if the photographs show the woman the client is actually in contact with, they may have been altered to make her appear more attractive. For instance, one Internet agency[15] warns that photographs may have been taken several years ago or that sometimes "the photo has been taken in a professional photographic studio and is therefore very flattering and not indicative of day to day reality." The agency also warns of pictures showing a closed-mouth smile since they "... can sometimes be a way of hiding gold or missing teeth."

As a relationship develops via e-mail and instant messaging, requests for money may be received. A relative may be seriously ill or the money may be needed to buy a computer so that the relationship can continue. The potential bride may also ask for money to buy an airline ticket so that a meeting can be arranged. As a precaution, some people may choose to send an airline ticket instead of money. However, it is often possible to claim a refund on a ticket or sell it to someone else.

An e-mail relationship may also provide a way to collect information that can be used for extortion. Although most fraud of this type is likely to be carried out on a small scale, this may change as organized crime takes more of an interest in the Internet. For instance, there is evidence that the Russian mafia is already involved in Internet dating fraud, as well as other Internet-related crime.[16]

If they are not already involved in these areas, organized crime groups may also become interested in other activities related to Internet dating fraud, such as *visa fraud* and *human trafficking*. This might provide many new criminal opportunities, for example a prostitution ring might use its involvement in Internet dating to recruit sex workers.

EMPLOYMENT FRAUD

Fake recruitment agencies use various ploys to collect fees from potential job candidates. Perhaps the most common fraud is charging a joining or administrative fee to new clients. Various inducements are offered to encourage payment of the fee. Clients may be told that the agency has a perfect job for them but can only supply details after the fee has been received. In countries where unemployment is high, the incentive to pay may be a guaranteed job. If the target group is made up of housebound people, such as the elderly or disabled, the incentive may involve work that can be carried out from home.

Schemes offering people the chance to work from home have existed for decades and have deceived thousands—if not millions—of people around the world. Figures from the National Consumers League[17] show that the third most common type of Internet fraud reported in 2000 was related to work-from-home schemes. Such schemes accounted for 2 percent of all complaints received by the organization. In general, the initial contact with victims was through Web sites (84 percent), e-mail (10 percent), and newsgroups (4 percent). By 2005, work-from-home schemes had become the seventh most common type of Internet fraud and accounted for only 1 percent of all complaints.[18] However, the average loss suffered by victims grew from $412 in 2000 to $1,785 in 2005. It is also worth noting that the use of e-mail to contact victims increased to 25 percent, while the use of Web sites decreased to 75 percent.

DIPLOMA MILLS

There are many different types of employment fraud and not all are perpetrated by questionable employment agencies. Those looking for work sometimes exaggerate in their C.V.s, hoping to gain an advantage over any competitors. However, some people go further by buying fake qualifications from *diploma mills* or *degree mills*. Diploma mills are universities that provide diplomas for little or no study. There are also other companies who can provide authentic-looking diplomas and transcripts from nonexistent universities, or who are able to produce counterfeit diplomas from genuine, prestigious universities.

Many diploma mills provide a range of additional services that are intended to make their degrees appear more authentic. For example, some offer a verification service that allows a suspicious human resource manager to check a prospective employee's academic record. Some diploma mills also produce merchandise, such as rings and coffee mugs, that add to the illusion of legitimacy being projected.

Faced with various pressures, such as competition for jobs, it is understandable that some people may feel forced into buying a fake degree. When even senior politicians are found to hold degrees from diploma mills,[19] it should not be surprising to learn that diploma mills represent a multimillion dollar industry. For instance, in 2003 it was estimated that there were more than 400 diploma mills and 300 counterfeit diploma Web sites in operation.[20] In addition, sales of fake diplomas were estimated at $500 million annually.

Many of today's work-from-home schemes are advertised under new names to reflect the influence of the Internet. Although ads may use terms such as teleworking, telecommuting, virtual offices, remote working, and outsourcing, they are still referring to the same swindles that have been used for decades.

Some of the most common work-from-home frauds involve the modern equivalent of *envelope stuffing*. This type of work used to involve mailing out hundreds of letters every week. The letters would contain several leaflets, each advertising a particular service or product. Joining the scheme meant paying a special administration fee in exchange for a starter pack. Each worker also had to buy or create a mailing list containing details of prospective customers. Of course, the company could usually provide a suitable list for a fee. Workers also had to bear all postage and stationery costs, including the cost of the leaflets. In return for their efforts, a commission would be promised for every reply received in response to the mailing. Invariably, the leaflets mailed out would include one offering people the chance to work from home.

Most *envelope-stuffing* schemes enable the companies behind them to generate money in several ways. Apart from charging an administration fee, a company can make profits by selling mailing lists and stationery to the workers. It may also provide a printing service for leaflets, generating large profits by recommending that workers buy leaflets in bulk. Alternatively, it may receive a commission in exchange for recommending a particular printing company to workers. The replies collected by workers allow the company to create mailing lists that can be sold repeatedly. Before selling them to others, the company may use the lists itself to recruit new workers. This effectively makes the lists almost worthless to other buyers. While companies have several ways of generating money, workers are seldom able to make a living from envelope-stuffing schemes because operating expenses are simply too high for them to be able to make any profit.

On the Internet, the electronic equivalent of an envelope-stuffing scheme relies on e-mail instead of the postal system. Mailing lists are replaced by collections of e-mail addresses on compact disc or DVD, while leaflets are replaced by Web sites hosted by the company behind the scheme for a monthly fee. The administration fee is sometimes replaced by the requirement to buy an e-book containing instructions and other information. In addition, instead of collecting the names and addresses of potential customers, workers gather e-mail addresses so that new e-mailing lists can be created.

Another common work-from-home fraud advertised via the Internet is based on assembling items for sale in large stores. As well as paying an administration fee, workers are made to buy raw materials and assembly kits from the company. For some products, workers may also need to buy special equipment. For instance, a sewing machine will be needed to make ties, baby clothes, and similar items. Some companies ask workers to produce a sample that the company will evaluate for a fee. Invariably, the sample will not be of acceptable quality, leaving the worker with a batch of raw materials that have been paid for but will never be used and allowing the company to retain any fees paid to it.

Assuming a worker is accepted by the company, money is earned by producing items and selling them back to the company at a small profit. However, while the worker is required to buy materials from the company, the company is not obliged to buy the finished products. If an excuse is needed, the company is likely to argue that the product is of unacceptable quality, no matter how well made it is. Even if the company buys the finished product, workers are likely to find that they are earning only a few cents per hour because their expenses are so high.

Work-from-home schemes often make outrageous claims in their advertising. Often, such claims are technically accurate, even if they are not very realistic. Some examples of genuine advertisements taken from Web sites, including spelling and grammatical errors, follow. Each example is accompanied by its true meaning and some additional information.

Earn $500.00 a week Typing At Home

This is a typical envelope-stuffing scheme that involves typing addresses onto labels or entering e-mail addresses into a bulk e-mail program.

EARN $200-$1,000 WEEKLY! Assembling products at home.

This is a typical piecework scheme where likely earnings will be in the region of a few dollars. Larger amounts will only be possible if several family members take part and long hours are worked.

Earn $14/hr using your word processor in the comfort of your home

Workers are offered secretarial or administrative work, such as handling routine correspondence or processing medical bills. After paying a joining fee, they receive a list of companies they can write to for work. Assuming they are able to find employment, many people find that the volume of work they are expected to handle is very high. While an experienced typist might achieve reasonable earnings, others will only make a few dollars per hour.

Work at Home as an Actor/Actress!

Workers are recruited to talk to people calling adult phone lines or psychic hotlines. The worker is responsible for locating customers and convincing them to pay for the service. Internet-based services use instant messaging, voice chat, and other methods to hold conversations with customers.

Earn $1000 a week in your sleep!

Virtually any scheme can be advertised using this headline. Workers create or buy a Web site that is used to advertise work-at-home schemes. Since the Web site is available 24 hours a day, the owner is able to attract business even while he is asleep.

It is worth remembering that Web sites advertising these schemes tend to record the e-mail address of anyone making an inquiry. Eventually, the address is likely to end up on a list of "opportunity seekers" to be sold on compact disc or DVD.

ADULT GOODS AND SERVICES

There are several common frauds associated with the purchase of adult goods and services via the Internet. Like many of the other types of fraud discussed in this section, perhaps the most common deception involves failing to provide goods or services after receiving payment.

A particular problem concerns adult Web sites that offer access to pictures, video clips, and other materials on a commercial basis. Some sites provide free previews that are intended to attract regular subscribers. However, in order to access the free samples, visitors to the site are asked to prove that they are 18 or older. This is usually done by providing credit card details, the underlying logic being that credit card companies do not issue cards to children.[21] In most cases, the Web site will contain a statement promising that credit card details will not be stored and that they will only be used to verify the visitor's age. The visitor will also be told that once his age has been checked, a password can be issued so that there is no need to provide credit card details in future. However, some weeks later, visitors find that their credit card statements show that they have been subscribed to the Web site or have paid a large fee for temporary membership. Since e-mails and phone calls to the Web site in order to cancel the subscription and obtain a refund are ignored, reluctant subscribers are forced to contact their credit card companies instead. Some people will choose to accept the loss of the membership fee, rather than face the embarrassment of pursuing a refund through the credit card company. For others, obtaining a refund through a credit card company can take a great deal of time, allowing the Web site to charge credit cards with additional fees. Even if some people manage to get their money back, it will probably be the credit card companies that bear the loss. This is because once it becomes necessary to issue refunds or credit card facilities are suspended, the company behind the site will be folded and the owners will start over.

A Refund to …?

People requesting refunds from adult Web sites and other services are sometimes surprised when they receive immediate agreement. However, there may be certain conditions attached that customers dislike. For instance, while the customer's original payment may have appeared on his credit card statement against an innocuous company name, he may be told that refunds are processed by a sister company with a more explicit name. The customer will also be reminded that the company name will appear against the refund on the customer's statement and might be seen by a number of people, including the customer's wife. In some cases, as a form of revenge against those who complain about the Web site or demand a refund, a receipt, or acknowledgment may be "accidentally" sent to the customer's wife.

In a variation on this kind of fraud, visitors to an adult Web site may be offered access to materials that are illegal, such as child pornography. Whether or not the content actually exists is largely immaterial, because the real purpose of the offer is to discourage complaints against the site. For instance, obtaining a refund from a credit card company would involve the card owner admitting that he was attempting to obtain access to child pornography. A similar confession would be needed in order to report the site to law enforcement agencies. It might be argued that those who seek illegal content deserve whatever happens to them. However, other people may also be vulnerable to this practice since they have no control over what is shown to them after they have gone through the age verification process. As an example, a person expecting to see legal content might be shown illegal images instead. Having supplied his credit card details in order to access the site, it would be difficult to convince someone that the material was shown against his will.

In some cases, online stores and adult Web sites may become involved in extortion. As an example, a man joining an adult Web site catering to gay men might receive messages threatening to reveal his sexuality to friends and family. It is important to remember that blackmail is not restricted to commercial Web sites and may occur at any adult-oriented Web site. As an example, a Chicago man, Brett Wohl, received a prison sentence in 2004 after being convicted of blackmailing men he met in Internet chat rooms.[22] Wohl visited gay chat rooms in order to find potential victims and gather information about them. Once a relationship was established, he encouraged the men to send compromising pictures of themselves. The pictures were used to blackmail the men by threatening to expose their sexuality to their wives.

PYRAMID SCHEMES

Most people are familiar with the concept of a *pyramid scheme*, where a small number of people each recruits a number of new members. In turn, each new member recruits a number of other people, who recruit others, and so on. Figure 7.1 shows part of a pyramid where each new member is required to recruit two people. The top level of the pyramid contains one person who recruits two members. On the second level, the two new recruits each find two new members, bringing the total number of people in the pyramid up to seven. Each new level added to the pyramid doubles the number of new members. Starting from the top of the pyramid, the growth in membership follows a pattern like this: 2, 4, 8, 16, 32, 64, 128, 256, and so on. Most pyramid schemes rely on members recruiting 10 or more people at a time, so the pyramid grows extremely quickly.

Virtually all pyramid schemes are based around the sale of various products, such as cleaning materials or cosmetics. Members earn a commission on every item they sell, as well as a smaller amount for every item sold by people they have recruited into the scheme. A small number of schemes forget about selling products altogether and take a more direct approach. New members are asked to send money to some of the people higher up in the pyramid. Payments are made directly, either by sending currency through the postal system or via electronic payment services, such as PayPal.

Pyramid schemes are often advertised with the promise that members can earn large sums of money in exchange for relatively little work. Since the reasoning behind such promises seems plausible at first glance, it is worth

Figure 7.1   Part of a Simple Pyramid Scheme`

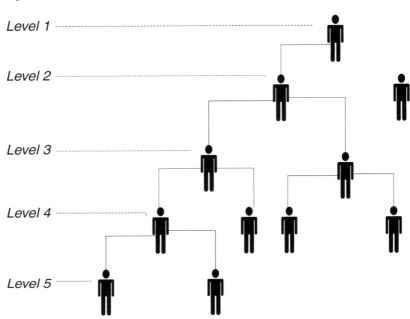

Level 1

Level 2

Level 3

Level 4

Level 5

looking at in more detail in order to expose a fundamental flaw. Members of any given scheme are promised payments up to a certain number of levels, usually three or more. Figure 7.1 can be used to show how this works. Imagine that a man at top of the pyramid receives a small sum of money for each person he recruits up to three levels below him. For everyone recruited to the first level below him, he will receive $5. This will fall to $4 for those recruited to the second level below him and $3 for the third level. There are two members at the second level, so the man receives $2 \times \$5 = \$10$. The people on the second level have recruited a total of four people, meaning that the man will receive an additional $4 \times \$4 = \$16$. Those on the third level have recruited eight more people, so the man receives $8 \times 3 = \$24$. The total received will be $50. Note that even though the amount of the payment decreases at each level, the number of payments increases and larger amounts are returned overall.

The logic behind such schemes starts to break down as soon as the pyramid increases beyond a certain size. Put simply, the pyramid becomes so large that not enough new members can be recruited in order to allow the existing members above them to make a profit. In a pyramid where each member is asked to recruit 10 other people, only 10 levels are possible: an 11th level would require an intake of new members larger than the entire population of the earth (10,000,000,000,000). However, in reality, pyramids are likely to break down well before they reach a significant size. This is because some people leave, others fail to recruit enough new members, and so on.

The further down the pyramid a person is located, the more likely they are to have difficulty in recruiting new members. Also, the further down the pyramid, the more chance there is of being affected by a breakdown in the pyramid's structure. This is because the lower the level, the more people on the levels above and below, so the greater the chance of a problem occurring. It is also worth noting that the operator of a pyramid scheme sometimes takes the place of some of the people who leave the scheme. This helps to fill any "gaps" in the pyramid's structure, but also allows the operator to claim any payments due to the person who has left. Taken together, the factors discussed here mean that only the people towards the very top of the pyramid are likely to earn a substantial sum.

There are two other problems associated with pyramid schemes that should be highlighted. First, all pyramid schemes are illegal in the United States, Europe, and other nations. Second, pyramid schemes generate millions of e-mail messages every day, contributing to the problem of spam (see later).

INVESTMENT FRAUDS

Common investment frauds include *Ponzi schemes* and a form of *stock fraud* called *pump and dump*.

Ponzi schemes are named after Charles Ponzi (1882–1949), a persistent criminal who carried out a number of major frauds throughout his lifetime. Ponzi is best known for a fraudulent investment scheme he operated between 1919 and 1920. In 1919, Ponzi began an investment business in Boston, promising his investors a return of 50 percent every 45 days. The only way Ponzi could keep his promise was by using the money he obtained from his most recent investors to pay what was due to his earlier investors. Within months, Ponzi found that his "robbing Peter to pay Paul" approach could not be sustained because he was unable to recruit enough new investors to cover his commitments. Ponzi declared bankruptcy in 1920 and eventually received several prison sentences before being deported from the United States. In all, it is estimated that 40,000 people invested in Ponzi's scheme, losing around $15 million among them.[23]

Most of today's Ponzi schemes promise regular returns on a given investment. The investor is asked to entrust a lump sum to the company for a fixed period of time. In exchange, he is promised regular interest payments until the end of the agreement, when the whole of his investment will be returned. For instance, investing $10,000 over two years might return $400 every month. By the end of the term, the investor will have received $9,600, almost doubling his investment. Investors usually receive a number of interest payments in order to build their confidence and trust. They are then given the opportunity to make a further investment or encouraged to introduce friends and family to the scheme. Eventually, the monthly payments stop and the investment company ceases to exist.

Occasionally, people are offered the chance to earn large returns by investing over a period of days or weeks. Typically, the investor is told of a company merger, property deal, or other event that is due to take place soon. In order to take advantage of the opportunity, the investment company needs to raise a large sum of money very quickly. In exchange for what is effectively a short-term loan, the company will share the profits with the investor. This means that the investor could earn as much as 50 percent interest over a few weeks. If the investor seems skeptical of the scheme, he may be offered the chance to invest a small sum, perhaps $1,000, to test the investment company's claims. When the investor receives the interest he was promised, it becomes easier to convince him to invest a much larger sum.

Ponzi schemes are attractive to criminals since they are easy to set up and require only a minimal outlay. Large expenses, such as interest payments, are easily funded by using the money gathered from new investors. Operating via the Internet allows a scheme to be monitored and controlled from almost anywhere. In addition, the Internet makes it harder to identify and locate the people behind the scheme.

Pump and dump schemes usually involves a criminal buying a large number of shares in a specific company. The criminal then attempts to increase the value of the shares by posting rumors to financial message boards, news-groups, Web sites, or anywhere else potential investors might see them. The rumors may mention a possible takeover, a surge in profits, a technological breakthrough, or the imminent introduction of a new product. When the value of the stock rises, the criminal sells all of his shares at a large profit.

A variation on this scheme involves decreasing the value of a given stock so that shares can be bought at a bargain price. As soon as the value of the stock returns to normal, the shares can be resold and a large profit realized. In general, only large companies are susceptible to this approach because only they have the resources needed to weather the effects of sudden, significant changes in share value.

One of the best-known examples of online stock fraud took place in August 2000 and involved Mark Jakob, a 23-year-old former student. Jakob planted fake information on the Internet about Emulex, a major company in the area of networking. Within an hour, the company's stock had fallen in value by $2.5 billion, but Jakob stood to make a profit of $240,000.[24] Thinking that there might be a wider problem within the industry, panicked investors began to sell their holdings, causing shares in other companies, such as Brocade and Qlogic, to fall in value too.[25]

I wrote about another example of online stock fraud several years ago:

In January 2001, Arash Aziz-Golshani and Hootan Melamed were both jailed for manipulating the stock of a printing company called NEI Web World. Over a period of time, the duo purchased thousands of shares in the company at between 5 and 13 cents each. They then posted numerous messages to bulletin boards that exaggerated the value of the company. When the company's stock climbed to $15 per share, they sold their holdings at a profit of $350,000. However, as soon as it was realised that the rumours circulated by the pair were false, the shares immediately fell in value by 25 percent, causing other investors to suffer losses.[26]

Online stock fraud is more difficult to carry out nowadays for three main reasons. First, people have become more suspicious of what they read on the Internet and are likely to verify rumors about the shares they hold before acting. Second, message boards, Web sites, and other places where disinformation can be posted have become more security conscious. For instance, it is no longer possible to post information anonymously to many of the most influential message boards, chat rooms, and Web sites. Many services now also verify the identities of their members, requiring them to provide personal information that is difficult to fake, such as credit card details, when they join. Finally, more people are monitoring places where financial information is posted in order to identify attempts at fraud. Around the world, law enforcement agencies, insurance companies, consumer protection organizations, financial organizations, and other agencies constantly monitor the financial information appearing on the Internet. Large companies also monitor the Internet, regularly checking Web sites, message boards, newsgroups, and financial chat rooms for any mention of themselves. This is done to protect the company against various online threats, including fraud.

SAFETY AND PREVENTION

The following guidelines are drawn from a number of sources including the FBI, eHow, National Consumers League, and the Federal Trade Commission.

BUSINESS USERS

Fraud of the kind described in this chapter is unlikely to affect business users.

INDIVIDUALS AND FAMILIES

- Adoption agencies, employment agencies, investment advisors, and pharmacies are all subject to scrutiny from various agencies. When dealing with any of these organizations, advice should always be sought from relevant professional associations, government agencies, or other bodies. Simply checking that a person or company holds a legitimate license may be enough to avoid being swindled.
- Always seek advice before purchasing high-value goods or making agreements of any kind. If making a large investment, for example, consult a financial expert. Similarly, if buying medicines online, always seek medical advice before adding nonprescription, herbal, or traditional products to your daily treatment.

- Only deal with reputable companies that have an established reputation. Larger companies with many branches are likely to be very reliable.
- Where possible, always pay for goods or services using a credit card that offers protection against fraud.
- Research companies before dealing with them. This is particularly important with regard to adoption agencies, dating services, and investment companies.
- Keep up-to-date with news about new types of online fraud. A number of Web sites provide information and advice that is regularly updated. See *Further Information* for some examples.
- Install and use appropriate security software, such as add-ons for your Web browser that warn of potential security problems.

FURTHER INFORMATION

Reading

Sindell, K., 2005. *Investing Online for Dummies*. Hoboken, NJ: Hungry Minds Inc.
Collier, M., 2003. *EBay Bargain Shopping for Dummies*. Hoboken, NJ: Hungry Minds Inc.

Online

The National Consumer League provides detailed guidance on avoiding many kinds of online fraud: http://www.fraud.org/tips/internet/internet/inttip/inttip.htm.
The Federal Trade Commission has information on common online frauds, including some not covered here: http://www.ftc.gov/ftc/consumer.htm.
Crimes of Persuasion provides a great deal of detailed information on computer crime: http://www.crimes-of-persuasion.com.
As well as supplying a great deal of general information on fraud, Hoaxbusters also provides a searchable index of known frauds: http://hoaxbusters.ciac.org.

Junk E-Mail

Every Internet user pays for the unwanted advertising that appears in their inboxes every day. Most people delete these messages without reading them. However, that badly spelled message offering unbeatable bargains may be more than just a minor irritation.

Indiscriminate advertising affects the entire infrastructure of the Internet. If Web sites load a little more slowly or e-mail messages take longer to arrive, part of the reason may be the enormous traffic generated by these messages every day.

However, the problem goes much deeper than an unresponsive Web site. The products sold through this kind of advertising are often fraudulent and sometimes dangerous—as discussed in the previous chapter. In addition, the profits that result from these messages often go to individual criminals, organized crime gangs, and terrorists.

Could it be that unsolicited advertising is not quite as innocuous as it seems?

WHAT IS SPAM?

Spam is a serious and growing problem that affects computer users in a number of different ways. Spam is perhaps best described as unsolicited e-mail that is usually commercial in nature. For example, most spam consists of advertising. Spam is comparable to the "junk mail" most people receive every day. Those who send *junk e-mail* are normally called *spammers*.

Spam can also refer to advertising posted to newsgroups, message boards, and Web sites. In recent years, spam has also started to appear in entries posted to the *guest books* that some people host on their sites.

SPAM WITH EVERYTHING

The term "spam" is taken from a comedy sketch performed by the *Monty Python* team. The sketch is set in a diner where every item on the menu includes at least one portion of spam. The term reflects the idea that e-mail users are forced to receive unsolicited advertising, just as the diner's customers are forced to have spam as part of their meals.

THE EXTENT OF THE PROBLEM

In 2004, the International Telecommunication Union estimated that spam cost businesses approximately $23.5 billion a year worldwide.[1] It was also estimated that spam accounted for more than 60 percent of all e-mail traffic, amounting to approximately 15 billion messages each day.[2] These figures were supported by research carried out by the Radicati Group, which reported that around 76.8 billion e-mail messages were sent each day in 2004.[3] Of these messages, more than three-quarters (83 percent) were business related. In addition, spam accounted for nearly half of all e-mail traffic, or approximately 38 billion messages each day.

More recent figures from the Radicati Group show a huge growth in the use of e-mail and the volume of spam sent each day.[4] The company predicts that spam directed towards corporate e-mail systems will rise to 83 billion messages a day by 2009, up from 44 billion messages a day in 2006. Similarly, spam directed at individual Internet users will grow to 145 billion messages a day by 2009, up from 72 billion messages per day in 2006.

With regard to individual Internet users, some estimates[5] suggest that the average person receives at least six spam messages every day, amounting to an annual total of 2,200 messages.

Bill Gates, founder of Microsoft, is sent four million spam e-mails every day. However, his e-mail filtering software is so efficient that he actually only receives 10 junk e-mails.

Source: The Tesh Media Group (www.tesh.com)

All of the figures given here are of particular significance to North American Internet users, who represent almost a quarter (22 percent) of the world's e-mail users.[6] This makes the United States seem a particularly attractive target to spammers, and means that the country stands to suffer the highest losses.

However, as well as being a major target for spam, the United States is also considered the single largest source of spam e-mail. For instance, the Commtouch Detection Center monitors spam outbreaks around the world, often analyzing hundreds of millions of e-mail messages for its reports. According to Commtouch's figures for January 2006, 43.18 percent of global spam originated from U.S.–based sources.[7] Other significant sources of spam included China, Korea, and Germany. Another source of frequently updated information is the Spamhaus Project,[8] which provides a top-10 list of countries responsible for what it terms "spam issues." Figures for March 2006 showed that the United States was responsible for 2,284 incidents. Other entries on the list included China (416), Russia (289), Japan (259), and Taiwan (192).

Analyzing the content of spam messages shows that most messages focus on a relatively small number of topics. Figures from Commtouch[9] show that more than half of the messages (52.46 percent) analyzed in January 2006 concerned medical products, such as pharmaceuticals. Other popular subjects included gifts (14.08 percent), adult products (13.38 percent), software (6.34 percent), and pornography and dating (5.28 percent). A small proportion of messages (0.88 percent) involved attempts at fraud. Although other estimates for 2006 use different categories from that of Commtouch, they tend to show similar trends. For instance, it was suggested that spam related to adult goods and services (e.g., products, pornography, and dating services) represented approximately 19 percent of all spam sent in the first part of 2006.[10]

> The Commtouch Detection Center provides a spam outbreak monitor that operates in real time. Users can see the details of spam outbreaks around the world as they happen: http://www.commtouch.com/site/ResearchLab/map.asp.

THE COST OF SPAM

The cost of spam to businesses and individuals is often underestimated. Although numerous estimates exist that conflict with one another, there is general agreement that spam results in losses that can be measured in billions of dollars each year.

For businesses, most losses tend to arise from lost productivity. However, there are also a variety of other costs associated with spam. These include lost *bandwidth,* increased software and hardware costs, increased labor costs, and increased storage costs. In a large company, for instance, millions of spam e-mails might be received each day. Dealing with these messages can place significant demands on the company's network. As these demands grow and network performance begins to decline, it may be necessary to buy new hardware so that the company's normal business activities do not suffer. In addition, specialized filtering software may be needed to automate part of the process of identifying and deleting spam messages. In turn, the adoption of filtering software may create the need to hire additional support staff to deal with problems related to e-mail, such as the accidental deletion of genuine messages.

In terms of global losses, it was estimated that companies lost $50 billion in 2005.[11] However, such a figure seems somewhat low when compared with some of the other estimates available. For instance, a 2002 estimate from the European Union suggested that spam costs $8–$10 billion each year in bandwidth costs alone.[12]

With regard to the United States, a number of estimates of the productivity losses resulting from spam have been published. One of the most conservative estimates suggests that U.S. businesses suffered productivity losses of around $4 billion in 2004.[13] At the other end of the scale, the highest estimate of annual losses to U.S. businesses is $87 billion.[14] A more believable estimate places annual losses due to spam rising from $10 billion in 2003 to $17 billion in 2005.[15] This seems reasonable because it is broadly in keeping with other estimates, such as those given by ISPs:

> In March 2004, the major U.S. service providers—Microsoft, America Online, Yahoo, and EarthLink—joined forces in filing lawsuits against what the companies said were major spammers in the United States and Canada. In their suits, the companies claimed that spam costs business in North America $10 billion US each year in lost productivity, network upgrades and destroyed or lost data.[16]

Another way of measuring the cost of spam is in terms of the annual cost per employee. Several sources have suggested that the annual cost per employee to businesses in the United States is in the range of $50 to $1,400.[17] However, it is worth noting that most estimates are based on a number of assumptions, such as how much employees earn. This means that there may be a great deal of variation in any figures given. For example, companies in the computer industry are likely to make more use of e-mail than, say, firms involved in food production. The more employees rely on e-mail, the greater the amount of spam they are likely to encounter. In addition, salaries in the computer industry tend to be relatively high, so productivity losses are likely to cost more. This can help to explain why some people suggest that the annual cost per employee of spam is as little as $50, while others suggest it is almost $2,000.[18]

The cost per employee can also vary according to local labor conditions. Salaries are likely to be higher in locations such as Silicon Valley or Seattle since these areas are home to a number of major technology companies, such as Microsoft. The effect of local labor conditions also works on an international scale. For instance, the annual cost of dealing with spam in the United States is approximately $170 per employee. In Germany, however, labor is more expensive, so the cost per employee is estimated at $241.[19]

Commtouch provides a simple tool[20] that can be used to calculate the cost of spam to a company. This tool helps to illustrate where some costs arise and can produce some startling results. As an example, imagine a company with 1,000 employees, each earning an average of $40,000 per year. Each employee receives 25 e-mail messages a day, of which 20 percent are spam. The calculator shows the cost of direct productivity losses is $48,260. In addition, the cost of responding to spam amounts to $29,246.79, while the cost of storing it is $17,520. In all, the annual cost of spam to the company is $95,026.79.

It is worth emphasizing the fact that all Internet users pay something towards the cost of dealing with spam. As well as companies, home users also face increased costs. This is because all major ISPs attempt to control the amount of spam passing through their networks. For instance, AOL and MSN have reported that they block 2.4 billion spam messages every day. This is equivalent to around 67 messages per user each day, or up to 80 percent of all incoming e-mail traffic.[21] The cost of dealing with spam tends to be passed on to subscribers, adding an average of $2 per month to their bills.[22]

As well as paying higher monthly charges, some home users may also be paying for the dubious privilege of downloading spam messages. Many ISPs impose a limit on how much data can be downloaded each month. Each spam e-mail received takes up some of the user's monthly allowance. If messages are fairly small, this may not have much of an impact on the user's allowance. However, the size of some spam e-mail messages can increase significantly if images, animations, sound effects, and other data are included. In these cases, a few hundred spam e-mail messages received over the period of a month can take up a significant part of a user's allowance.

Spam also causes a great deal of frustration and distress to many Internet users. Minor irritations might include having to wait longer for e-mail to download or having to waste time sorting genuine messages from unwanted advertising. More serious problems occur when people receive offensive materials, such as racist literature, or when children are sent sexually explicit advertisements.

Ultimately, the cost of spam may even include human lives. This is because spam is associated with the activities of certain criminal gangs and terrorist groups. Products sold through e-mail advertising may fund activities that range from human trafficking to terrorist attacks.

WHY SPAM EXISTS

E-mail provides a simple and cheap way of advertising goods and services. According to PC World,[23] hiring someone to send out bulk e-mail can cost as little as $300–$400 per million messages. Costs can be reduced even further if the company is willing to carry out the work itself. For a few hundred dollars, it is possible to buy specialized software to automate many of the tasks involved in sending out e-mail in bulk.[24]

Since sending out bulk e-mail is inexpensive, only a small *response rate* is needed to recover costs and generate a profit. It is estimated that a response rate as low as 0.001 percent[25] is enough to make spamming worthwhile.[26] In other words, only 1,000 responses out of every million messages sent are needed to make a profit.

But how many people actually respond to spam? Describing research carried out by the Pew Research Center in 2003, *PC World* reported:

> Seven percent of e-mail users, or more than 8 million Americans, say they have ordered a product or service offered in an unsolicited e-mail. One in three users say they have clicked on a link in unsolicited e-mail to get more information.[27]

The clickthroughs mentioned in the quote also provide some spammers with an income stream. Sometimes, bulk e-mail companies are able to earn a small fee for each Internet user who arrives at the client's Web site by following a link contained in an e-mail message. Although each individual clickthrough might only be worth a fraction of a penny, it is still possible to earn fairly large sums by sending out millions of e-mail messages each day.

A good example of the kind of the income that can be generated using spam concerns an American company, Amazing Internet Products. In 2003, details of orders received by the company were accidentally revealed to the public. In response to hundreds of thousands of e-mail messages, the company received 6,000 orders over a period of four weeks. The orders were for an herbal supplement, Pinacle, which was diplomatically described by one journalist as "male anatomy enlargement pills."[28] The number of orders received is surprising for three main reasons. First, the product cost $50 per bottle. Second, customers included a number of intelligent and well-educated people, such as company presidents and a mutual fund manager. Third, customers seemed unperturbed by the fact that the company's Web site did not contain any contact details, such as a postal address, e-mail address, or telephone number.[29]

DEALING WITH SPAM

Sending spam is illegal in many U.S. states, the European Union, and many other countries. It is possible to report spam to various agencies that may take action against the sender. The Federal Trade Commission[30] allows businesses and individuals to file complaints against spammers online, providing that the messages received are intended to deceive people. Spam can also be reported to other organizations, such as SpamCop,[31] who will attempt to take action on behalf of Internet users.

E-mail filtering can be used to identify and delete spam messages automatically. Filtering can be carried out at two different levels: at the server or at the desktop. At the server level, all of an organization's incoming e-mail is scanned for spam. After all spam has been removed, the remaining messages are distributed to individual users. One of the problems associated with server-based filtering is that it is sometimes difficult to recover genuine messages that have been accidentally identified as spam. At the desktop level, each user receives all of his messages and relies on the software installed on his individual machine to filter out spam. Although this approach gives individual users greater control over their e-mail, it tends to be more difficult and expensive to implement than server-based filtering.

There are a number of different ways of filtering e-mail. One of the simplest methods involves scanning for keywords, such as "xxx," "sex," or "$$$." However, it is relatively easy to defeat this method by spelling words differently. For instance, "sex" might become "s-e-x" or "Viagra" might become "vlagra." Keyword filtering may also result in false positives, causing genuine messages to be deleted because they contain one or more keywords.

More sophisticated methods are based on heuristics and *Bayesian filtering*. Heuristics uses a series of rules in an attempt to identify spam. A typical rule, for example, might flag any messages that have no return e-mail address. Bayesian filtering is a statistical method based on the frequency of certain words or phrases. Both methods provide high levels of accuracy and can be tailored to meet individual needs.

A third way of identifying spam is by using a *blacklist* or a *whitelist*. A blacklist contains details of e-mail or IP addresses suspected of being used to send out spam. Any message originating from an e-mail address or domain on the blacklist will be rejected. On the other hand, a whitelist contains a list of trusted e-mail addresses. Only messages originating from an e-mail address or domain on the whitelist will be accepted. All other messages will be rejected. Blacklists can be difficult to keep up-to-date and are relatively easy to work around, for example by using "throwaway" e-mail accounts. Whitelists are much harder to circumvent but may prevent the receipt of genuine messages from people not on the list.

SAFETY AND PREVENTION

The advice that follows is derived from a number of sources including Bocij et al. (2005), Bocij (2004), Martin (2005), Goodman, Heckerman, and Rounthwaite (2005), JunkMailStopper.com, ScamBusters.org, Learn the Net, the Federal Trade Commission, and many others.

BUSINESS USERS

- Invest in appropriate filtering software that can be used to combat spam. In terms of per-user cost, server-based filtering is over 60 percent cheaper than desktop filtering and more than five times cheaper than leaving employees to filter e-mail manually (Keizer, 2005).
- Make sure that company resources are not "hijacked" and used to send out spam. This requires some way of monitoring the traffic passing through the company's e-mail servers.
- Encourage staff to delete spam messages without reading them. This not only saves time but may also avoid problems related to programs or data that are sometimes embedded in messages.

THE TELLTALE PIXEL

There are a number of good reasons why spam should be deleted without reading it. For instance, Internet users sometimes receive e-mail messages that appear to be blank. However, some messages may not be blank and might contain a single pixel. A *pixel* is one of the small dots used to create certain types of images. For instance, an icon like the Recycle Bin will be made up of small dots arranged in a grid measuring 32 × 32 or 64 × 64. The pixel embedded in the e-mail message will usually be white so that it is invisible against the white background used by most e-mail packages.

When the message is viewed,[34] the e-mail program treats the pixel like any other image and attempts to download it so that it can be displayed. The act of downloading the pixel tells the spammer that he has found a valid e-mail address. Depending on the Internet user's security, other information might also be made available to the spammer, such as details of the user's computer system.

INDIVIDUALS AND FAMILIES

- Use any filtering tools supplied by your ISP. For instance, some providers of free e-mail accounts provide an online control panel that allows users to configure spam filtering.
- *Parental control software* can sometimes be used to prevent young people from viewing sexually explicit messages. Such programs can also stop young

people from following any embedded links that may lead to Web sites featuring adult content.

- Never respond to spam. This will help to make e-mail less effective as a sales tool, ultimately reducing the volume of spam sent out each day.
- Use multiple e-mail addresses. Free e-mail accounts are easily available and can be used when posting to newsgroups, message boards, guest books, and so on.

> Spam e-mail sometimes contains instructions on how to remove your name from the company's mailing list. Note that only a small number of these offers are genuine. In most cases, following the instructions simply tells the spammer that his message has been read and that your e-mail address is valid. This usually results in more spam being sent to your e-mail address and can help the spammer to make additional profits by selling your details to other spammers.

When the account begins to attract a large amount of spam, it can be discarded and a new one can be established. Your "main" e-mail address should only be given to people you know and trust. In addition, this address should never be used to post messages where they may become publicly accessible, for example on a message board. This is because many spammers use specialized software to construct mailing lists by harvesting e-mail addresses from these places.

- Most popular e-mail programs allow users to create e-mail filters. In Outlook Express, for example, the Message Rules item on the Tools menu allows users to create relatively complex rules for handling incoming messages. In addition, the program also features a Blocked Senders list that works as a simple, but effective, blacklist.
- Consider installing specialized antispam software. It is also possible to subscribe to services that filter e-mail on your behalf.
- Install a virus scanner and keep it up-to-date. Spam is sometimes used to distribute viruses.

RESOURCES FOR DEALING WITH SPAM

Free e-mail accounts are available from a number of sources. However, it is also possible to obtain free accounts that are specifically intended to help people deal with spam. Spamgourmet is an example of such a service: www.spamgourmet.com.

It is necessary to identify the source of a spam e-mail message before any action can be taken against the spammer. StopSpam.org provides a simple guide to deciphering e-mail headers that is used by thousands of people around the world: http://www.stopspam.org/email/headers.html.

A number of free or low-cost antispam programs are available. Some examples include the following:

CREATING AN E-MAIL FILTER IN OUTLOOK EXPRESS

These instructions demonstrate how to create a simple e-mail filter that will automatically dispose of all messages containing common terms found in spam messages, such as "Viagra," "xxx," and "$$$."

1. From the Tools menu, select Message Rules followed by Mail.
2. In the New Mail Rule dialog box that appears, check the item titled Where the Subject line contains specific words.
3. In the Rule Description text box at the bottom of the dialog, the text "Where the Subject line contains specific words" contains a hyperlink. Click on this link to display a new dialog box titled Type Specific Words.
4. Type a word or phrase into the text box at the top of the dialog. Click on the Add button to insert the phrase into the Words box. Repeat this process for each term you want to filter on. Suggestions for suitable keywords include viagra, sex, xxx, $$$, OEM, meds, medicines, drugs, and invest.
5. When you have finished adding keywords, click on the OK button to return to the New Mail Rule dialog.
6. In the section titled 2. Select the Actions for your rule, check the item titled Mark it as read.
7. In the section titled 4. Name of the rule, enter a suitable name for the new filter, such as "Basic Spam Filter."
8. Finally, click on the OK button to return to the first New Mail Rule dialog box, then click on OK again to return to Outlook's main screen.

This filter does not delete any messages—it simply marks them as read. When you are sure that the filter is working properly, it can be altered so that spam is deleted automatically or moved to a folder you create especially for spam. The filter can also be made more effective by adding new keywords that you identify from the spam messages that get past it.

- SpamAssassin runs on a server to identify and remove spam before it reaches users. The software is an Open Source project, meaning that it can be used free of charge. It is worth noting that many commercial products are based on SpamAssassin's code: http://wiki.apache.org/spamassassin/StartUsing
- POPFile scans incoming e-mail and classifies according to rules set by the user. The software is available in a number of versions that cater to different operating systems and languages. The software is an Open Source project, meaning that it can be used free of charge: http://popfile.sourceforge.net
- SpamFighter works with Outlook and Outlook Express to identify and remove spam. The standard version of the program can be used free of charge: www.spamfighter.com
- E-mail Remover attempts to identify spam messages before they are downloaded. Any messages identified as spam are deleted automatically, saving users from downloading them: www.email-remover.com

- SpamPal checks incoming e-mail and marks any messages considered spam. The user can process marked messages in various ways. SpamPal can be used free of charge: www.spampal.org
- FrontGate MX works with all popular e-mail programs and provides a broad range of antispam tools. The program is free of charge: http://www.presorium.com/en_au/products/fg/index.shtml

FURTHER INFORMATION

Reading

Fallows, D., 2003. "Spam: How It Is Hurting Email and Degrading Life on the Internet." October 22, 2003. Washington, D.C.: Pew Internet and American Life Project. Available online at: http://www.pewinternet.org/pdfs/PIP_Spam_Report.pdf.

Walker, A., 2005. *Absolute Beginner's Guide to Security, Spam, Spyware and Viruses.* Indianapolis, Indiana: QUE.

Feinstein, K. and McAneny, M. (eds.), 2004. *How to Do Everything to Fight Spam, Viruses, Pop-ups and Spyware.* Emeryville, CA: Osborne McGraw-Hill.

Online

Marjolein Katsma operates a Web site that has a comprehensive list of organizations to which complaints about spam can be made: http://banspam.javawoman.com/index.html.

HowStuffWorks provides a comprehensive guide to spam: http://computer.howstuffworks.com/spam.htm.

SpamLaws provides detailed information on antispam legislation in the United States, Europe, and many other countries: www.spamlaws.com.

Intellectual Property Theft

Software piracy is one of the most common crimes associated with computers. However, in recent years there has also been a trend towards downloading music, movies, and other copyrighted materials using methods such as peer-to-peer networking. In view of this, some people have proposed that a broader term, *copyright theft*, should be used to describe all of these activities. In some cases, it has been suggested that the term *intellectual property theft* (IP theft) is more appropriate, since this encompasses all forms of creative work, including products that are not protected by copyright.

The realm of software piracy and other forms of copyright theft has become known as the warez scene. *Warez* refers to any copyrighted material, such as software or music.

SOFTWARE PIRACY

Software piracy first became a problem for software companies at the very start of the personal computer boom that took place in the early 1980s. The launch of the IBM PC and later the Apple Macintosh brought computers within the reach of even the smallest companies. This created an almost instant demand for productivity packages among a new group of business users. At the same time, the arrival of inexpensive home computers such as the Commodore Amiga, Atari 800, Sinclair Spectrum, and many others created a demand for leisure software. In response, thousands of small software houses appeared, often made up of just one person working from home. These companies quickly became known as kitchen-table software houses within the computer industry.

As the number of computer users grew, more people began to make illegal copies of popular programs and tools they felt were useful. During this period, software was usually distributed via floppy disk or magnetic tape. Since few developers made use of *copy protection* techniques, many programs were easy to copy. Part of the problem was that small software companies did not have the resources needed to develop effective copy protection mechanisms. In addition, although some larger companies devised powerful copy protection tools, many customers found them awkward to use. This had an impact on sales and discouraged the use of some of the most effective methods.

COPY PROTECTION

Copy protection can be implemented in software or hardware. The most common software method is the registration code or serial number. Unless the correct code is entered, the software will not work. To prevent people from passing on their registrations codes to others, some programs phone home every now and then. This involves the program contacting a server located on the Internet from time to time in order to check the validity of the registration code being used. If several copies of the program are using the same code, or the code exists on a blacklist, the program stops working.

One of the most common physical copy protection tools is the *dongle*, a small device that plugs into the printer port or a USB port. Whenever the software runs, it checks to make sure that the dongle is present. If the dongle is not detected, the program ends. Dongles are normally used to protect specialized, high-value programs, such as CAD packages.

Compact discs and DVDs are sometimes protected by creating deliberate faults, such as physical damage. The software checks to make sure that the damaged section of the disc exists and contains the correct data before it runs. This is a reasonably effective technique because it takes advantage of the fact that CD-writers and DVD-writers are usually incapable of duplicating the damaged sections of a disc.

Further difficulty was caused by the introduction of various tools capable of circumventing copy protection techniques. Music systems with twin cassette decks were often capable of copying computer software and were sometimes even able to make *multigenerational copies*. These were copies made from other copies, for example a third-generation copy would be a copy of a copy of the original media. Some companies also distributed hardware and software tools that were marketed as legitimate backup products. These products were designed to circumvent common copy protection techniques, allowing users to create as many copies of the program as they wanted. A combination of low cost and ease of use helped these tools to sell in large quantities, significantly increasing overall levels of software piracy.

The introduction of CD-ROM as a means of distributing software temporarily frustrated casual software piracy. Copying a CD-ROM required costly hardware and could also be expensive in terms of media costs; it might take several attempts to copy a disc, with each try costing several dollars. It was also impractical to copy the huge quantity of data held on compact disc to tape or floppy disk. However, as the cost of hardware fell, piracy began to increase again. The availability of low-cost CD-writers also had the effect of encouraging music piracy, allowing people to make copies of entire albums for just a few cents. In recent years, a similar trend has been seen with DVD-ROM. However, the situation is considered more serious because even the most inexpensive DVD-writer can allow DVD movies to be copied.

As software piracy became more common, some people saw an opportunity to make money by selling pirated software via mail order. A constant demand for the latest programs was met in several ways, for instance by dealing with cracking groups. Cracking groups were made up of skilled computer users who gained satisfaction by defeating the copy protection methods used by software companies. *Crackers* often released collections of the programs they had removed antipiracy protection from. In some cases, this was done only to demonstrate the cracker's skills. In others, the software was sold to others who would distribute it further. Another way of obtaining new programs was by importing counterfeit software from countries without effective copyright legislation, or where governments saw software theft as unimportant.

The growth of the Internet allowed people to distribute pirate software in new ways. Software could be attached to messages posted to newsgroups, allowing anyone with a newsreader program[1] to download files at their leisure. In addition, many people established private *FTP sites,* sometimes using the resources of an unsuspecting employer or university rather than paying for their own storage space. These sites could house thousands of applications and were accessible to any user with a FTP client—which could be obtained free or at low cost.

Web sites providing links to pirated software, music, and movies also began to appear. Some sites specialized in supplying software fixes, called cracks, that could be used to defeat the copy protection routines used in various programs. This allowed people to download a legitimate trial version of a program, then use a crack to make it behave like the full, unrestricted version. Other sites specialized in supplying *keygens,* small programs that could be used to generate fake registration codes for a variety of programs. Again, this allowed people to convert a trial version of a program into the full, unrestricted version.

The use of cracks and keygens resolved a major problem for those who wanted to distribute pirated software on a large scale. Previously, it had been necessary to distribute pirated software in its entirety. This was costly in terms of storage space and bandwidth, making it difficult for the pirates to operate on a large scale. Now, however, people could download a trial version of the software from the developer's Web site, then use a small crack or keygen to unlock all of the program's functionality. In this way, the software developer could be made to bear the expense associated with downloading the software. Over the past few years, the cost of distributing software and cracks has been reduced further by the availability of free online storage space. Companies such as RapidShare, Savefile, Bigupload, and Megaupload provide accounts that let people share photographs, make backups of important files, access work-related files from home, and so on. Software pirates have been quick to abuse these services by using them to store copyrighted materials, such as software and music.

Another recent development has been a trend towards using peer-to-peer networking as a means of obtaining pirated software, music, and movies. Peer-to-peer (P2P) file sharing enables computer users to connect their systems together directly so that they can communicate with each other and share files. Modern P2P systems do not need to rely on a central server, making it difficult to identify and locate individual users. Some of the client programs used to share files include LimeWire, BearShare, Morpheus, and WinMX. One of the most controversial P2P networks is based on the BitTorrent tool created by Bram Cohen in 2002. The BitTorrent protocol uses a special file called a torrent to describe where a particular program, piece of music, or movie is located. Collections of torrents are published on Web sites and in newsgroups, making it easier for users to download copyrighted materials.

As more people have looked towards the Internet as a source of pirated software, many of those who previously sold CDs and DVDs via mail order have been forced to change the way they do business. Today, instead of buying a disc, customers pay for passwords and Internet addresses that will provide access to large collections of software. Since these sites generate large amounts of traffic, additional revenues are earned by selling advertising space and by forming links with other businesses. Adult Web sites, for instance, often pay a commission to those able to recruit new subscribers.

The Extent of the Problem

One of the best sources of information regarding software piracy is the annual *Global Software Piracy Report* produced on behalf of the Business Software Alliance (BSA). Over the years, the report has shown repeated increases in the losses resulting from software piracy. For instance, global losses grew from $12 billion in 1999 to $30 billion in 2003.[2] The 2005 report estimated that total losses from software piracy over the course of 2004 were in the region of $32.6 billion.[3] However, the losses predicted until the end of the decade seem far more serious:

> Globally, businesses and consumers will spend more than $300 billion on PC software over the next five years, according to IDC estimates. Given the current piracy rates, IDC predicts that, during the same five-year period, almost $200 billion worth of software will be pirated.[4]

Table 9.1 Priacy Rates for 2004 by Country—the Five Highest and Five Lowest Rates

Lowest Piracy Rates			Highest Piracy Rates		
Country	Piracy Rate(%)	Losses ($ million)	Country	Piracy Rate %)	Losses ($ million)
United States	21	6,645	Vietnam	92	55
New Zealand	23	25	Ukraine	91	107
Austria	25	128	China	90	3,565
Sweden	26	304	Zimbabwe	90	9
United Kingdom	27	1,963	Indonesia	87	183

Source: Business Software Alliance and International Data Corporation, 2005.

The *piracy rate* provides a useful way of measuring software piracy on national, regional, and global levels. This value describes the percentage of all installed software that is pirated. A piracy rate of 75 percent, for instance, means that three out of every four pieces of software are pirate copies.

The global piracy rate in 2004 was estimated at 35 percent. However, this value may be a little misleading since regional figures show large differences between the richest and the poorest parts of the world. For instance, the piracy rate for North America in 2004 was 22 percent, compared with a rate of 66 percent for Latin America. The gap between the developed world and emerging markets can also be illustrated by looking at which countries have the highest and lowest piracy rates. Table 9.1 shows the five countries with the lowest piracy rates in 2004, together with the five countries with the highest piracy rates.

As Table 9.1 shows, the highest piracy rates do not necessarily equate to the highest financial losses. For instance, the table shows that the U.S. piracy rate is more than four times lower than China's. However, since the U.S. market is much larger than China's, losses from the United States were almost twice as high as losses from China in 2004.

MOTIVES BEHIND SOFTWARE PIRACY

Software piracy has a number of attractions for home users. First is the opportunity to acquire expensive software packages at very low cost. Since most modern personal computers arrive equipped with a DVD-writer, the cost of acquiring a new program can be as low as the price of a blank disc. Even buying ready-made software compilations from Web sites or online auctions is inexpensive, since many items cost just a few dollars.

Second, some users collect software to trade with other people. Some people, like students, may trade with their peers in order to gain popularity.

Others may exchange software with others in order to make sure they always have access to the latest games and applications. Users may also collect software to support their hobbies, such as programming or genealogy.

Third, some users create and sell illegal copies of software in order to produce a small income that can be used to support their hobbies. A young person who plays computer games, for instance, might sell software at school to finance the purchase of the latest titles.

Many computer users are unaware that software piracy is a criminal offense in most countries. Those who are aware of the law often believe that piracy is a trivial offense and that individuals copying software for their own use are unlikely to be prosecuted. While there may be some truth to this, recent years have seen thousands of high-profile prosecutions take place as a way of publicizing the problem of software piracy and warning users of the risks they face.

There are three main arguments put forward in support of software piracy. First, it is claimed that some software companies do not provide enough information about their products, preventing the customer from making an informed buying decision. In some cases, a customer may buy an expensive product only to find that it does not meet his needs and that no refund can be made. By copying software, the user can make a full and careful evaluation of the product. If the program meets his needs, the user is likely to buy a legitimate copy in order to receive manuals, technical support, and other benefits. On the other hand, if the software is unsuitable, the user will not want to use it and is likely to delete any copies that were made.

SOFTWARE LICENSES

When an individual or a company buys a software package, they are usually only buying a license to use the program. The software remains the property of the software developer, as do any accompanying discs, manuals, and other materials. The license can be thought of as a kind of rental agreement.

Companies try to reduce costs by negotiating discounts when they buy multiple software licenses. Usually, only one set of installation media is supplied to the company, together with a set of license documents—the software can be installed on as many computers as there are licenses for.

Second, some people feel that software companies place restrictive license conditions upon their products. The license may prohibit users from making a backup copy of the software, or might include statements disclaiming responsibility if the software does not work properly. If users feel that these types of restrictions are unreasonable, they may simply disregard them. For instance, restrictions on making backup copies of a software application may be ignored because users believe they are entitled to safeguard their investment in the software.

Third, some users believe that software companies deliberately overcharge, placing some packages out of the reach of individuals and small businesses. Copying the software is harmless since the user would never have bought it anyway.

In order to balance the discussion, it seems appropriate to look at some of the counterarguments made by software companies.

Perhaps the simplest and most compelling argument they make is that software is protected under international copyright laws. In most countries, the copying of software is regarded as theft and exposes the individual to both criminal and civil liability.

THE THEFT ANALOGY

Recent research has concluded that many Internet users see nothing wrong with copyright theft, such as software and music piracy.[5] In many cases, people see making illegal copies of computer programs or music files as a normal part of their leisure activities. Why is this?

Part of the answer may involve the idea that Internet software piracy is seen as a victimless crime. If some Internet users believe there is a victim, it is usually a faceless corporation that is more than capable of bearing the loss of a single sale. However, this tends to change when people are asked to think of downloading a game or music album in the same way as stealing a CD or DVD from a store. This is because the analogy changes perceptions about copyright theft, emphasizing the fact that every download of a copyrighted file represents a crime. In addition, it reminds people that they are personally responsible for online copyright theft, just as they would be if they stole a music CD from a local store.

Another argument focuses on software pricing, especially with regard to business applications. The costs involved in the development of a sophisticated computer program can be extremely high. The effort needed to create an application is normally measured in terms of *labor hours*. In the case of a word processor, for instance, a large team of programmers might take several years to develop a sophisticated product. This represents millions of labor hours that need to be invested before the software can be released. In addition, additional labor hours will be needed after release to provide support services and develop the software further. This means that the price of the software must be set at a level that will recover the initial cost of development, fund further development, and allow research into new products. Once the company's investment has been recovered, the price can be lowered a little. However, software piracy acts to reduce the income generated from sales of the program. This jeopardizes any further development of the program and obstructs the introduction of new products. In many cases, a cycle begins where piracy causes the price of the software to increase, leading to more piracy and further price increases. In this way, those who make illegal copies of software are claimed to be directly responsible for the higher prices faced by legitimate customers.

As well as individuals, organizations can also engage in software piracy. The most common form of corporate software piracy occurs when a company makes more copies of a program than allowed for by the software license. In small companies, this is usually the result of trying to save money on IT expenditure. In larger companies, this often occurs accidentally and is usually caused by a failure to monitor the use of software licenses.

CONSEQUENCES OF SOFTWARE PIRACY

For individuals, the legal consequences of software piracy are largely the same as for other crimes and include fines, imprisonment, and the confiscation of equipment. Those who work in the computer industry also face the possibility of their reputations being damaged.

The use of pirated software significantly increases the risk of virus infection. This is because many "cracked" programs and cracks are distributed by virus writers in an attempt to infect as many computers as possible in a short time.

The use of programs that have been altered by cracking groups also raises the possibility of damage to data. Whenever a program is modified, there is a risk that it will stop working properly. However, some problems are not immediately noticeable and may remain undiscovered for weeks, months, or even years. If this happens, errors may accumulate throughout all of the data files used by the program. For individual users, this may mean the loss of personal files, such as word-processing documents. For businesses, however, it may mean the loss of accounts data, customer records, and other information critical to the company's operations.

Business users also face a number of other difficulties related to the use of pirated software. Some of these include:

- Financial penalties, such as fines. The company might also be exposed to both criminal and civil action.
- Legal action taken by employees. If employees are encouraged to use pirated software, they might face action from unions, colleagues, and other parties. In such an event, an employee may take legal action against the company for exposing him to such risks.

- Negative publicity resulting from action taken by software companies or the Business Software Alliance. Such publicity would be likely to damage relationships with customers and suppliers. The impact on public confidence might also harm sales and overall profitability.
- Disruption to everyday activities caused by the company being deprived of its application software. In some cases, even a temporary disruption might harm overall profitability. For instance, relationships with clients might be harmed if the company fails to maintain high standards of customer service.
- Reduced morale across the company, causing productivity losses and other problems, such as labor disputes.

It is worth noting that the risk of facing action from the BSA or other agencies increases with the size of the organization. The bigger the organization, the higher the likelihood of finding illegal software on the company's systems. In addition, there is an increased risk that an employee may report the company to an antipiracy organization, especially since many of these organizations offer a substantial reward for information leading to a successful prosecution.

SAFETY AND PREVENTION

The following information is derived from a number of sources, including Bocij et al. (2005), Bocij (1992), the Business Software Alliance, the Federation against Software Theft, and Microsoft.

It is worth noting that terrorists, organized crime gangs, and radical groups all use software piracy as a way of raising funds.[6] Reducing software piracy offers one way of limiting the activities of these groups.

BUSINESS USERS

- Consider introducing a formal policy regarding the use of illegal software. Being seen to take an active stance against software piracy may provide a measure of protection against prosecution and can help to protect the company's reputation.
- Regular software audits should be carried out to monitor and control the software used within the company. The responsibility for this should be given to a senior member of staff, who should also keep records of the software licenses owned by the company. Software audits bring a number of benefits:
  a. Illegal or unauthorized programs can be identified and removed quickly.
  b. Eliminating illegal or unauthorized software will encourage employees to focus on their work. Games and Internet browsers, for example, are well-known distractions that cost organizations many millions of labor hours each year.

    c. Eliminating illegal or unauthorized software will also reduce the risk of virus infection. In turn, this will help to maintain productivity while reducing support costs.

    d. Ensuring that employees use only authorized software can help to protect the integrity of the company's data. It can also encourage employees to keep to formal standards and procedures regarding the use of the company's systems.

- Software to help manage the auditing process can be obtained free of charge or at low cost. Examples of free auditing packages include the following:

    a. The Business Software Alliance provides access to several free software audit tools: http://www.bsa.org/uk/antipiracy/Free-Software-Audit-Tools.cfm

    b. Belarc publishes Belarc Adviser, a tool which can be used free of charge by individual users: http://www.belarc.com/free_download.html

    c. Allied Business Systems supplies a free version of its Software Audit Protection Program: http://www.alliedhr.com/sapp.htm

- If it is necessary to reduce costs, consider adopting Open Source alternatives to commercial packages. Many Open Source packages are the equal of their commercial counterparts in terms of quality, and some are even considered superior. In addition, some Open Source programs share the look and feel of commercial packages, allowing costs associated with training and support to be reduced.

INDIVIDUALS AND FAMILIES

Thanks to the increased availability of *freeware, shareware, Open Source,* and budget-priced software, it is now harder than ever for anyone to justify the use of pirated software. Free or low-cost alternatives exist for almost every category of software, from games to programming tools. For instance, two of the most common kinds of software targeted by software pirates are operating systems and office suites.

In terms of operating systems, *Linux* is a free package based on Unix. More than 50 variants of Linux are in common use and are easily downloaded from Web sites such as SourceForge.net. A particular variant of Linux that has been packaged for distribution is called a *distro.* Distros often include hundreds—sometimes thousands—of additional programs, all of which are freeware or Open Source. These programs include word-processing programs, art packages, Web browsers, media players, e-mail programs, file managers, programming tools, and many more.

There are also numerous alternatives to commercial office suites such as Microsoft Office. For instance, OpenOffice is a powerful and respected Open Source package that is compatible with all major office suites, including Microsoft Office. In addition, the program supports several operating systems, including Windows, Linux, Sun Solaris, Mac OS X, and FreeBSD.

As these examples demonstrate, free and low-cost software offers a viable alternative to making illegal copies of programs.

MUSIC AND MOVIE PIRACY

Music piracy has become an important issue since the turn of the century. As the Internet has grown, sales of counterfeit CDs through online auctions, Web sites, newsgroups, spam, and other channels have increased significantly. The International Federation of the Phonographic Industry (IFPI) estimates that 1 billion counterfeit CDs were sold in 2002 and 1.7 billion discs in 2003. Although sales of counterfeit CDs fell to 1.2 billion in 2004,[7] this may have been because of a growth in the use of file-sharing programs. Rather than paying for counterfeit discs, users may prefer to download music free of charge and create their own CDs. Music can also be downloaded freely from newsgroups, Web sites, and other services.

The problem of music piracy has been compounded by the practice of distributing files in a highly compressed format. For instance, the well-known MP3 format can allow more than 200 tracks to be stored on a single CD. These formats also make it quick and easy to download files; a broadband connection enables a whole album to be downloaded in just a few minutes. Playing music downloaded from the Internet is also simple, since Windows and other operating systems arrive complete with powerful media players. If users dislike these programs, numerous alternatives are available free of charge, allowing almost any computer to be turned into a virtual jukebox. It is also possible to play music away from a computer with the use of portable MP3 players, most regular DVD players, some hi-fi systems, or special radio transmitters that "stream" music from a computer to a receiver in another room.

Movie piracy has also grown steadily over the past decade. The Motion Picture Association of America[8] estimates that the annual losses worldwide due to movie piracy grew from 2.2 billion in 1997 to $3.5 billion in 2002. The MPAA also estimates that the U.S. entertainment industry loses $3.5 billion each year due to movie piracy—and this figure does not include losses due to Internet piracy.[9]

File-sharing programs, newsgroups, and other Internet services have also had an impact on movie piracy. Like music files, movies can be compressed to relatively small sizes, usually without any noticeable loss of quality. Formats such as DivX and Xvid allow entire movies to fit on a single CD. Movies can be played back on a personal computer, standalone media player, or on some domestic DVD players. It is also possible to convert a downloaded movie into other formats so that it can be used with other equipment or burned to DVD.

Like crackers, organized groups of *rippers* compete with each other to become the first to release a movie. This means that new movies are often available for download within hours of theatrical release. In some cases, movies can become available months before release.

THE EXTENT OF THE PROBLEM

With regard to music, the IFPI[10] estimates that one in three of all music discs sold around the world is an illegal copy. This is based on figures that

Table 9.2   Top 10 Countries Designated as Priorities by the IFPI in 2004

Country	2004 Piracy Rate (%)
Paraguay	99
China	85
Indonesia	80
Ukraine	68
Russia	66
Mexico	60
Pakistan	59
India	56
Brazil	52
Spain	24

Source: International Federation of the Phonographic Industry, 2005b.

suggest 1.2 billion pirated discs were sold in 2004. The size of the annual global market for pirated music is approximately $4.6 billion.

The IFPI has also reported that sales of pirated music exceed sales of legitimate discs in 31 countries. As shown by Table 9.2, piracy rates greater than 50 percent exist in a number of countries.

Movies are also copied widely. The International Intellectual Property Alliance (IIPA) collates figures related to copyright theft involving music,

Table 9.3   Movie Piracy Rates and Losses for Selected Countries

Country	2005 Losses ($ million)	2005 Piracy Rate (%)
China	244	94
Russian Federation	266	81
Hungary	102	73
Poland	102	66
Mexico	483	62
Thailand	149	62
Taiwan	98	51
Sweden	253	32
Italy	161	22
Canada	118	8

Source: International Federation of the Phonographic Industry, 2005b.

movies, software, books, and other *intellectual property.*[11] Table 9.3 shows 2005 piracy rates for a number of selected countries, together with the overall value of these losses.

Although these figures do not relate directly to Internet piracy, they help to show that intellectual property theft should be regarded as a serious problem.

PIRACY FINANCES TERRORISM

There is a great deal of evidence to suggest that profits from software, music, and video piracy may sponsor terrorist groups. As an example, Interpol has reported that profits from music and software piracy help to finance terrorist groups, such as Al Qaeda and Hezbollah.[12] Similar views have also been expressed in a number of other countries. For instance, *The Hindu,*[13] one of India's leading newspapers, reported, "The former Director-General of Police (Punjab), Julio F. Ribeiro, said … that a portion of the proceeds from the music and video piracy trade could be ending up in the hands of terrorist organizations."

Organized crime also benefits from activities such as music piracy. For instance, with regard to the United States, research by the Recording Industry Association of America (RIAA) claims that "CD-R reproduction in the eastern half of the United States is now dominated by organized criminal syndicates intent on monopolizing the illicit market share by operating on high volume and very low profit margins."[14]

No accurate figures exist regarding how many movies, music files, and other copyrighted materials are downloaded each year. However, it seems likely that the total far exceeds the number of counterfeit CDs and DVDs sold around the world. A number of file-sharing services claim more than a million members, and the very largest may have more than a hundred million active users. For instance, Kazaa reported having more than 140 million users in 2002.[15] In addition, there is no real way of knowing how many people download music and movies from newsgroups, Web sites, and other sources each day. However, what is known is that hundreds of music tracks and movies are posted to Usenet and elsewhere each week. If only a small proportion of those who read newsgroups or use file-sharing programs download a few songs or movies every week, this might amount to billions of files each year.

Although the music industry is adamant that file sharing reduces music sales, the evidence supporting this view is not conclusive. While a number of studies have concluded that file sharing has an impact on the sale of CDs, others have challenged this opinion. Some examples of relevant research supporting each viewpoint follow.

Some of the research supporting the view that file sharing affects music sales include:

- A 2004 study from Harvard concluded "... this paper finds that file sharing has had large, negative impacts on industry sales."[16]
- A 2004 conference article by academic Stan Liebowitz[17] concluded "... the evidence to date strongly suggests that file-sharing harms the sound recording industry."
- A European study carried out in 2005 by Jupiter Research found that consumers were three times more likely to download music files illegally, rather than use a legal download service.[18]

Studies that dispute the belief that file sharing impacts music sales include the following:

- A 2005 survey from the Leading Question, a music research company, reported that people who illegally share music online spend 4 1/2 times more on digital music than people who do not share music.[19]
- A 2004 study carried out at the Harvard Business School has suggested that downloading music from the Internet has no effect on sales of CDs.[20]
- An empirical Japanese study carried out in 2004 concluded "... downloads do not reduce CD sales and student surveys show that the use of file sharing does not reduce CD purchases."[21]

While sales of CDs seem to be declining, online music services have seen tremendous growth. This seems to suggest that customers are still willing to buy music but want the convenience and flexibility offered by online services.

THE SUCCESS OF ITUNES

The Apple iTunes service is a good example of a successful online music retailer. Launched in April 2003, the service offered customers the opportunity to download music from a library of 200,000 tracks for 99 cents per song. Within 16 days of launch, more than two million songs had been sold.[22] Four months after launch, sales had reached a total of ten million songs.[23] In 2005, iTunes became one of the best-selling music retailers in the United States, selling more titles than traditional retailers such as Tower Records, Borders, and Sam Goody. In addition, the company was also the largest online music retailer, responsible for 7 out of every 10 online music sales.[24] In February 2006, iTunes reported that it had sold one billion tracks since launch and that three million downloads were being recorded each day.[25]

In order to compete effectively, traditional music retailers will need to adapt to a changing market and embrace new business models.

A number of entertainment companies have already started to change the way they do business. Some have formed alliances with companies offering telephone and Internet services, allowing all of the partners to access new markets and share the profits. Video-on-demand, for instance, allows computer users to download and watch movies on their computers. However, this type of service needs the participation of three companies: one to provide the content, one to provide Internet services, and one to provide the telephone line the data will travel over.

FURTHER INFORMATION

Reading

International Federation of the Phonographic Industry, 2005b. *The Recording Industry 2005 Commercial Piracy Report.* June 2005. London: International Federation of the Phonographic Industry. Available online at: http://www.ifpi.org/site-content/library/piracy2005.pdf.

Business Software Alliance and International Data Corporation, 2005. *Second Annual BSA and IDC Global Software Piracy Study.* May 2005. Washington, D.C.: Business Software Alliance and International Data Corporation. Available online at: http://www.bsa.org/globalstudy/upload/2005-Global-Study-English.pdf.

Online

The International Intellectual Property Alliance publishes detailed information regarding rates of music, video, and software piracy in a number of different countries: http://www.iipa.com/countryreports.html.

The Recording Industry Association of America represents the interests of the U.S. recording industry. Its Web site contains information on a wide variety of topics, including piracy, consumer trends, legal cases, and more: http://www.riaa.com/issues/piracy/default.asp.

The Business Software Alliance represents software companies around the world. Its Web site provides access to detailed information on software piracy and free software-auditing tools: www.bsa.org.

Part 4

Online Relationships and Deviance

Cyberstalking

This chapter and those that follow look at the impact of the Internet on different kinds of human relationships. As will be discussed later on, our use of chat rooms, message boards, newsgroups, and other online services often reflects certain aspects of our lives. For instance, a constant presence on a message board who responds to virtually every post on every subject may not be the friendly, outgoing person they appear to be. In fact, such a heavy reliance on a message board for contact with other people may indicate a person who is socially isolated and desperate for company.

If the Internet can sometimes reveal something of a person's nature, it can also help to hide the most unpleasant parts of their personality. This can make it difficult to know who to confide in and who to trust. The helpful chat room user who offers comfort to someone who is receiving threatening or abusive messages may only be doing so to check the results of his own handiwork. Similarly, the eligible bachelor who seems to be thinking about marriage may already have a wife and children, or may be dating several women at the same time.

There are so many ways in which the Internet influences society that a book of this nature can only offer an overview covering a selection of areas. However, the range of topics discussed is felt to illustrate some of the most extreme forms of human online behavior, from cannibalism and suicide clubs to Internet addiction and cults. This chapter focuses on cyberstalking, a relatively new phenomenon and one that is the focus of my own ongoing research.

What Is Cyberstalking?

Cyberstalking has only existed since the late 1990s, when the first major cases came to widespread public attention. In essence, cyberstalking describes the use of *information and communications technology (ICT)* in order to harass one or more victims. Acts of harassment can include the transmission of offensive e-mail messages, identity theft, and damage to data or equipment.[1] In the context of cyberstalking, ICT refers to any form of technology, including computers, e-mail, fax machines, cell phones, and even handheld games consoles. In addition, harassment means any behavior that causes the victim distress, whether intentional or not.

Cyberstalking incidents take a variety of forms and can involve multiple victims and multiple perpetrators. Some incidents can also involve an organization as the victim or perpetrator and are usually described as *corporate cyberstalking*. The online activities of pedophiles, such as *grooming*, are also considered to be related to cyberstalking. As an example, an official report on cyberstalking prepared by the U.S. Attorney general links cyberstalking with the sexual abuse of children. The report states:

> Although the Internet and other forms of electronic communication offer new and exciting opportunities for children, they also expose children to new threats. For example, Federal law enforcement agencies have encountered numerous instances in which adult pedophiles have made contact with minors through online chat rooms, established a relationship with the child, and later made contact for the purpose of engaging in criminal sexual activities.[2]

There is some debate as to whether or not cyberstalking is an entirely new form of deviant behavior. Some writers and criminologists believe that cyberstalking is simply an extension of offline stalking.[3] This point of view sees technology as just another tool used by a stalker to pursue his victim. This approach sees defamatory posts to a message board as comparable to poison pen letters, while abusive e-mail is equivalent to a threatening phone call. Another perspective sees cyberstalking as a completely new form of crime, one that has only existed for a decade or so and that is still evolving. Some of the arguments in favor of this view are difficult to refute, for instance there is evidence to show that the motives behind cyberstalking can be very different to those behind offline stalking.[4]

A number of common behaviors are associated with cyberstalking, including the following:

- Making threats: Most cyberstalking incidents involve threats made against the victim, usually made by e-mail or via instant messaging.
- False accusations: Many cyberstalkers attempt to harm the reputation of a victim by posting false information about them.
- *False victimization:* Some cyberstalkers attempt to escape blame for their actions by falsely claiming that their victims have harassed them.

- Abusing the victim: Many cyberstalkers send their victims abusive or offensive messages by e-mail or via instant messaging. E-mail messages are often accompanied by pornography or other offensive materials.
- Attacks on data and equipment: Cyberstalkers may sometimes attempt to damage a victim's computer system, usually by transmitting a computer virus or other destructive program.
- Attempts to gather information about the victim: Cyberstalkers use a variety of different methods in order to gather information about their victims. In some cases, they have even been known to hire private detectives or advertise for information via the Internet.
- Impersonating the victim: Cyberstalkers often attempt to impersonate their victims with the intention of humiliating them or encouraging other people to take part in the harassment.
- Encouraging others to harass the victim: Many cyberstalkers find ways of using third parties to harass their victims. A common technique involves posting the victim's details to message boards dealing with prostitution or rape fantasies. Victims may receive hundreds of telephone calls and e-mail messages. In some cases, people have arrived at the victim's home expecting a sexual encounter. Involving third parties in harassment is usually described as *stalking-by-proxy*.
- Ordering goods or services on behalf of the victim: Some cyberstalkers cause nuisance or distress by ordering items on behalf of the victim. In some cases, cyberstalkers attempt to humiliate their victims by ordering embarrassing products, such as sex toys, and having them delivered to the victim's place of employment.
- Arranging to meet the victim: There have been many cases where cyberstalkers have traveled to meet their victims, or where victims have gone to meet the cyberstalker.
- Physical assault: Although such incidents rare, cyberstalkers have sometimes gone on to attack their victims.

THE EXTENT OF THE PROBLEM

There are no reliable estimates regarding the number of cyberstalking incidents that take place each year. In addition, it is not known how many cyberstalkers are currently active, and how many victims there are.[5] Some people have made a direct comparison between offline stalking and cyberstalking, making some huge leaps in logic in order to arrive at some dubious figures. It is these figures that are often cited in the media, somehow gaining more credibility each time they are published.

Although it is felt that offline stalking and cyberstalking are not directly comparable, they are clearly related and share many characteristics. This means that knowing something of offline stalking may help to improve our understanding of cyberstalking.

Findings from a National Violence against Women Survey that took place in 1998 are often quoted in the media and official reports. The survey was the first major inquiry into stalking in the United States and remains one of the largest studies of its kind. In all, 8,000 men and 8,000 women took part in a nationally representative telephone survey that gathered detailed information on respondents' experience of violence. The report suggests that 1 in 12 women and 1 in 45 men have experienced stalking at some point in their lives.[6] In the year preceding the survey, 1 percent of all women and 0.4 percent of all men were stalked. Although these figures may seem small, they refer to millions of Americans. For instance, the figures describing the lifetime incidence of stalking translate to 8.2 million women and 2 million men.[7]

It is interesting to note that the statistics for the United States are comparable with other countries, such as the United Kingdom, Canada, and Australia. For example, the 1998 British Crime Survey found that 11.8 percent of the population had been stalked at some time in their lives,[8] a figure that is in keeping with the value of 10.3 percent reported by the National Violence against Women Survey.

If, as some people argue, these figures can be translated to cyberstalking, this would mean a global population of almost half a million cyberstalkers pursuing around 3.5 million victims.[9] In the United States, there would be approximately 132,000 cyberstalkers and around one million victims.

Such estimates are based on a number of assumptions and cannot be considered precise. As an example, other estimates claim that the number of cyberstalking victims worldwide could lie between 474,000 and 18.75 million. Since all of these estimates are based on similar assumptions, it is difficult to decide which is most accurate. Perhaps a better way of helping people to understand the extent of cyberstalking is by looking at the potential number of cyberstalkers and victims. In 1999, the Department of Justice published a report entitled *Cyberstalking: A New Challenge for Law Enforcement and Industry*. The report was careful to avoid offering firm figures, preferring to state:

> Assuming the proportion of cyberstalking victims is even a fraction of the proportion of persons who have been the victims of offline stalking within the preceding 12 months, there may be potentially tens or even hundreds of thousands of victims of recent cyberstalking incidents in the United States.[10]

The accuracy of published estimates has also been challenged in the media. As an example, the report from the Department of Justice mentioned estimates obtained from an online safety organization. Referring to these figures, Lewis Koch, a technology writer, wrote:

> The alleged number of stalkers in the U.S. is 200,000. That number has been floating around for eight years. The reporter who first reported it in 1992 can't exactly recall his source. Oprah Winfrey and Sally Jessy Raphael picked it up that year.[11]

Although it is not possible to provide any firm figures regarding the extent of cyberstalking, it is still possible to gain an insight into the severity of the problem by looking at the number of cases dealt with by online safety organizations. Two of the very largest online safety organizations are Working to Halt Online Abuse (WHOA) and CyberAngels. Curtis Sliwa, who also founded the Guardian Angels, founded CyberAngels in 1995. CyberAngels has reported dealing with up to 500 cyberstalking cases each day, of which 65–100 represent genuine incidents.[12] WHOA was founded by Jayne Hitchcock as a way of helping others following her own experience as a victim of harassment. Several years ago, WHOA's Web site[13] reported that the organization dealt with up to 100 cases each week. More recently, the site has reported that 50 cases a week are dealt with.

Web Police was one of the oldest and largest Internet safety organizations. Originally established in 1986 and with branches located around the world, the organization dealt with all forms of computer crime. Figures published in 2004, prior to the demise of the Web Police Web site, reported that 3,704 criminal and civil complaints were received each day. Of these incidents, only 31 percent were considered valid in terms of being related to the Internet. This amounted to 1,148 complaints each day, grouped into a number of categories. These categories included child pornography (195), stalking (126), harassment or threats (103), and chat room abuse (23). It was unusual that Web Police saw these behaviors as separate from one another, but taken together, they amounted to 447 complaints each day that could be linked with cyberstalking. Interestingly, Web Police reported a success rate of 87 percent, meaning that most valid complaints were resolved satisfactorily.

WHO ARE THE CYBERSTALKERS?

Since so little is known about cyberstalking there are no accepted typologies of cyberstalkers. However, typologies of offline stalkers are sometimes helpful in understanding the behavior of some cyberstalkers.

A complete discussion of stalking typologies is beyond the scope of this book, but two of the best-known and potentially useful come from researchers in the United States and Australia. Michael Zona and his colleagues carried out a review of case files from the Threat Management Unit of the Los Angeles Police Department.[14] They found three basic types of stalker: erotomanics, love obsessionals, and simple obsessionals.

Erotomanics are those who are convinced that they are loved by the people they stalk. Most erotomanics are female and there will have been no prior relationships with the people stalked. The attention of erotomanics tends to focus on celebrities. Love obsessionals also tend to believe that the people they stalk love them. However, love obsessionals are different from erotomanics because their delusions come from a more serious psychotic illness, and they sometimes understand that the victim does not love them in return. Most love obsessionals are male and most focus on celebrities. Simple obsessionals tend to pursue people with whom there has been a previous relationship of some kind. Although many victims are ex-intimate partners, other groups are also represented such as neighbors and work colleagues. This group is made up of equal numbers of males and females.

Australian researcher Paul Mullen and his colleagues[15] proposed a classification made up of five categories of stalkers: rejected, intimacy seeking, incompetent, resentful, and predatory. A rejected stalker pursues an ex-intimate, such as a former spouse or girlfriend. Rejected stalkers are motivated by a desire to achieve some kind of reconciliation or a desire for revenge against the victim. The intimacy seeker hopes to establish a relationship with the object of his affection. He often believes that the victim feels the same way, and that a romantic relationship is destined to happen. Unlike other stalkers, the incompetent stalker is not in love with his victim and is simply trying to establish contact with her, perhaps by asking for a date. This type of stalking seldom lasts very long but may be repeated frequently with a new victim each time. The resentful stalker is seeking revenge for some kind of hurt or injury, whether real or imagined. The stalker wishes to frighten the victim so that he feels that he has exacted revenge. Resentful stalkers sometimes present themselves as victims in the same way that some cyberstalkers try to use false victimization as a defense for their actions. The predatory stalker is often regarded as the most dangerous type of stalker. This person uses stalking as a way of preparing for an attack the victim. Assaults are usually sexual in nature and can involve a great deal of violence.

Another way of examining stalking and cyberstalking is by looking at some of the behaviors displayed by stalkers. Brian Spitzberg,[16] a professor at San Diego State University, analyzed 103 studies of stalking and developed a classification of the behaviors commonly found in stalking incidents. These behaviors take one of seven basic forms:

1. hyperintimacy, or behaviors displaying excessive interest in developing a relationship
2. proximity/surveillance, or following types of behavior
3. invasion, in which the stalker trespasses on the victim's property, space, or privacy
4. proxy, in which the stalker involves associates of the victim or third parties to pursue the victim
5. intimidation and harassment, whereby the stalker threatens or otherwise attempts to psychologically manipulate the victim
6. coercion and constraint, through which the stalker controls the victim through extortion, threat, or force
7. aggression, which takes the form of violence, whether sexual or nonsexual

Spitzberg's classification is important because it can also be applied to cyberstalking incidents with little difficulty. For instance, "invasion" might describe attempts to compromise the victim's computer system.

WHO IS MOST AT RISK?

As mentioned, there are very few sources of information regarding cyberstalking. One of the best-known sources is WHOA's online harassment figures,[17] which are published each year.

It must be stressed that the data provided by WHOA is not representative, since it consists of information obtained from self-selected stalking victims. In addition, in many cases the data is incomplete, usually because victims of stalking have been unwilling or unable to provide various pieces of information. Finally, there are methodological issues related to the collection and analysis of the data that may influence reliability and validity. Despite these problems, WHOA's figures remain the only widely accessible statistics.

The 2005 figures are based on a total of 443 cases dealt with by the organization and cover a number of areas. Since all of WHOA's data is easily accessible online, only a brief summary is provided here. Note that a number of incomplete responses mean that percentage values will not always total 100.

The largest groups of victims were aged 18–30 (38 percent), 31–40 (25 percent), and 41 or older (30 percent). WHOA has noted that the proportion of victims aged 41 or older has been increasing since 2003. This might be explained as the result of increased computer literacy among younger people. As young people become more able to protect themselves against online harassment, the number of younger victims is likely to fall. On the other hand, the number of victims aged 41 or older is likely to remain fairly constant, or might even start to increase as the Internet becomes more accessible. If this line of reasoning is correct, the proportion of victims aged 18–30 or younger should fall, while the proportion of victims aged 41 or older should rise. WHOA's figures appear to support this view, since they show that both groups are changing as described. However, it may be a number of years before there is enough data to confirm this argument.

Some other characteristics of victims include the following:

- As might be expected, most victims were female (67 percent), with men only making up a quarter (25 percent) of all victims.
- In terms of marital status, a large proportion of victims was single (37 percent). Almost a third of victims were married (31 percent) and a further one in ten were divorced (11 percent).
- In terms of ethnicity, the majority of victims were Caucasian (73 percent). Smaller groups were Hispanic (5.5 percent), African-American (4 percent), Asian (4 percent), or Native American (2.5 percent).
- In general, most victims lived in the United States, with smaller groups located in Canada and the United Kingdom. In the United States, the largest groups of victims were located in California (11 percent), New York (5.75 percent), Florida (5.25 percent), Virginia (4.25 percent), Pennsylvania (4.25 percent), and Texas (3.25 percent).

- In order, most cases of harassment began via e-mail, message boards, instant messaging, chat rooms, or Web sites. Other methods of harassment included mailing lists, gaming Web sites, guest books, viruses, and blogs.
- Almost half of victims (49.5 percent) did not know the identity of the cyberstalker. When the cyberstalker was known to the victim, it was as an ex-intimate (33 percent), online acquaintance (26 percent), colleague (12 percent), friend (11 percent), an ex-intimate from an online relationship (6 percent), school friend (4 percent), or relative (3 percent).
- Asked if the harassment escalated, most victims (60 percent) responded that it did. Almost a quarter (22 percent) of victims reported that they received threats offline or that the harassment moved offline.
- In order, most of the cases WHOA resolved were handled by contacting the cyberstalker's ISP, advising the victim to change her online identity, other advice, referring the victim to law enforcement, or referring the victim to a lawyer.

As part of my own research into cyberstalking, I carried out a survey of 169 Internet users in order to learn more of how cyberstalking affects its victims.[18] Since this was an exploratory study, it must be stressed that the sample used was not representative and that the findings are considered only tentative.

Allowing for cases that may have involved more than one stalker, approximately a third of respondents (33.9 percent) could be considered genuine victims of cyberstalking.

Most cyberstalking victims were female (62.5 percent) and aged 30 years or older (60.7 percent). Only 19.6 percent of respondents were aged below 20, and a further 19.6 percent were aged between 21 and 30. More than three-quarters of respondents (76.5 percent) were married or living with a partner.

Most respondents lived in the United States (46.4 percent) or the UK (43.9 percent). In terms of ethnicity, most respondents described themselves as being of UK origin (40.3 percent) or as African-Caribbean (33.9 percent).

A large group of cyberstalking victims (42.1 percent) did not know the identity of the person who harassed them. It was noted that only a small number of respondents claimed to have been harassed by a work colleague (1.75 percent) or a former partner (8.77 percent). Almost a quarter (23.81 percent) of respondents stated that their cyberstalker encouraged others to take part in the harassment. Almost 42 percent of those who did not know the identity of their cyberstalker said that the cyberstalker had encouraged others to take part in the harassment.

Although the harassment experienced by many users had ceased, 26.3 percent reported that they were still being harassed at the time they completed the questionnaire. Respondents were asked to state how long the harassment they had experienced had lasted. The shortest period of harassment was two weeks, the longest 38 months. The average was 7.95 months, but most cases of harassment (63.2 percent) ended within six months.

While some of the statistics presented differ from WHOA's figures, there is sufficient agreement to identify some important risk factors. A crude "profile" of a typical cyberstalking victim could be this: Cyberstalking victims are likely to be female, Caucasian, aged 40 or below, and living in the United States. Approximately half of all victims will not know the identity of the cyberstalker. However, the cyberstalker is likely to be an ex-intimate, possibly from an online relationship. Although the harassment may escalate online, there is only a one-in-four possibility that it will move offline.

NEW AND EMERGING FORMS OF CYBERSTALKING

It was mentioned earlier that cyberstalking is still evolving as a form of deviance. Some new and emerging types of this abnormal online behavior include the following:

ONLINE GAMING

Although no research has been carried out in this area, accounts of harassment carried out in online gaming environments are beginning to appear on Web sites, blogs, message boards, and elsewhere.

Online games take place in an environment populated with interactive computer-controlled characters (called *NPCs* or *non-player characters*). Anyone with an Internet connection can take part in a game, although most require the payment of a monthly subscription. The latest online games operate on a large scale, allowing hundreds of human players to take part at any given time. Every player is free to interact with other human players or computer-controlled players. Players can carry out a wide range of activities, such as forming alliances, spying, sabotage, bartering, negotiating treaties, and so on.

Online games can contribute to harassment by allowing players to group together in order to victimize another player. As an example, members of the group may continually attack the victim's online character (called an *avatar)*, making it impossible for him to take part in the game. Alternatively, the group may refuse to communicate with the victim, "freezing" him out of the game.

Groups may also insult or threaten the victim while they play the game. Many online games allow people to communicate with each other as they play. Some players have headsets that allow them to speak to each other, while others use instant messages. This feature is sometimes used to send threats or offensive messages to another player. It is also possible for a player to rename his game character or use his own graphic for an avatar. Players sometimes choose a name or graphic intended to upset or frighten another person. In some cases, for example, avatars have been named after the victim, using prefixes such as "Death to …" or "Die …" The avatar's graphic has also been changed into an image of a skull, the Grim Reaper, or a skull and crossbones.

Although this kind of behavior may not seem particularly serious, it should be remembered that victims tend to be young people who may experience more distress than adults in this kind of situation. In addition, a number of factors may serve to increase the victim's distress. For instance, the harassment may be an extension of bullying that is taking place elsewhere, such as at school. The victim may start to feel that he is under constant pressure because the bullying does not stop when school finishes. Even at home, where he should be safe, the bully can still reach him and can still ruin his leisure time.

It is also worth noting that the behaviors described here can also take place with some kinds of multiplayer games, such as those played via games consoles.

CELL PHONES

As cell phones have become more powerful and more affordable, some people have started to use them to harass others. Most harassment takes the form of threatening text messages or calls. However, many modern phones are equipped with built-in cameras, allowing the use of photographs and video clips as a way of victimizing others. At one level, someone may capture an unflattering photograph of a friend and decide to send it to a small number of others. At another, several people might stage a violent incident, record it, and then make the video available to millions of viewers via the Internet.

MOSHZILLA

The potential harm caused by distributing photographs taken with a cell phone is illustrated by the following example:

> ... 19-year-old student Alex Stram took his new digital camera to a San Diego hardcore rock show, snapped a slew of pictures and posted them to his online photo gallery. One funny but arguably less-than-flattering picture of a young woman moshing [jumping and or bumping into other members of the audience] sparked the imaginations of viewers, who Photoshopped the mosher into a range of poses, including dancing in an iPod ad, walking on the moon, and duking it out in the boxing ring with Homer Simpson. Creative, to be sure. But some images were less innocuous, depicting the girl, for example, in sexually compromising positions.
>
> Within a few weeks, the photos had spread to multiple message boards, some of which were attracting a quarter of a million hits and 30 responses a page.[19]

In the United Kingdom and Europe, the practice of filming violent attacks has become known as *happy slapping*. Since 2004, the number and severity of such incidents has started to increase because of competition among those who participate in attacks. Since 2005, an increasing number of incidents have seen victims severely beaten, raped, and even killed. Table 10.1 provides some examples of serious incidents from around the world.

Table 10.1   Some Examples of "Happy Slapping" Incidents from Around the World

Year	Location	Incident
2005	United Kingdom	Three 14-year-old boys were arrested in connection with the rape of an 11-year-old girl. A video of the attack was video-taped and sent to peers at her school.[a]
2005	United Kingdom	A girl had surgery to remove a pellet from her leg after a young man shot her with an air rifle while his friend photographed the attack with his mobile phone.[b]
2005	United States	In California, a high-school student was charged with felony assault for punching a class-mate in a school locker room. The incident was recorded and posted on the Internet. The 17-year-old victim ended up with a crushed jaw and a black eye.[c]
2005	Germany	Two youths—one Italian and one Spanish—each received a nine-year prison sentence for beating a disabled British man to death and recording the attack using a cell phone.[d]
2005	Spain	Two youths were arrested for a series of happy slapping attacks, including assaults on a 50-year-old man and an 18-year-old.[e]
2005	Saudi Arabia	Two Saudi men raped a 17-year-old girl and distributed a video made with a camera phone via the Internet. Both men were sentenced to be flogged and jailed.[f]

Table 10.1   (continued)

Year	Location	Incident
2005	Italy	Two men used a camera phone to record the rape of a 17-year-old girl, then distributed the video to their friends.[g]
2006	Germany	A mobile phone was used to record an attack on a 15-year-old girl by 15 youths.[h]

[a]Katz, 2005.
[b]Katz, 2005.
[c]Katz, 2005.
[d]Carabott, 2005; Saunders, 2005.
[e]*The Spain Herald,* January 19, 2006.
[f]Reiter, 2005.
[g]PicturePhoning.com, 2005.
[h]Connolly, 2006.

Not all serious incidents involving cell phones need involve violence. There have been many cases where harassment has led to a variety of serious outcomes. Some examples include:

- In 2000, Gail Jones, a 15-year-old schoolchild from the United Kingdom, died after being harassed via her cell phone. After receiving as many as 20 silent calls in half an hour, Gail committed suicide by taking an overdose. Ironically, Gail left a suicide text message on her phone before she died.[20]
- In 2005, Shaun Noonan, a 14-year-old from the United Kingdom, committed suicide by hanging himself after becoming a victim of bullying, including a happy slapping incident.[21]
- In 2004, an Indian schoolboy recorded a sexual encounter between himself and a 16-year-old girl using his mobile phone. The video clip found its way to the Internet, where copies were sold via an auction site. When tried for his actions, prosecutors demanded the boy should be placed in psychiatric care for displaying "animal instincts." Eventually, the boy was made to undergo counseling and his parents made to submit weekly behavioral reports. The girl involved in the incident was sent to live in Canada by her parents.[22]

The extent of harassment by cell phone in the United States is not known. Much of the relatively scant research into this form of harassment has been carried out in the United Kingdom, and the figures that have been published suggest a serious and growing problem. For instance, a survey by National Childrens' Homes found that 14 percent of the young people they interviewed had received text message that they found distressing.[23] Of equal interest are the survey's findings concerning parents, those that young people are expected to call upon for help. Some 37 percent of parents were unaware of the danger of harassment via cell phones, and 19 percent thought that this kind of harassment was not common or never happens.[24]

It seems only a matter of time before the trends seen in Europe begin to appear in the United States, especially since ownership of sophisticated camera phones is steadily increasing. For instance, while only 3 percent of Internet users in the United States owned a camera phone in 2004, more than a quarter (27 percent) owned one by the end of 2005.[25] As phones become more sophisticated, it is likely that new ways of using them to harass others will emerge. As an example, as ownership of phones with *Bluetooth* (wireless) technology has started to rise, accounts of harassment carried out using this facility have started to appear.

BLOGS AND PHONES

The link between cell phones and the Internet has been strengthened with the introduction of moblogs. A blog is an online journal, a diary that is published on a Web site. A *moblog* allows new entries to be published in a journal directly from a cell phone. Material can be made available to Internet users within moments of taking a photograph or entering a few lines of text into the phone. Moblogs have been linked with happy slapping incidents because they allow the "proof" of a successful attack to be published almost instantly.

REACTIVE STALKING

My own research into cyberstalking proposes that former victims of harassment may sometimes go on to victimize others as a direct result of their experiences, a behavior I have termed *reactive stalking*.[26] Although my research has focused on reactive stalking in the context of cyberstalking, there seems to be no reason why the material should not apply equally to offline stalking. For this reason, I have chosen a single term to refer to all forms of this behavior.

The reasoning behind reactive cyberstalking is that victims of any form of stalking have direct knowledge of a number of behaviors intended to harm, control, or terrorize others. Knowing how these behaviors have been used against them, and knowing how effective they can be, some people use these methods against those they see as a threat.

Some forms of reactive stalking involve a self-perpetuating cycle of fear, paranoia, and extreme behavior. Fear leads to a constant lookout for evidence of some kind of threat. If no threat exists, perfectly innocent events may be reinterpreted to validate the reactive stalker's fear. Having created a threat, the stalker feels justified in taking action against those considered responsible. In turn, the need to take extreme action reinforces the stalker's fear, causing the cycle to repeat. Reactive stalking becomes most serious when like-minded people come together and begin to reinforce each other's fears and beliefs.

In order to avoid any misunderstanding, it must be made clear that reactive stalkers should not be seen in the same light as other stalkers. In most cases, reactive stalkers genuinely believe that they are acting in defense of themselves and their families.[27] Furthermore, there is seldom a deliberate intent to cause harm to others since many of the stalker's actions may be carried out unconsciously. When dealing with reactive stalking, our first instinct should be to offer help, not mete out punishment.

I obtained firsthand experience of reactive stalking while researching a case where a group of people harassed a writer and some of her friends. The group's harassment of the writer included attacks on her reputation, threats, and false allegations. In one incident, the group accused the writer of fraud with the result that she lost her job. In another, it was alleged that the group attempted to convince a second stalker to target the writer. The writer had befriended another victim of stalking, and it was believed that the group had managed to contact the friend's stalker in order to persuade her to harass the writer.

When I began to research this case, I encountered many of the same behaviors seen by the writer. Like the writer, I was subjected to threats, false allegations, and attempts to harm my employment. The group also attempted to use stalking-by-proxy by involving Jayne Hitchcock—arguably the world's most famous Internet safety advocate—in their activities. However, although Hitchcock initially appeared to be taken in by the claims made by the group, she quickly realized that the group might be trying to manipulate her and withdrew. It is interesting to note that the group's behavior became more extreme over time, largely because the members tended to reinforce each other's fantasies. For instance, the group's initial allegations focused on my credentials as a writer and academic. Within days, it was being claimed that I was colluding with the stalkers of those who had responded to an anonymous online questionnaire I had developed. For this claim to be true, I would have needed to identify, locate, and then make agreements with more than two hundred individual stalkers.

SAFETY AND PREVENTION

The single most important way in which people can protect themselves against cyberstalkers and other predators is by controlling their personal information to ensure that it does not become accessible to others. Many Internet users are shocked to learn that a great deal of information about them is available free of charge to anyone with a little time and patience. The more active a person has been as an Internet user, for example by using newsgroups and chat rooms, the more information is likely to be available.

Many cyberstalking cases begin with arguments that take place in chat rooms or newsgroups. Before joining in a chat room conversation or posting to a newsgroup, it is a good idea to watch for a while, so that you can learn how the group functions. Watching a newsgroup or chat room like this is often called *lurking*. Although some people dislike lurkers, explaining that you are trying to learn how the group functions before joining in usually avoids any hostility.

Cyberstalking cases can also begin from simple misunderstandings, making it important to learn how to behave appropriately when posting to newsgroups or taking part in chat room conversations. The "rules" that describe how to behave correctly when using chat rooms, newsgroups, and other services are often called *netiquette*. Learning netiquette serves several purposes and may help to protect against those who become aggressive or abusive towards you. For instance, in the event that you become harassed by another user, you are likely to receive support from other people because you will have been seen to have acted properly at all times.

Business Users

I am not aware of any published guidelines for organizations that deal with cyberstalking. The following advice is drawn from a wide variety of sources, including the general computer security advice offered by various writers and researchers. It is also worth noting that the guidelines that follow are of most relevance to small organizations. This is because larger companies will have a team of dedicated security specialists and will have already implemented most of the advice given here.

- Implement an acceptable use policy (AUP). Make sure that all employees are aware of the AUP and are familiar with its content. Many companies make compliance with the company's AUP part of the conditions of employment for new members of staff.
- Take regular *software audits*. This involves checking company computer systems to make sure that no illegal content is being stored, such as pornography or pirated software.
- Try to predict some of the threats the company is most likely to face. Plan how the company can maintain normal operation in the event of a serious problem, such as a denial of service attack. *Business continuity planning* is essential since no security measures are ever completely foolproof.
- Ensure that regular backups are made of important data. Although employees should be encouraged to make backups of their own data, someone should be given overall responsibility for ensuring that data stored on a network is backed up at regular intervals.
- Consider placing controls on the use of company facilities for e-mail and Web browsing. This can be done in many different ways. For instance, some companies use specialized software that controls access to certain Web sites

and maintains a log of user activity. In some companies, personal use of company e-mail and Internet facilities by employees is banned.

- Consider monitoring the Internet traffic—including e-mail—that passes through the company's systems. This may help to detect incoming or outgoing messages containing inappropriate content, such as threats.

INDIVIDUALS AND FAMILIES

With regard to e-mail, chat rooms, message boards, and newsgroups, a number of additional points are also relevant. The following advice is derived from a large number of sources, including the U.S. Department of Justice (Reno, 1999), National Center for Victims of Crime, WHOA, and others.

- Always avoid becoming involved in arguments of any kind. As soon as a discussion begins to involve personal attacks of any kind, you should withdraw.
- Avoid disclosing personal information. There are many ways you can disguise or hold back personal information. For instance, when asked where they live, some people name a city near to them. This allows them to talk about their locality while making it a little harder for anyone to locate them.
- Use a gender-neutral nickname. Do not use a nickname that might be considered provocative in any way.
- Consider opening a new e-mail account (called a *throwaway* account) that can be used for posting to newsgroups or visiting chat rooms. There are many providers of free e-mail accounts, making it possible to discard an e-mail address if it becomes targeted for abusive messages.
- Never complete personal profiles on services such as ICQ, MSN, and Yahoo. This is likely to be one of the first places a cyberstalker will look for information.
- Do not give out personal information, such as your real name or telephone number. This can provide a cyberstalker with a starting point for gathering more detailed information.
- Never send out pictures of yourself, since these could be modified and posted on Web sites or in newsgroups.
- Do not flirt with other users. According to organizations such as Wired-Patrol, this is how many cyberstalkers first come into contact with their victims.
- Never agree to meet someone in person unless you are completely comfortable in doing so. If you choose to meet someone, arrange the first few meetings so that they are short and take place in a public location. In addition, make sure a friend accompanies you and that other people know where you are and when you are expected to return.
- Never send rude or offensive e-mail. In general, never say something in an e-mail message that you are not prepared to say face-to-face.
- Make sure that your e-mail signature does not contain information that you do not want made public. The help files that accompany your e-mail program will provide information on how to edit or delete a signature.

FURTHER INFORMATION

Reading

Bocij, P., 2004. *Cyberstalking: Harassment in the Internet Age and How to Protect Your Family.* Westport, CT: Praeger Press.

Bocij, P., 2003. "Victims Of Cyberstalking: An Exploratory Study of Harassment Perpetrated Via the Internet." *First Monday* [online] *8,* no. 10. Available at: http://www.firstmonday.dk/issues/issue8_10/bocij/index.html.

Reno, J., 1999. *Cyberstalking: A New Challenge for Law Enforcement and Industry.* Washington, D.C.: U.S. Department of Justice. Available online at: http://www.usdoj.gov/criminal/cybercrime/cyberstalking.htm.

Online

Cyberstalking Info is owned and operated by the author of this book as a nonprofit organization dedicated to research and victim support: www.cyberstalking.info.

Caslon Analytics provides an overview of cyberstalking, complete with numerous references: http://www.caslon.com.au/stalkingnote.htm.

Although Bully Online is a British organization, the articles, advice, and information it provides are suitable for an international audience. The site covers all aspects of bullying and harassment, including technological forms of harassment, such as that carried out with the use of cell phones: www.bullyonline.org.

Online Relationships

As complex as human relationships are, the Internet makes matters more difficult by allowing entirely new kinds of relationships to develop. Relationships can be formed and maintained over long distances in a way that is more immediate than sending a letter or waiting for someone to pick up a phone. Relationships can also exist entirely online, with people able to find new friends without ever leaving their homes. It is even possible to meet a lover and consummate an affair without the partners ever physically meeting in the offline world.

However, while chat rooms, message boards, webcams, and other technological tools can enrich the lives of many people, they can also be abused, causing tremendous pain and suffering. As this section has shown, people can be deceived in many different ways. A person with the very best intentions might be tricked into helping a cyberstalker by providing him with information or by taking part in stalking-by-proxy.

Romantic relationships pose a particular problem for many Internet users. In an online relationship, for instance, everything one partner knows about another is based on trust. On the Internet, men can become women, the old can become young, the poor can become rich, and the plain can become beautiful. A photograph sent by a woman to a man might show a young, attractive woman with a bright smile. In reality, the photograph is of a friend or has been culled from a magazine or Web site—the real woman talking to the man is someone who is overweight, middle-aged, and simply looking for attention. In a similar way, the man who claims to be single can turn out to be married with children and may even have dozens of other online lovers. Ultimately, even the most basic facts known about another person met online may need to be questioned. For instance, there have been many cases where men have posed as women online in order to humiliate other men or as part of a crude extortion scheme.

Once a relationship of some kind has been established, other risks may need to be faced. The sympathetic ears that listen patiently to someone's problems may not be as concerned as they seem. Instead, they may be waiting for an opportunity to recruit the troubled person into a cult or far-right group.

Despite all of these dangers, it is possible to carry out safe and fulfilling social and romantic relationships via the Internet. However, in order to do so, equal quantities of caution and common sense are needed.

As with many of the other areas discussed in this book, it is not possible to provide detailed coverage of every aspect of an area such as this. An in-depth discussion of online relationships could be—and has been—the subject of an entire book. Instead, some selected areas have been chosen because they raise a number of issues considered important to Internet users.

Social Isolation

Web sites, blogs, and message boards carry literally thousands of accounts of failed online relationships. Many of these accounts describe infidelity, emotional abuse, fraud, and blackmail. Despite having experienced these things, some people continue to move from one online relationship to another, often ignoring any warning signs that suggest history may be about to repeat itself. Why is this?

Perhaps part of the answer lies in the notion of social isolation, which can be described as loneliness brought on by not being able to interact with other people or take part in social events. Many such people come to rely on the Internet for social interaction; for some it is the only way they can communicate with other adults.

People may become socially isolated for a number of reasons. For instance, a lone parent caring for a disabled child is likely to have limited opportunities to engage in social activities and form new friendships. Elderly and disabled people can also become isolated if they find it difficult to travel within the local community, or if children and relatives live far away. Other factors, such as unemployment, living in a rural location, or being unable to speak English are also likely to play an important part.

It is difficult to estimate how many people can be described as socially isolated in the United States. Although social isolation has been looked at in the context of specific groups, such as the elderly, little—if any—research has attempted to examine the extent of the problem across the entire population. At best, we can only hope to indicate whether or not a serious problem exists by looking at the potential number of socially isolated adults in the United States.

Those most likely to become socially isolated are lone parents, the elderly, and those with disabilities. The U.S. Census Bureau[1] publishes a great deal of statistical information that can be viewed or downloaded free of charge. Figures from the 2004 American Community Survey estimated that almost 38 million Americans aged five years and over have a disability. This amounts to approximately 14.3 percent of the population. The survey also estimated that approximately 34 million Americans are aged 65 or over, amounting to approximately 12 percent of the population. With regard to lone parents, 27 percent of children lived in single parent families in 2001.[2] However, since several children might live with a single adult, the proportion of lone parent households is likely to be significantly smaller.

Although these figures do not allow the total number of socially isolated adults to be calculated, they do suggest a problem that might affect millions of people. As an example, a number of studies have shown that the sense of loneliness normally associated with social isolation affects 20–60 percent of the elderly.[3]

The crude figures discussed here suggest that social isolation is a serious and growing problem in the United States. In addition, there seems to be no reason to believe that the situation is significantly different in other similar societies. For instance, the proportion of people living alone and aged 65 or over in the United States is similar to that in the United Kingdom and a number of European countries.[4] Similarly, the proportion of single parent families in the United States is in keeping with countries such as the United Kingdom[5] and Australia.[6]

If we accept that social isolation seems likely to affect relatively large numbers of people, then it also seems reasonable to suggest that many people turn to the Internet as a way of dealing with their loneliness. Once again, however, there are no figures that can be used to estimate Internet usage among socially isolated adults. As before, general figures related to Internet use can provide only a vague idea of how many socially isolated adults make regular use of the Internet in order to interact with others.

The number of people who make regular use of the Internet is similar across countries such as the United States, the United Kingdom, and Australia. As an example, NUA Internet Surveys[7] has collected a number of estimates concerning the number of Internet users throughout the world and within individual countries. According to the company, the total number of Internet users in the world stood at more than 600 million as of September 2002. In the United States, more than half of the population were regular Internet users (59.1 percent), as of 2002, a figure in keeping with countries such as the United Kingdom (57.24 percent), Australia (54.38 percent), Canada (52.79 percent), and New Zealand (52.7 percent). Use of the Internet by different groups is also similar across countries. In the United States, for example, around a quarter of all adults aged 65 or over make regular use of the Internet,[8] compared with up to 18 percent of UK adults aged 65 or over.[9]

Although there are differences in the way that people from different cultures/countries use the Internet,[10] people tend to engage in the same basic activities, such as sending e-mail, visiting chat rooms, and searching for information. The Pew Internet & American Life Project studies the impact of the Internet of the lives of Americans. The project carries out extensive surveys and other research that is made available to the public free of charge. According to the project, on an average day more than half of Americans go online (53 percent).[11] Once online, their social activities include sending e-mail (45 percent), using instant messaging (12 percent), playing a game (9 percent), taking part in an online group (6 percent), using a chat room or taking part in an online discussion (4 percent), or using an online dating service (2 percent).

These figures seem to suggest that relatively few people use chat rooms or dating services. This is somewhat misleading, since even a small proportion of Internet users can represent many thousands—or even millions—of people. In the case of chat rooms, for instance, it was estimated that there were more than 1.25 million chat rooms worldwide in 2003.[12] The suggestion that only two percent of users visit online dating services may also be a little misleading. For instance, at least one online dating service based in Europe claims to have more than 6 million members.[13]

It is accepted that some of the points made here may seem somewhat tenuous because of a lack of accurate and appropriate statistical data. Despite this, it is held that the overall argument is sound. Commonsense reasoning supports the view that if there are millions of socially isolated adults in the United States and beyond, at least some will use the Internet for social interaction.

Although people will hope that the Internet provides a way to establish and maintain social relationships, it may actually increase social isolation in some cases. As an example, a study by the Stanford Institute for the Quantitative Study of Society (SIQSS) carried out in 2000 found that the more people use the Internet, the more socially isolated they are likely to become.[14] Similar findings were made in a study of adolescents by Sanders et al.[15] The activities people carry out while using the Internet may also act to increase social isolation. Schnieder,[16] for instance, found that people who take part in cybersex may become socially isolated through a variety of factors, such the breakdown of key relationships. However, other writers argue that the Internet is beneficial in terms of building and maintaining social relationships. McKenna and Bargh,[17] for instance, suggest that the Internet provides a wealth of new opportunities "... to explore aspects of identity and to interact with members of socially sanctioned groups, such as lesbians and gay men or fringe political groups." A similar view is expressed by Bradley and Poppen,[18] who studied a group of elderly, disabled, and housebound people given access to the Internet. Subjects were able to make friends with people in similar circumstances to themselves, resulting in significant changes in their lives.

Once people begin to use the Internet as a primary means of communicating with others, they become vulnerable to a number of risks. While many of these risks have parallels in the offline world, some are unique to the Internet. Insincere suitors (often termed *love rats* or *love cheats*), for example, are common both online and offline.

LOVE CHEATS

A study carried out by the University of Florida looked at the impact of online relationships on married couples. A total of 76 men and 10 women were interviewed about their use of chat rooms and their reasons for forming an online relationship. Most people said that they went into chat rooms because of boredom, a partner's lack of sexual interest, or a desire for variety and fun.[19] Almost a third of those interviewed eventually met the person they communicated with. Of this group, all but two ended up having an offline affair. In one case, a man had 13 affairs with women he had met over the Internet.[20]

Although all Internet users are vulnerable to online predators to some extent, those who are socially isolated often present targets that are particularly attractive. Such victims tend to have such a deep need for acceptance and friendship that it overrides their natural caution. This is often manifested by a willingness to believe in even the most ludicrous stories, or to forgive offensive behavior. It can also be argued that such victims are especially appealing to cyberstalkers and other abusive people. This is because the victim's reliance on the Internet is likely to amplify the anxiety and distress she suffers. At the same time, she will also be reluctant to give up her primary means of social interaction. Her isolation also means that there are fewer people she can call on for help and support, effectively decreasing the risk of capture to the cyberstalker.

Social isolation can help to explain why some people enter destructive relationships even when they suspect the person they are in contact with is insincere.

WHITE KNIGHTS

The image of a white knight is often used to represent a person who saves someone from danger or harm.[21] Often, the knight is presented as noble-minded and benevolent, a person without any motive other than a desire to rescue those in distress. This metaphor can be found in a wide variety of settings, from literature and film to business and politics. In business, for example, a white knight can be described as a potential buyer chosen by a company in order to avoid a hostile takeover.[22]

On the Internet, some users have begun to refer to the *white knight syndrome* (sometimes also known as *Florence Nightingale syndrome*) in order to describe two distinct forms of behavior associated with some of those seeking romantic relationships via chat rooms and other methods. Even a cursory search using Google returns over 900,000 results related to "white knight syndrome." Some typical examples include the following:

In an entry about long-term relationships, a personal blog (online diary) comments:

> Guys like crazy girls. I call it "The White Knight Syndrome." Many of my guy-friends have experienced it and I've had to watch them go through it, with my mouth shut. They think the girl needs help and they think that they can help her.[23]

SocialGrid describes itself as "… a free online dating service and decentralized social networking community that helps people meet through Google." In a section on dating tips,[24] the site states that the idea of entertainment value "… explains why some people are attracted to troubled people. Some people enjoy rescuing or fixing up screwed-up people (Florence Nightingale or White Knight syndrome)."

The Global Psychics Web site features a section on relationships that states:[25] "So many women are waiting for some white knight to come along and rescue then from their lives … I'm appalled and sometimes even a little ashamed of us as a species … "

In a message board devoted to personal relationships, one post reads:

> I am 56 and I am looking for someone in her fifty's who is attractive, young at heart, and who wants me without necessarily "needing" me. My therapist says I have the "White Knight" syndrome and she will hammer me if I look like I am rescuing a damsel in distress.[26]

As a final example, a blog created by a counselor makes the following comment:

> My extensive training in counseling mostly overcame that conditioning. Mostly. Two of my relationships were with women who were clinically depressed. I suffered from the White Knight syndrome, something not documented in the DSM IV-A. I tried to rescue them, even though they did not want to be rescued. That is another story.[27]

As the examples show, becoming a white knight for a man usually involves "rescuing" a woman—the proverbial "damsel in distress"—from some form of peril.[28] This peril can take many different forms and is largely a matter of interpretation on the part of the male involved. In some cases, for instance, a white knight may wish to rescue a woman from what he perceives as an abusive relationship. In others, the peril might take a more abstract form, such as poverty or disability.

A good example of this form of behavior involves men who seek to free women who work in the sex trade. Often, the Internet is used to locate information about where to find women who might be amenable to being rescued. The Mango Sauce Web site,[29] for instance, is a popular resource for expatriates and potential visitors to Thailand. According to the site, many Western males visit Bangkok with the aim of finding a girlfriend or wife and often form relationships with Thai prostitutes. Such relationships are common enough for the site to comment that "Ex-hooker wives and girlfriends seem to be the norm here." In explaining this, the site suggests "Could it be White Knight Syndrome? Planeloads of lonely, kind-hearted guys arrive in Thailand each day and there are plenty of damsels apparently in distress to choose from."

A further example involves the Dutch sex trade. The Channels Web site[30] offers a virtual tour of Amsterdam and features a knowledge base containing questions and answers compiled from a message board hosted at the site. One article contains a request for information on the sex trade from a man wishing to locate a sex worker that he hopes he can "… offer a better life somewhere else." Most of the responses are negative and point out how unrealistic the man's aims are. For instance, one person suggests: "In professional terms, you have what's called the 'white knight' syndrome—you wish to rescue a young woman who will be forever grateful to you. Forget it buddy. What you are proposing here is a fantasy and little else."

White knight syndrome can also be applied to women. Often, the term is applied to a woman who expresses a wish to be rescued from difficult circumstances she may be experiencing, such as problems within her current relationship. As indicated by the examples given earlier, sometimes the wish to meet a white knight is stimulated by a desire for excitement or a need for major lifestyle changes. However, the desire to meet a white knight can sometimes result in a woman being victimized by an insincere suitor. This may occur for several reasons; for instance the need to overcome her feelings of social isolation may cause a woman to overlook warning signs that she would otherwise act upon.[31] Alternatively, the would-be white knight may have developed ways of overcoming his target's natural caution, perhaps by developing an online persona with extremely attractive qualities. The case of Col. Kassem Saleh provides a fairly typical example of the emotional distress that can be caused by this kind of victimization.

Col. Kassem Saleh came to international attention in 2003, after it was found that he had started online relationships with up to 50 women across the United States and Canada. Saleh had even proposed to some of the women he romanced, although he was reportedly still married at the time.[32] Some of those he proposed to said they had turned their lives upside down by preparing to sell their homes and buying wedding dresses in preparation for marriage.[33]

Saleh was described as "... a Taliban-battling soldier with the soul of a poet who wrote intoxicating love letters home."[34] At 51 years old, Saleh's record was very impressive: He had headed reconstruction and humanitarian efforts for the U.S.–led military operation in Afghanistan and had 29 years of service.[35]

Saleh was accused of fabricating a number of stories in order to form relationships with women. For instance, he often claimed to be divorced and called himself the "monk warrior" because he said that he had not had sex for ten years.[36] In one case, he met a woman through www.tallpersonals.com, explaining away his 5'9" height by claiming that parachute jumps had caused to him to shrink down from 6'5".[37]

Following an enquiry, Saleh was found guilty of violating military regulations by disclosing sensitive information, committing adultery, and engaging in conduct unbecoming an officer.[38] He was also fined $7,000 in pay.

It is worth noting that Saleh's behavior should not be considered unusual. The work of Monica Whitty,[39] for example, demonstrates that men have very different attitudes to women regarding romance and infidelity. For instance, men are less likely than women to see sexual acts—whether offline or online *(cybersex)*—as a breach of fidelity. Whitty's research[40] also suggests that men are prone to lying about themselves in chat rooms in order to appear more attractive to women. However, perhaps the most convincing evidence that the behavior described here is commonplace is the existence of Web sites such as Infidelity Check.[41] This site provides statistics, case studies, and other resources concerning Internet relationships, especially "... Internet infidelity and destructive behavior resulting in the break down of family and intimate relationships." According to the statistics given on the site, less than half of men believe that online affairs are adultery, and one-third of divorce litigation is caused by online affairs.

Although the women described in this example undoubtedly endured a great deal of emotional distress, there are many other forms of victimization that they might have suffered. There are many personal accounts published on message boards, Usenet and personal Web sites that describe how white knight syndrome can ultimately result in outcomes such as blackmail, fraud, stalking, and cyberstalking. The Safer Dating Web site,[42] for instance, contains many personal accounts of this nature.

In extreme cases, white knight syndrome may also lead to murder. For instance, it can be argued that John Robinson, the serial killer known as Slavemaster, deliberately presented himself as a white knight to several of his victims. Robinson was sentenced to death in early 2004 for eight murders, although it is suspected that he may have been responsible for more. Robinson met most of his victims via the Internet and lured them to meetings through various inducements. In one case, Robinson met one of his victims, Lisa Stasi, at a refuge for battered women. Although separated from her husband, the woman told his family shortly before her disappearance that Robinson had put her up at a local hotel and had promised to set her up with a job in the Chicago area.[43] Another victim, Sheila Dale Faith, had recently become widowed and was caring for her disabled daughter when she met Robinson. Before her disappearance, Sheila told her friends that she had found her "dream man." Robinson had promised her that she would never have to work, that he would take her on a cruise, and that he would take care of her daughter, even offering to teach her to ride horses in Kansas.[44]

The murder of Kerry Kujawa demonstrates that men can also be taken advantage of with little difficulty. In 2000, Kerry developed an online relationship with a young woman named Kelly McCauley.[45] Kerry became attached to Kelly and eventually arranged a face-to-face meeting. A week or so after the meeting, Kerry's relatives and friends received an e-mail supposedly written by Kerry himself. The message stated that Kerry was fine and had decided to stay with Kelly a little longer. However, Kerry had been murdered by Kenny Wayne Lockwood and his body disposed of. The messages to Kerry's friends and family had been sent by Lockwood as a means of delaying suspicion. Lockwood had created the identity of Kelly as a way of meeting young men. The deception was assisted by a story that many men would find appealing: Kelly was in a destructive relationship and needed someone to help her. To complete the illusion, Lockwood sent photographs of an attractive young woman that was supposedly Kelly.

HERO SYNDROME

Like white knight syndrome, a person suffering from *hero syndrome* seeks to become a hero by saving people from danger. However, unlike White Knight Syndrome, the hero sometimes manufactures the threat he wishes to avert.

In the business world, hero syndrome is often used to refer to people who tend to take on too much work in order to please supervisors and colleagues. Heroes are driven "... by the need for approval, recognition, and being wanted and valued."[46] This means that they often become indispensable to their employers even though they may not be the most efficient or reliable employees.

For the emergency services, hero syndrome is often associated with arson. It is known that some people—including firefighters themselves—start small fires in order to gain recognition for averting a disaster.[47] With regard to firefighters, a report from the United States Fire Administration states:

> ... one of the primary motives for firefighters who commit arson is to be seen as a hero. They may be the first to call in a fire, the first on the scene, and one of the most eager, excited, and enthusiastic members of the response team. Their main reason for lighting the fire is so they can appear as a hero, either by being the first to spot the flames, or by rescuing people and saving property.[48]

The concept of hero syndrome became popularized in 1996, following an explosion in Centennial Olympic Park, Atlanta, during the 1996 Olympics. The explosion killed two people and injured 111 others.[49] A little before the explosion, Richard Jewell, a former law enforcement officer, told the FBI that he had seen a suspicious knapsack near a tower that was later damaged by the explosion. Jewell helped FBI agents move civilians away from the area and was initially praised for helping to save lives.[50] However, just three days later a newspaper published a story reporting that the FBI suspected Jewell of having planted the bomb in order to gain attention. Newspaper stories and television shows discussed the concept of hero syndrome, quoting various experts, including a former FBI behavioral scientist.[51] Jewell's guilt was assumed for almost three months until the FBI officially cleared him in October 1996. Another man, Eric Rudolph, was later arrested and charged with multiple crimes, including the 1996 bombing.[52]

It is worth noting that Jewell probably became a suspect for the bombing because of an earlier incident that took place during the 1984 Olympics in Los Angeles. In this incident, a police officer planted a pipe bomb on a bus and then took credit for disarming it. The police officer, Jimmy Wade Pearson, later admitted planting the bomb himself.[53] Following the incident, he resigned and was placed on probation for five years, fined $10,000, and ordered to undergo counseling.

It is relatively easy to locate many examples of hero syndrome in relation to the Internet. Typical cases usually involve a person starting a campaign of harassment targeted at one or more individuals. The "hero" then consoles the victim or offers his assistance in helping to end the harassment. Bocij, Bocij, and McFarlane[54] provide a good example of such behavior in their discussion of a serial cyberstalker who targeted a number of young, socially isolated women. In this case, a serial cyberstalker adopted three distinct online identities in order to disguise his activities. Each identity had a specific purpose with regard to the harassment. The first identity was that of a female who had a number of things in common with the victim, such as being a single mother. This identity was used for a number of purposes, such as gathering information about the victim or convincing her to take advice that seemed genuine but was of no practical value. The second identity used by the cyberstalker was that of a mature male who behaved sympathetically towards the victim, for example by offering encouragement. It can be argued that this identity represented the "hero" who came to each victim's assistance. The third identity was that of a young male who was responsible for most of the harassment experienced by victims. This identity clearly represented the threat or danger that victims needed to be "rescued" from.

Another example concerns the case of David Cruz, a U.S. citizen living in the UK, who began a campaign of harassment against an acquaintance, Chloe Easton, after she turned down his romantic advances.[55] Over a period of seven months, Cruz relentlessly harassed Easton and her family. In one incident, Cruz advertised Easton's personal details on a prostitution-related Web site with the result that she received more than 30 calls asking about her services. In another, Cruz contacted Easton's employers, posing as a business client and claiming that she had offered sexual services to him for a price. Cruz also targeted Easton's parents, for example by trying to convince them that she had appeared in pornographic videos, or by "warning" them that she was about to be gang-raped by a group of men waiting near her work. Throughout much of the harassment, Cruz gave the appearance of a concerned friend who was trying to help Easton find the person stalking her. For instance, he would use various nicknames to enter chat rooms and post made-up details of Easton's sexual activities. He would then tell Easton that he had accidentally found this information and offer to show it to her.[56] Following his conviction in 2003, Cruz received a prison sentence of five months.

FURTHER INFORMATION

Reading

Baker, A., 2002. "What Makes an Online Relationship Successful? Clues from Couples Who Met in Cyberspace." *CyberPsychology and Behavior* 5, no. 4 (August 2002). Available online at: http://oak.cats.ohiou.edu/~bakera/ArticleH.htm.

Baker, A., 2005. *Double Click: Romance and Commitment Among Online Couples.* Cresskill, NJ: Hampton Press Inc.

Silverstein, J. and Lasky, M., 2004. *Online Dating for Dummies.* Hoboken, NJ:Hungry Minds Inc.

Online

Online Dating Magazine provides articles, information, advice, and safety tips concerning online dating: www.onlinedatingmagazine.com.

SelfHelp Magazine provides a complete guide to handling online relationships, with a special emphasis on safety: http://www.selfhelpmagazine.com/articles/relation/booklet/cdintro.html.

Deviant Subcultures

The previous chapters in this section were largely concerned with romantic relationships; even cyberstalking can sometimes be viewed as an expression of one person's infatuation with another, no matter how abnormal. This chapter focuses on the hatred and depravity that controls how some people treat others. Although much of the material presented here is somewhat disturbing, its purpose is to educate readers about the very darkest parts of the Internet.

CULTS AND HATE SPEECH

Cults[1] have been active on the Internet since the mid- to late 1990s. As an example, the Aum Shinrikyo group, which was responsible for poison gas attacks on the Tokyo underground in 1995, was known to be using the Internet to recruit new members as early as 1998.

Although much has been written about the sophisticated brainwashing techniques employed by some cults, some people believe that simpler methods are used more commonly. Modern cults use many of the same techniques used to influence people every day, such as the methods used by advertising agencies to persuade us to buy a particular product.[2] Some of these methods are easily incorporated into the design of a Web site or into the wording of an e-mail message. Others require a little more work but can be highly effective.

Of particular interest is the "love bombing" technique favored by numerous cults[3] since it is often employed via the Internet. The Watchman

Fellowship[4] describes itself as "... an independent Christian research and apologetics ministry focusing on new religious movements, cults, the occult and the New Age." Although social isolation is not mentioned explicitly, the Fellowship's Web site explains how someone can become vulnerable to exploitation by a cult:

> The vulnerable person is someone who lacks something very important. That something can be a network of supportive people like family and friends. It can be someone who has suffered a significant loss like the death of a loved one, or a marriage, or a job. The sense of loss causes a person to seek something to fill the void. The college freshman who may be homesick, or out of contact with family and friends, is a good example of someone who is vulnerable. The motivations to find friends who will relieve the feelings of isolation are very strong and can overcome good judgment about finding the right kind of friends.

Love bombing involves creating a relationship where the victim becomes emotionally (and sometimes physically) dependent on another person. As long as the victim behaves as required, he will continue to receive attention and affection. In the case of a cult, when the recruit has been indoctrinated and is considered loyal, the attention paid to him can be gradually reduced. This frees the recruiter to locate another potential convert. The Watchman Fellowship says this about love bombing:

> Love bombing is an all-pervasive expression of caring for the individual and others ... In a cult the love stops when the individual is being corrected ... Love bombing also becomes a tool to keep people in the cult. The thought of losing the powerful sense of being loved by the group can dissuade the doubter from leaving.

As might be expected, love bombing is considered so effective that terrorist groups and far-right groups have also adopted it as part of their recruitment strategies.

The use of the Internet by extremist groups is well known and has been documented extensively. For instance, a great deal of attention has been paid to the use of racist Web sites as a means of promoting racism and recruiting new members. As the Internet has grown in popularity, so too has the number of Web sites operated by far-right organizations and other extremist groups. According to the Simon Wiesenthal Center, there was just one hate Web site in 1995, but this number had grown to 600 by the end of 1997.[5] By 1999, there were 1,426 hate sites, and there were more than 3,300 by June 2002.[6] The sophistication of hate sites has also increased over time. Early sites seldom made use of multimedia, such as sound or animation, and the materials made available to visitors were often badly written. Modern sites, however, are targeted at specific groups, such as children, and often contain materials intended to attract visitors, such as MP3 music and online games.[7] Research has also found that some Web sites use storytelling as a way of persuading adolescents to accept the values of certain groups.[8]

Not all attempts to spread racist messages or recruit new members are made by organized groups or through Web sites. As chat rooms have become more popular, some people have started to use them to recruit new members for the groups they belong to.[9] In many cases, attempts to find new members are made on a personal basis, rather than as part of an organized recruitment drive.

In some online communities, those who seek to recruit new members have become known as *headhunters*. A typical headhunter begins by attempting to form a friendship with someone considered a potential recruit. As the relationship develops, the headhunter uses discussion and persuasion to encourage the recruit to develop extreme views. Eventually, the recruit is introduced to other members of the extreme group and encouraged to join.

Sometimes, a headhunter may recruit people as his own followers before introducing them to the far-right group. By ensuring that new members are loyal to him before allowing them to join the group, the headhunter is able to increase his own influence and standing within the group. In some cases, a headhunter may not belong to any organized far-right group but will recruit followers to his own informal group.

A good example of a headhunter was reported to me by a message board user and research participant who was able to support her account with a range of corroborating evidence, such as records of chat room conversations. BurningRage[10] was the nickname used by a regular visitor to a chat room devoted to discussions of philosophy and sociology. When new users entered the chat room, BurningRage would usually ask if they were black or Jewish. If they were, they would be subjected to a constant stream of racist abuse until they left the chat room. Another tactic involved entering the room and making a racist comment in order to see how other users would react. Anyone challenging the comment would be threatened or subjected to abuse; anyone else would be considered an ally. Clearly, such behavior went far beyond simple attention-seeking, such as the "provocative comments" described by various writers[11] that are sometimes used as a means of stimulating reciprocal communication.

Sometimes, if several other people who might object to his behavior occupied the chat room, BurningRage would adopt a different strategy and strike up a seemingly innocent conversation concerning topics like economics, religion, or politics. However, the conversation would quickly be manipulated so that BurningRage could put forward a racist viewpoint. Any conversation about economics, for instance, would quickly turn into an attack on blacks and Jews, blaming all of the world's economic problems on the stereotypes and urban myths associated with these groups. This would continue until his targets became uncomfortable enough to leave the chat room.

BurningRage also paid attention to other chat room users, especially those who remained neutral when he attacked members of minority groups. Sometimes, he would ask people directly if they agreed with his views. If they did not, they would be called racist names like "nigger lover" or "kike whore" and subjected to abuse until they left. BurningRage also claimed to have advanced ICT skills, so he often made threats based around technology. Some threats were relatively simple; he would transmit a computer virus to his victim's computer, or would *mail-bomb* the victim's e-mail account. Other threats, however, were more serious; he would invade the victim's computer, locate his or her personal information, and then give this to neo-Nazi groups near to the victim's home in order to encourage a physical attack. Proof of BurningRage's technical skills came from his ability to control aspects of the chat room environment, for instance by expelling people from the room ("booting"), changing his screen name repeatedly within the space of a few moments, or by including expletives in his screen name or in messages to people.[12]

In some cases, BurningRage continued to harass individuals even after they left the chat room. A number of individuals were pursued for several months at a time and claimed that BurningRage was responsible for a range of technology-based acts of harassment. For instance, some people received threatening messages by anonymous e-mail, while others reported that their identities had been used to post offensive messages to chat rooms and message boards. BurningRage seemed to have a particular dislike for those with disabilities and reserved his most extreme behaviors for them. For instance, in at least one case he was accused of making death threats.

Those who shared BurningRage's views or who at least did not openly disagree with him would be treated courteously and would receive a great deal of attention. These people received frequent compliments and praise. Often, as a friendship developed, a person would confide in BurningRage and tell him about his or her personal problems. BurningRage never failed to appear understanding and always offered as much encouragement and advice as possible. Sometimes, BurningRage would also offer help and advice with technical problems, even going as far as sending software and music files via e-mail. Since many of those using the chat room were socially isolated, it can be argued that BurningRage's approach encouraged them to become emotionally dependent on him. Once a firm friendship was established, BurningRage could use this dependence to recruit the person as a follower.

BurningRage also used a variety of other techniques to develop relationships with potential converts. Other followers were often used to strike up conversations with a possible convert so that they could gather information about his or her background. These conversations would also be used to create a positive image for BurningRage before introducing him as a close friend. On some occasions, BurningRage made romantic advances to females, even taking part in cybersex in order to strengthen the relationship. He would also fabricate elaborate stories intended to gain the sympathy of those he communicated with. Sometimes, he would manipulate the chat room environment in order to keep a captive, silent audience for his stories. By taking control of the messenger program used to coordinate communications, BurningRage could stop other people "talking" and could even prevent them from leaving the conversation by ending the program.[13]

Those who became BurningRage's followers were made to signify this by adding "88" to their screen names, in order to show their support for neo-Nazi ideals.[14] Some followers remained part of BurningRage's informal group, but others were also encouraged to join the far-right organization he belonged to.

It is possible to explain much of BurningRage's behavior in terms of a model of hate crimes carried out by groups that has been developed by the FBI.[15] In brief, this model suggests that hate groups move through seven stages:

- In Stage 1, a hater sets out to find others who feel like they do in order to form a group.
- In Stage 2, the hate group defines itself "… through symbols, rituals, and mythologies, which enhance the members' status and, at the same time, degrade the object of their hate."[16]
- In Stage 3, the group disparages the target in order to bind the group together and establish a common cause.
- In Stage 4, the group begins to taunt the target.
- In Stage 5, the group attacks the target without weapons.
- In Stage 6, the group attacks with weapons.
- In Stage 7, the target is destroyed, whether physically, psychologically, or otherwise.

Each of these stages can easily be identified in relation to the Internet and the behaviors displayed by BurningRage. For example, the use of "88" in screen names allows the group to define itself (Stage 2), while the use of technology-based attacks, such as viruses, is equivalent to attacking the target with weapons (Stage 6). It can also be argued that Stage 7 is reached when the target leaves the chat room, or has been harmed in other ways, such as through the use of identity theft.

The creators of the model, Schafer and Navarro,[17] also discuss the concept of a reactive offender, traditionally described as one who attacks because of some perceived transgression, such as an insult or interracial dating. In the model they propose, the reactive offender attacks because of secondary justification, which is perhaps best explained through the use of an example:

… a group of skinheads encounter a mixed-race couple and shout racial slurs. If the couple reacts in a manner other than a submissive one, the skinheads perceive that behavior as an act of aggression. The skinheads later tell the police they merely defended themselves against aggressors. The skinheads, of course, leave out the fact that they acted as the instigators.[18]

Secondary justification can be clearly seen within BurningRage's online behavior. For example, it was mentioned earlier that he often made racist comments immediately upon entering the chat room. If anyone challenged these comments, he or she would be victimized.

Another interesting aspect of BurningRage's behavior concerned his willingness to take part in lengthy conversations on topics such as philosophy and history. Several users remarked upon his ability to put forward relatively sophisticated and intelligent arguments in support of his racist views. His arguments were so convincing that he was sometimes able to persuade people to accept even his most extreme beliefs, such as his claim that the Holocaust never took place. However, some people noted that some of his responses seemed identical to earlier postings and sometimes appeared very quickly on the screen. This suggests the possibility that BurningRage may have been following some kind of script, such as those used by high-pressure salespeople to anticipate and deal with any resistance to buying their products. In addition, BurningRage may also have been using a keystroke replacement program[19] to automate the task of entering parts of the script. The use of such a program would explain the speed with which BurningRage was able to enter relatively long passages of text.

As the example of BurningRage shows, headhunters appear to engage in two forms of behavior: recruiting new members to a formal or informal group, and victimizing individuals perceived as enemies. In many cases, these behaviors are inextricably linked. For example, the headhunter may choose to demonstrate his power to a potential recruit by victimizing another person.

DEVIANT SUBCULTURES AND ADDICTION

One of the best and worst aspects of the Internet is that it allows like-minded people to find each other and form online communities. In some cases, this can be of great benefit; for example, there are many self-help groups that give advice and support to those suffering from rare diseases. In other cases, groups can form to pursue deviant or criminal interests; for example, a number of online pedophile networks exist.

Once more, since an in-depth discussion of this area is beyond the scope of this book, the material covers selected deviant subcultures.

SUICIDE CLUBS

Internet suicide clubs are thought to have originated in Japan between 2002 and 2003. Having come to the attention of the international media in 2003, similar clubs quickly started to appear in Europe, the United States, and Australia.

A *suicide club* provides people with the information and advice needed to take their own lives. Some clubs do nothing more than supply information, but others provide additional help, such as keeping the suicidal person company until they pass away. Some examples of suicide clubs include the following:

- In Japan, seven people were believed to have committed suicide after meeting in an Internet chat room in 2004.[20] The young people died from carbon monoxide poisoning after sealing themselves in a car and lighting charcoal burners.
- In January 2003, Brandon Vedas, a computer technician from Arizona, took an overdose of prescription drugs in front of his webcam.[21] Vedas, aged 21, was encouraged to take the overdose by 12 of his online friends, who watched the entire incident live via the Internet. Instead of attempting to help Veda, the twelve voyeurs continued to watch until he lapsed into a coma and died.
- In 2005, an Oregon man, Gerald Krien, was charged with trying to solicit aggravated murder after attempting to organize a mass suicide intended to take place on Valentine's Day.[22] As many as 32 people apparently planned to log in to a chat room on Valentine's Day so that they could keep in contact with each other as they committed suicide.

Wesley J. Smith, a well-known author who writes about euthanasia, has described groups that help people to commit suicide as being involved in IAS, or *Internet-assisted suicide*. He cites the case of Suzy Gonzales, a 19-year-old student who committed suicide with the help of an online discussion group. Smith criticizes the group for assisting Gonzales' suicide instead of encouraging her to seek psychiatric help. The *San Francisco Chronicle*[23] also described the incident, saying of the group: "Gonzales found people who told her that suicide was an acceptable way to end her despair, and who gave her instructions on how to obtain a lethal dose of potassium cyanide and mix it into a deadly cocktail." Remarkably, Gonzales was able to buy a pH meter and potassium cyanide online, using a trick recommended to her by the group. Perhaps more disturbing is the *Chronicle's* inclusion of a long list of examples of people who committed suicide with the help of the group and the following comment:

> Gonzales' death is the 14th confirmed suicide associated with the online discussion group ... An additional 14 suicides are listed by the group as "success stories" but cannot be verified because the individuals used anonymous screen names, and the group has refused to disclose their true identities.[24]

Although some of the examples given here mention groups, Internet suicide pacts can also involve smaller numbers of people, often just two. Sometimes, a suicide pact may have a sexual component. As an example, a Houston man, Edward Frank Manuel, was arrested in 2003 after arranging to strangle a woman during sex.[25] After killing the woman, Manuel was supposed to place a yellow rose on her chest before burying her in a Texas forest. Manuel agreed to meet the woman at a Houston bus terminal but was immediately arrested when he arrived. When the police searched Manuel's car, they found yellow roses and a device that was to be used to strangle the woman.

In many cases, people enter into a suicide pact because they feel a need for human company at such an important time. For instance, the first Internet suicide pact in the United Kingdom took place in 2005. A man and a woman committed suicide within two days of meeting in a chat room. Their bodies were found in a car parked outside of a London store. The woman was found sitting behind the driver's wheel wearing a white shroud with the name and telephone number of a friend written on her shoulder.[26]

INTERNET ADDICTION

Internet addiction (sometimes called Internet dependence) occurs when excessive Internet use begins to impact on other areas of a person's life. As an example, many people have reported experiencing marital problems because of compulsive Internet use.

The exact proportion of people affected by Internet addiction is unclear, but research seems to indicate that approximately 5–15 percent of U.S. users are affected. For instance, a 1998 study of 18,000 Internet users who visited the *ABC News* Web site found that 5.7 percent of people met the criteria for compulsive Internet use.[27] However, a different study involving 531 students at the University of Texas at Austin reported that 13 percent could be classed as Internet dependent.[28] More recently, it has been estimated that between 6 percent and 10 percent of Internet users in the United States "... have a dependency that can be as destructive as alcoholism and drug addiction."[29]

Although roughly equal numbers of men and women use the Internet, males seem more prone to addiction than females.[30] For example, in a study of 1,300 students, 103 were found to meet the criteria for Internet dependence, and of this group 91 were male.[31] In addition, the study carried out at the University of Texas at Austin found that 71 percent of those classed as Internet dependent were male.[32]

The most common activities carried out by those addicted to the Internet include using chat rooms, viewing pornography, shopping, and e-mail. Some studies have found the use of pornography to be particularly high. As an example, the study of those who visited the *ABC News* site found that 64 percent of dependent Internet users spent an average of four hours a week viewing pornographic Web sites.[33]

A simple Internet addiction test can be found at http://www.netaddiction. com/resources/internet_addiction_test.htm.

As one would expect, Internet addicts spend more time using the Internet than nonaddicts. A study at the University of Pittsburgh looked at 396 users who described themselves as dependent on the Internet and 100 nondependent users.[34] The study found that the dependent users spent an average of 38.5 hours online each week, compared with less than five hours for the nondependent users. However, it is worth noting that other studies have found smaller differences in Internet use between dependent and nondependent users.

Internet addiction appears to have most impact on relationships, sometimes causing them to break down. In the University of Pittsburgh's study mentioned a moment ago, it was found that more than 90 percent of dependent users had suffered "moderate" or "severe" impairment in their academic, interpersonal, or financial lives.[35] In addition, 85 percent said that their work had also suffered. None of the nondependent users reported similar difficulties. A similar study, this time carried out by Carnegie Mellon University in Pittsburgh and involving 169 nondependent Internet users, stated: "Greater use of the Internet was associated with declines in participants' communication with family members in the household, declines in the size of their social circle and increases in their depression and loneliness."[36]

Internet addiction is not unique to the United States. As an example, it has been estimated that there are approximately one million Internet addicts in Germany, amounting to about three percent of the online population.[37] Concern over Internet addiction in Germany is such that Europe's first camp for young people suffering from Internet addiction was opened there in 2003.

There has been some debate as to whether Internet addiction represents a genuine condition. However, the popular view is that it is an illness similar to other kinds of addiction. In addition, some countries now recognize Internet addiction as a medical condition. For instance, in Finland, young people can be excused from compulsory military service if they are considered to be suffering from Internet addiction.[38]

The seriousness of Internet addiction can be highlighted by using the example of online games. Addiction to online games has become a serious problem in South Korea, where almost three-quarters of the population has access to a broadband Internet connection,[39] and there are more than 10 million online gamers from a total population of approximately 48 million.[40] Online games are considered so addictive that the South Korean government has even started to send psychologists into Internet cafes to warn players of the dangers of addiction.[41] A number of deaths have resulted from addiction to online games. Some examples include the following:

- In 2001, Shawn Woolley, a 21-year-old from Wisconsin, committed suicide after his advances were rejected by another player in the online game he played every day.[42]
- In October 2002, 24-year-old Kim Kyung-jae collapsed and died after playing computer games at a South Korean Internet café almost nonstop for 86

hours. The police reported that the only breaks he took were to buy cigarettes and use the toilet.[43]

- In 2005, a young Korean couple left their four-month-old daughter alone while they went out to play an online game at a local Internet café. When they returned, the child had died from suffocation. The couple was booked on criminal charges.[44]
- In August 2005, a 28-year-old man collapsed after playing online computer games for almost 50 hours. Although the man was moved to a hospital, he died three hours later.[45]
- In 2004, a 16-year-old youth entered an Internet café and drank a quantity of pesticide. Prior to drinking the pesticide, he had played online games for 11 days at the Internet café. Despite all attempts to save him, the young man died two days later.[46]

Recognizing Internet Addiction

The advice for dealing with Internet addiction is very simple:

- Be aware of behaviors that may indicate Internet addiction.
- Without exception, always seek professional advice when dealing with Internet addiction.

SOME COMMON SYMPTOMS OF INTERNET ADDICTION

Some signs that may indicate Internet addiction include the following:

- Constantly looking for opportunities to use the Internet.
- Feeling happy or excited when using the Internet, but moody, irritable, and unhappy when offline.
- Unable to reduce or control Internet use.
- Complaints from friends or family regarding the amount of time spent online.
- Losing track of time when online.
- Inability to predict the amount of time spent using the Internet.
- Attempts to hide or disguise the amount of time spent online.
- Less involvement with a partner, children, or friends because of the amount of time spent online.
- Avoiding social gatherings.
- Spending less time on routine activities, such as eating, in order to use the Internet.
- Spending less time on hobbies or other leisure activities.
- Performance is affected at work or school.
- Changes in sleep patterns, perhaps staying up late at night in order to use the Internet.
- Physical problems, such as eyestrain or backaches.

SEXUAL DEVIANCE

Sex and the Internet have always gone hand in hand. Whatever the fantasy or fetish, there appears to be a Web site, newsgroup, or message board to cater to it. A good example of this involves *Usenet,* a worldwide system of discussion groups that carries more than 100,000 newsgroups. Although not every ISP carries every group, and many groups are inactive, Usenet remains a huge repository of information. Despite difficulties in estimating the size of Usenet, it has been suggested that the volume of data passing through Usenet each day is around 280 gigabytes, equivalent to approximately 140,000,000 pages of text. Another measure is the size of the database stored by Google Groups. The company maintains an archive of Usenet messages dating back to the 1980s and reports that its database is made up of more than a billion posts.[47]

Even a cursory search of Usenet results in hundreds of groups devoted to adult topics.

Each group can be placed on a continuum that moves from mild to extreme in terms of the material it contains. The "mild" material deals with the least explicit content, such as pictures of swimsuit models. Somewhere towards the middle of the continuum are groups that deal with topics such as telephone sex, exhibitionism, bondage, and group sex. The "extreme" material deals with the most explicit content. The behaviors depicted may be abusive, dangerous, or illegal, covering acts such as bestiality and incest. In addition, there are also at least 20 active groups devoted to pedophilia.

Some groups cover behaviors that might be described as bizarre rather than harmful. Examples include groups devoted to tickling, fantasies about cartoon characters, and the wearing of diapers (infantilism).

Virtually every newsgroup has an equivalent Web site, chat room, or message board. Those interested in pedophilia, for example, have the choice of an estimated 23,000 Web sites devoted to this topic.[48]

Throughout this book, numerous examples have been given showing how a person's online behavior can sometimes spill over into the offline world. It is known, for instance, that some people form online relationships and eventually go on to meet in person. It has also been shown how some forms of deviant behavior evolve in order to take advantage of new technology. This is also the case with some of the new forms of sexual activity that have started to appear over the past few years. As an example, *dogging* is a relatively new trend that started in the United Kingdom but has quickly spread to Europe and beyond. Dogging involves people meeting to have anonymous sex in a public place. Notice of an encounter is usually displayed on a Web site a few hours ahead of the meeting time. This is to make it difficult for the police or any other agency to intervene. Once people arrive at the meeting place, they divide into smaller groups according to their sexual preferences. Any number of people and any combination of men and women is allowed. There are various rules that govern the meeting. Voyeurs, for instance, may not be excluded from viewing any activity they choose. In addition, married couples must take part separately or must involve at least one other person in the sex act.

Occasionally, some of the sexual fantasies of Internet users are so extreme that they can lead to injury or even death. For instance, if a rape fantasy spills over into the offline world, a woman may find herself attacked in her own home:

> A man enacting a rape fantasy game with a "victim" he met in an Internet chatroom broke into the wrong apartment and assaulted an innocent woman …
>
> Howard met his intended target on a "rape fantasy" chat site. In September last year, he forced his way into what he believed to be her apartment, and attacked the female occupant. Howard had, however, got his wires crossed. He hit the terrified woman, who fought back by shouting and "attacking his testicles." She testified that she believed she was going to be killed.
>
> Luckily, Howard then asked for her chatroom handle. She protested she had never been in a chatroom and did not even own a computer.[49]

The case of the Rotenburg Cannibal (or the Master Butcher) is perhaps one of the best-known incidents where an online sexual fantasy led to a death. In 2001, a German man, Armin Meiwes, placed an ad on the Internet that read "Wanted: young well, built 18–30 year old for slaughter."[50] One of those who responded was Bernd Jürgen Brandes, a computer technician looking to fulfill his fantasy of being butchered and eaten. After corresponding with Meiwes over several months, Brandes wrote his will, sold his car, and took a one-way train journey to Rotenberg, where Meiwes lived.[51]

At his trial, a video recording made by Meiwes was shown to the jury. The recording showed what took place that evening over a 4 1/2 hour period. The video began by showing Brandes undressing in Meiwes' kitchen. Although he seemed a little unsteady, there was no evidence that Brandes was acting under duress. After Brandes said "Slice the thing off now," Meiwes was shown cutting off Brandes' penis.[52] Next, Meiwes bandaged Brandes with towels and then began to cook the penis. A little later, Brandes tried to eat his own flesh but was unable to. Brandes was then given 20 sleeping tablets and a bottle of cough medicine to dull his pain. Once Brandes was unconscious,

> Meiwes took Brandes to the bathroom, leaving him in the bath to "bleed out" while Meiwes went back downstairs to watch a movie. Finally, Meiwes took Brandes to "the butchery," a room at the top of the house that had been painted in black and red. The room was also equipped with a table and various ropes and meat hooks. Meiwes stabbed the semi-conscious Brandes to death before hanging him on a meat hook and cutting out some of his organs.[53]

After Brandes' death, Meiwes advertised for further victims and met with five potential candidates. One person was rejected because he was considered too fat. Another, Jorg Bose, got as far as allowing himself to be hung naked on a meat hook before backing out. A third man backed out after seeing a video of Bose being prepared to be butchered.[54] None of the people Meiwes met with were harmed.

Meiwes was caught when an Austrian student saw one of his advertisements and reported him to the police.[55] In a magazine interview that took place shortly before his trial, Meiwes seemed oddly reminiscent of Hannibal Lecter from *Silence of the Lambs*. In the interview, Meiwes described how he had cooked parts of Brandes with olive oil, garlic, pepper, and nutmeg, then ate him with sprouts, potatoes, and a bottle of South African red wine.[56]

> In 2004, *GQ* magazine reported rumors that a movie about Meiwes was being prepared, starring Hugh Grant as Meiwes and Brad Pitt as Brandes.

At his trial on January 30, 2004, Meiwes received a prison sentence of 8 1/2 years for manslaughter. After sentencing, the supervising judge stated:

> We have seen people growing accustomed to a sub-culture that we could not imagine existing before this trial. We opened a door we would rather close again but we have shown how many people in need of help are out there fuelling their fantasies on the internet.[57]

Following the trial, German police reported that an estimated 800 people were thought to be taking part in online forums devoted to cannibalism. In addition, Meiwes was known to have been in contact with at least 400 of them.[58]

SAFETY AND PREVENTION

The following advice is drawn from a variety of sources including the American Academy of Child and Adolescent Psychiatry, the *New York Times*, PedoWatch.com, Cyberstalking Info, and others.

BUSINESS USERS

The information given for individuals and families may be helpful in identifying employees who might benefit from additional support.

INDIVIDUALS AND FAMILIES

How can we tell if someone is contemplating suicide, suffering from Internet addiction, or taking part in other deviant or antisocial activities? In general, people experiencing these difficulties tend to indicate their anxiety or distress through one or more warning signs.

It is worth remembering that different sources of distress may share similar warning signs. An inability to sleep, for instance, might be associated with thoughts of suicide, bullying, sexual abuse, and so on. In addition, the presence of one or more signs does not necessarily prove that some kind of problem exists. An inability to sleep might suggest that a young person is being abused, but it might also indicate a young person who is a little nervous about a quiz that is coming up at school. In a similar way, just because a given behavior does not appear in the list, it should not be dismissed out of hand.

Whenever there is cause for concern, professional help should be sought immediately.

The list that follows applies to a broad range of Internet users, young or old, male or female. In no particular order, some of the warning signs that may indicate a person is at risk of harm include the following:

- Changes in sleeping patterns
- Changes in eating patterns
- Reduced performance at school or at work
- Fatigue and lack of motivation
- Self-neglect; for example, not taking care of personal appearance
- Inability to concentrate
- Increased use of alcohol, tobacco, or drugs
- Reckless or dangerous behavior
- Personality changes, especially outbursts of temper, moodiness, and withdrawal
- Changes in social behavior; for example, avoiding social occasions
- Signs of mental illness; for example, hallucinations or delusions
- Increase in physical complaints; for example, stomach upsets, headaches, tiredness
- Loss of interest in hobbies and other pastimes
- Ignoring responsibilities; for example, chores or child care
- Demands for increased privacy
- Sudden fear or dislike of certain people or places

FURTHER INFORMATION

Reading

Jewkes, Y. (ed), 2003. *Dot.cons: Crime, deviance and identity on the Internet.* Cullompton, Devon: Willan Publishing.

Young, K., 1998. *Caught in the Net: How to Recognize the Signs of Internet Addiction— A Sure-fire Strategy for Recovery.* Hoboken, NJ: John Wiley & Sons Inc.

Online

The International Cultic Studies Association provides information about cults and psychological manipulation: www.csj.org.

The Rick A. Ross Institute of New Jersey provides an archive of materials about cults, destructive cults, controversial groups, and movements: www.rickross.com.

The Youth Suicide Prevention Program provides a list of resources dealing with suicide prevention for young people and parents: http://www.yspp.org/resources-Links/links.htm.

Psych Central provides a list of resources dealing with suicide prevention: http://psychcentral.com/resources/Suicide_and_Crisis.

Glossary

Acceptable use policy (AUP). A formal document that sets out rules describing how a computer system or a service may be used. The AUP also sets out what behaviors are not allowed and the penalties that may be imposed if the rules are broken. Many organizations have AUPs, including ISPs, schools, colleges, large companies, and government departments. In many organizations, the AUP forms part of a formal security policy. See also *Formal security policy.*

Advertising-supported software. See *Adware.*

Adware. Sometimes known as advertising-supported software, a type of software designed to display advertising to users. Adware is often linked with spyware, since some applications collect information about users in order to target advertising more accurately. See also *Spyware.*

Air gapping. Critical computer systems are often protected from hackers and other online hazards by ensuring that they are physically disconnected from any network, including the Internet.

Algorithm. A term used in computer programming to describe the method used to carry out a task. Also used to describe a specific way of encrypting data. See also *Encryption.*

Analytical attack. An approach towards discovering an encryption password by relying on the way in which we use language. For instance, knowing that a password is made up of English words, a dictionary might be used to identify the word or phrase. See also *Brute force attack.*

Anonymous e-mail. Messages that have had identifying information removed. All e-mail messages contain information that identifies where the message originated. There are a number of ways in which this information can be removed from a message so that the sender cannot be identified (or located).

Armored virus. A virus that has been designed to be difficult to take apart for analysis.

Attack. An attempt to disrupt a computer system or network. Also used to describe an attempt to defeat an encryption algorithm. See also *Encryption, Brute force attack*, and *Analytical attack*.

Autoexec macro. A special macro that runs as soon as a document or data file is opened. See also *Macro*.

Avatar. An image used to represent an Internet user in chat rooms, message boards, online games, and so on.

Backup facility. A location where organizations duplicate their key systems. If a disaster occurs, such as an earthquake, the organization can switch to the duplicate site straight away.

Backup regime. A regular routine for making and testing backups.

Bandwidth. The amount of information that can be sent over a network in a given period of time. Bandwidth is usually measured in bits per second (bps); the higher the bps, the faster information can be sent or received.

Bayesian filtering. A statistical means of identifying spam based on the frequency of certain words and phrases.

BBS. See *Bulletin board system*.

Binary file infectors. See *Parasitic virus*.

BIOS (Basic Input/Output Software). The special software needed to control a computer's keyboard, display screen, disk drives, serial communications, and a number of other functions. Without a working BIOS, a computer is unable to start up.

BitTorrent. A popular peer-to-peer network. See also *Peer-to-peer networking*.

Blacklist. A list of e-mail addresses (or domains) from which messages will not be accepted. See also *Whitelist*.

Blog. An online diary that is usually hosted with a free service. The term is a contraction of "Web log" and was popularized by Blogger, producers of what is arguably the best known and most popular blogging software.

Bluetooth. A technology that allows devices, such as cell phones and handheld games consoles, to communicate wirelessly over relatively short distances.

Boot sector. The sector of a disk that can hold instructions that are carried out whenever the computer is started or reset. The boot sector of a floppy disk is automatically read whenever the disk is inserted into the drive.

Boot sector virus. A type of virus that is stored in the boot sector of a disk. See also *Boot sector*.

Bot. Short for robot, automated programs that can be used for a variety of purposes, from carrying out searches on the Internet to sending out advertising messages by e-mail. Bots are often used to carry out distributed denial of service attacks. This involves flooding a company's Web or e-mail services with so much fake traffic that they become overloaded. See also *Denial of Service* and *Zombie*.

Botnet. A group of zombie computers capable of being directed towards various tasks, such as launching denial of service attacks. See also *Zombie*.

Browser hijacker. A program that attempts to force a web browser to visit a particular web site.

Brute force attack. An approach towards discovering an encryption password by trying every possible combination of letters, numbers, and special characters. See also *Analytical attack.*

Bulk e-mailer. Specialized e-mail software used to create and send personalized e-mail messages on a large scale.

Bulletin board system (BBS). An early form of the message boards seen today. Some BBS hosted file libraries containing various pieces of software that users could download.

Business continuity planning. Trying to predict the problems that may affect an organization, ranging from labor disputes and natural disasters to cash flow problems and hacking, and then planning how best to overcome these difficulties. Evidence of careful business continuity planning is often needed for insurance purposes. See also *Disaster recovery planning.*

Chain e-mail. The electronic equivalent of chain letters. Often used to carry out hoaxes. See also *Dying child hoax* and *Virus hoax.*

Chat room. A Web site or part of a Web site where people can hold real-time conversations. In most chat rooms, users communicate with each other by typing messages. However, some chat rooms allow users to speak to each other (using microphones attached to the sound cards in their computers) and some allow video conferencing (using *Webcams*).

Checksum. A unique number calculated by examining the contents of a file. Recalculating the checksum will produce a different value if the file has been changed. This provides a quick and simple way of verifying the integrity of a file.

Cipher text. Data that has been encrypted, which converts plain text into cipher text. See also *Encryption.*

Clickthrough agreement. Details of the program's software license that are usually displayed on the screen when new software is installed. Installation halts until the user agrees to the terms of the license by clicking on an "OK" button.

Command and control. Organizing and directing people, equipment, and resources in order to accomplish a task.

Computer virus. A small computer program that copies itself from one computer to another. A single computer may be capable of "infecting" many others within a very short time. Many viruses are programmed to carry out various actions, such as deleting data, once a set of specific conditions is met. All computer viruses should be considered destructive.

Cookie. A small file saved onto a user's hard disk drive when a Web site is visited. The file contains information about the Web site, such as user ID and preferences, so that the Web site "remembers" a user from one visit to another. Cookies are considered a potential security risk since they are sometimes used to store personally identifiable information.

Copy protection. Any method used to discourage or prevent illegal copies being made of a computer program.

Copyright theft. Illegal copying of software, music, video, and other copyrighted materials.

Corporate cyberstalking. A cyberstalking incident involving an organization as the victim or perpetrator. See also *Cyberstalking.*

Crack. A small software patch that can be used to circumvent the copy protection method used by a given program.

Cracker. A person who disables the copy protection routines used by software companies to prevent piracy.

Cracking. Removing or defeating the copy protection routines used to protect computer programs, such as games.

Crew. A group of virus writers, hackers, or crackers. See also *Hackers* and *Crackers.*

Cryptanalysis. The art of "breaking" the methods used to encrypt data. See also *Encryption.*

Cyberattack. The use of technology, especially the Internet, to attack a company, government agency, or other organization. Cyberattacks are targeted against a country's physical and information infrastructures. See also *Physical infrastructure* and *Information infrastructure.*

Cyberhooliganism. Destructive acts perpetrated through computers, such as Web site defacement or distributing viruses.

Cybersex. A sexual act carried out via the Internet where partners usually send each other explicit text messages. Occasionally, webcams and other technology may also be used.

Cyberstalking. The use of technology in order to harass one or more victims.

Cyberterrorism. The use of the Internet to further political or ideological goals, usually through attacking Web sites and computer systems belonging to governments and large organizations. Cyberterrorism is often described as a criminal act that is (a) perpetrated through computers, (b) politically motivated, and (c) intended to result in death, violence, or destruction.

Data mining. Searching for patterns within a body of data, or trying to separate useful information from the irrelevant. At the simplest level, data mining can be carried out using a search engine.

Degree mill. See *Diploma mill.*

Deleting. Removing a file such that only the directory entry specifying its location is deleted. The data that makes up the file remains untouched until overwritten by new data. This means that if the file is accidentally deleted, it can often be recovered.

Denial of Service (DoS). A form of cyberattack that involves flooding an organization's Internet services (Web site, e-mail, etc.) with large volumes of fake traffic until the targeted systems grind to a halt.

Detection rate. A measure of how well a virus scanner is able to find viruses.

Dialer. This type of program alters the settings used to make dial-up connections to the Internet, usually with the aim of calling premium rate numbers at the expense of the user.

Digital Pearl Harbor. An unexpected attack upon important computer systems that results in massive damage, possibly including human casualties and deaths.

Diploma mill. Sometimes called a *degree mill*, a company or person who provides counterfeit degrees in exchange for a fee.

Disaster recovery planning. Developing plans and procedures that try to anticipate and respond to different situations, such as an attack on a company's computer systems, so that normal operation can be resumed as quickly as possible.

Disinfection. When an antivirus program detects a virus, it will attempt to remove the virus without damaging any data.

Disk imaging software. Software used to make a complete copy of a computer's hard disk, effectively creating a snapshot of the computer at a specific date and time. When the disk image is copied back onto the computer's hard disk, the computer is restored to its exact state at the date and time the image was created.

Distributed denial of service (DDoS). An attack that uses other computers on the Internet to generate fake Internet traffic and direct it towards a specific company. These computers are often used without the knowledge or consent of their owners, having been compromised by specialized programs that can generate e-mail or Web traffic when activated by the attacker. These programs, often called bots or zombies, can be placed on computers many weeks or months before they are needed. See also *Bot* and *Zombie*.

Distro. A unique collection of the Linux operating system distributed with a large number of additional applications.

Dogging. People meeting to have anonymous sex in a public place.

Domain name. An identifier of the owner of a Web site. For instance, a domain name such as greenwood.com indicates that the Web site belongs to the Greenwood Publishing Group.

Domain name server. A computer that converts human-friendly Web addresses (URLs) into a computer-friendly numeric format (IP address). See also *URL* and *IP address*.

Dongle. A hardware device used to prevent users from copying a program. When the program runs, it checks for the presence of the dongle. If the dongle is not found, the program terminates.

Downtime. The period of time a computer is unavailable due to a breakdown, virus infection, or other problem.

Drive-by download. Describes a way of downloading software, usually malware, to a computer without the user's consent. Often, just visiting a web page causes the download to take place.

Dumpster diving. Searching a person's trash in order to find information about them.

Dying child hoax. A hoax wherein people are asked to help a terminally ill child achieve her dying wish of spreading a message telling people to live life to its fullest. See also *Chain e-mail.*

E-mail filtering. The use of special software to scan incoming e-mail messages in order to identify and delete spam.

E-mail virus. A type of computer virus distributed via e-mail.

Encryption. Encoding information so that it can only be read by someone with the right password or pass phrase. See also *Algorithm, Plain text, Cipher text, Key.*

Envelope stuffing. A work-from-home scheme that involves sending out large mailings in order to recruit others to the scheme.

Erasing. Destroying a file completely. Both the directory entry specifying the file's location and the data that makes up the file are overwritten with new data.

Escrow. An impartial third party who manages a transaction on behalf of a buyer and a seller, ensuring that the buyer receives his goods and the seller receives payment.

False positive. A virus scanner mistakenly identifying a legitimate program as a virus.

False victimization. A cyberstalker falsely claiming that he is being harassed by the victim.

File attachment. Any data file, such as word-processing documents, databases or spreadsheet files, attached to an e-mail message.

Filter. Software that allows e-mail messages to be marked for special attention. In general, a filter checks for a series of conditions, such as if the message contains certain words, or if it comes from a specific e-mail address. Any messages matching the filter conditions can be dealt with in different ways, for example, by deleting them automatically or by moving them to a different place.

Firewall. A computer program or hardware device that monitors and controls all traffic entering or leaving a network. If any unauthorized traffic is detected, it is automatically stopped and an alert is issued. On a smaller scale, personal firewalls monitor Internet traffic entering or leaving a personal computer. Again, unauthorized traffic is stopped automatically and the user is alerted. In addition to monitoring traffic, some firewalls also provide "stealth" functions that effectively make the computer invisible to the tools used by hackers.

Florence Nightingale syndrome. See *White knight syndrome.*

Force multiplier. A factor that significantly increases the effectiveness of a force, sometimes allowing a smaller force to defeat a much larger one.

Formal security policy. This formal document that sets out all of a company's security arrangements and often contains detailed procedures for dealing with particular situations, such as backing up data.

419 fraud. A common e-mail fraud where victims are offered a commission in exchange for helping to smuggle large sums of money out of Nigeria or another West African nation.

Freeware. Software that can be copied, distributed, and used free of charge. Although there may be some restrictions on the use of a specific program, the author does not require payment for his work.

FTP (file transfer protocol) site. A collection of files stored on a computer connected to the Internet. Using an FTP client, these files can be listed, viewed, or downloaded.

Grandfather, father, son method. A method for making backup files that allows several versions of the data to be kept.

Grooming. A gradual process preparatory to sexual abuse, where a pedophile befriends a young person and attempts to gain his trust.

Guest book. A mechanism that allows visitors to post comments and greetings that can be viewed by other visitors and the owner of a Web site.

Hacker. A person who is able to cobble together complex computer programs very quickly and easily. Nowadays, hackers are commonly thought of as computer criminals; people who break into computer systems or cause all sorts of other damage. It is worth remembering that not all hackers are criminals and not all hacking is illegal.

Happy slapping. Using a cell phone to record an assault on someone so that the resulting video clip can be posted to the Internet.

Headhunter. A person who recruits Internet users to an organized group of some kind, usually a far-right organization.

Hero syndrome. Some people seek attention by manufacturing a threat and then preventing a disaster. As an example, a fireman might start a small fire so that he can take credit for discovering and extinguishing it.

Heuristics. Use of a set of simple rules by a virus scanner to help detect virus activity.

Home-page hijacker. See *Browser hijacker.*

Human trafficking. Recruiting people through fraud, threat of violence, coercion, or other means and transporting them to another country where they are forced to work in the sex trade, as laborers, and so on.

ICT. See *Information and communications technology.*

Identity theft. Impersonating someone, often by using his or her personal information, usually with the aim of obtaining money, goods, or services at the expense of the victim.

Incremental backup. Once a full backup has been made, all subsequent backups, which only need to record what has changed since the last time the backup procedure was used.

Information and communications technology (ICT). A collective term used to describe any form of computer technology or any form of technology used for communications, such as fax machines and mobile phones.

Information assets. Any source of information owned by an organization that is considered important or valuable.

Information infrastructure. The data held within computer systems used to manage public services. The data is often critical to the operation of the service. For instance, a hospital would find it difficult to function if its patient records were lost or destroyed. See also *Physical infrastructure.*

Information overload. When too much information is supplied, making it difficult to focus on the specific items needed. In some cases, all of the information supplied may be relevant, but most will be unimportant.

Information warfare. The offensive and defensive use of information and information systems to deny, exploit, corrupt, or destroy an adversary's information and information systems while protecting one's own. Such actions are designed to achieve advantages over military, political, or business adversaries.

Instant messaging (IM). Messaging that allows two or more people to hold a conversation in real time, with none of the delays associated with e-mail. Typically, most users communicate with each other by typing text messages, but some programs also allow them to speak to each other or use video conferencing.

Intellectual property. A broad term used to describe any kind of creative work, including software, music, movies, poetry, novels, trademarks, and images.

Intellectual property theft (IP theft). The illegal copying of any form of creative work, including software, music, prose, images, and so on. IP theft is broader than copyright theft, since it encompasses a wider range of works that can be copied, including works that cannot be protected via copyright. See also *Copyright theft* and *Software piracy.*

Internet addiction. Similar to any other addiction, this describes compulsive Internet use.

Internet-assisted suicide. When an online group provides information, advice, and other assistance to someone wishing to commit suicide.

Internet service provider (ISP). A company that provides clients with access to the Internet. Typically, customers access e-mail, the World Wide Web, Usenet, and other services via a modem that connects to the ISP's computer systems.

IP (Internet protocol) address. A Web address given in a numeric, computer-friendly format, e.g., 65.215.112.149. See also *URL.*

ISP. See *Internet service provider.*

Junk e-mail. See *Spam.*

Key. A password or pass phrase that is used to encrypt or decrypt data. See also *Encryption.*

Keygen. A small program that generates a valid, but illegal, registration code for a given program.

Key logger. A program that records every key pressed by a computer user, allowing passwords and other sensitive data to be collected secretly.

Labor hour. A simple way of measuring the effort needed to develop a computer program.

License agreement. A document describing the terms under which a piece of software may be used. As an example, many license agreements specify that users may not copy the program under any circumstances, even for backup purposes.

Linux. An Open Source version of the Unix operating system. See also *Open Source*.

Logic bomb. A program, often a computer virus, designed to trigger on a certain date or time.

Love bombing. Creating a relationship where the victim becomes emotionally (and sometimes physically) dependent on another person. As long as the victim behaves as required, he will continue to receive attention and affection.

Love cheat (or love rat). A person who carries on several online relationships at a time.

Lurking. Watching a chat room, newsgroup, or message board without taking part.

Macro. A simple program that carries out a sequence of commands in order to automate a common or repetitive task.

Macro virus. A virus written using the built-in programming languages now found in many software packages and stored within a data file, such as a word-processing document, that runs whenever the file is opened. Macro viruses have become the most common form of virus in circulation. See also *Macro*.

Mail-bombing. Flooding an e-mail account with millions of messages with the intention of causing the account to be closed. Also known as *E-mail bombing*.

Malware. A general term used to describe any piece of malicious software. A program is considered malicious if it causes disruption of any kind, or if it steals, changes, conceals, or destroys information stored on a computer or network system.

Message board. A forum for computer users to exchange ideas and discuss common interests. Users are able to read messages posted by other people and can post their own messages in response.

Moblog. An online diary allowing new entries to be posted via a cell phone. See also *Blog*.

Motherboard. A computer's main circuit board. The motherboard houses the computer's processor, memory, expansion cards, and other vital components.

Multigenerational copy. It is often possible to make a copy of computer program from another copy. The quality of each copy degrades with every generation until the computer can no longer load the program. This does not apply to some kinds of media, such as DVD or CD-ROM, where every copy is identical to the original, allowing an unlimited number of generations.

Multimedia messaging services (MMS). Using modern mobile phones to send messages containing multimedia data to other users. These messages can include pictures, sound and even video.

Multipartite virus. A virus that uses a combination of methods to infect a computer.

Netiquette. A set of informal rules that describes how a person should behave when using Internet services, such as e-mail and newsgroups. These rules tend to reflect practices that experienced Internet users commonly agree are both responsible and polite.

Newsgroup. A forum where people can read messages posted by others, reply to them, or post their own comments. There are many newsgroups available, and they can be accessed via the Web or by using a special program called a newsreader. The whole system of newsgroups is often referred to as *Usenet*.

Non-player character (NPC). An interactive, computer-controlled character that appears in a game.

Online pharmacy. Allows prescription medicines to be ordered online, usually at a discount.

Online stock fraud. Using the Internet to carry out stock fraud. See also *Pump and dump* and *Ponzi scheme*.

Open Source. Software that is supplied completely free of charge. Open Source programs are supplied complete with source code, allowing users to modify the software as they see fit.

P2P. See *Peer-to-peer networking*.

Parasitic virus. A type of computer virus that embeds itself within a program.

Parental control software. A range of services offered by ISPs that can be used to protect young people from inappropriate content, such as pornography. Many ISPs provide tools that allow parents to screen out bad language, violence, and other unsuitable materials. Although parental control software can be helpful, it is not completely effective and should not be relied upon as the only way of dealing with unsuitable content.

Patch. A small piece of software used to update an operating system or other program.

Payload. The actions that a computer virus will carry out when activated.

Peer-to-peer networking (P2P). Enables computer users to connect their systems together directly so that they can communicate with each other and share files.

Personally identifiable information (PII). Information that can be linked to a specific individual.

Pharming. Redirecting the victim's Web browser to a fake Web site.

Phishing. Using fake e-mail messages and Web sites to trick people into revealing confidential information, such as bank account details.

Phone home. A method of copy protection where a computer program occasionally contacts a server via the Internet to verify that it is a legitimate copy. Can also describe the act of a Trojan sending stolen information back to its owner. See also *Trojan*.

Physical infrastructure. The equipment, software, and services needed to manage public services, such as power stations, airports, and hospitals. Can also refer to the equipment needed to operate and control information systems, such as company networks, the Internet, and e-mail systems. See also *Information infrastructure.*

Piracy rate. A way of measuring software piracy based on the percentage of all installed software that is pirated. A piracy rate of 75 percent, for instance, means that three out of every four pieces of software are pirated copies.

Pixel. Short for "picture element." Some images, such as newspaper photographs, are made up of small dots arranged in a grid. A pixel represents a single dot.

Plain text. Data to be encrypted. Encryption converts plain text into cipher text. See also *Encryption* and *Cipher text.*

Poisoning. Changing the information held on a local domain name server so that Web browsers are automatically directed to a fake Web site.

Polymorphic virus. A type of virus capable of modifying its structure to avoid detection.

Ponzi scheme. A type of investment fraud that uses the money from new investors to pay high rates of interest to older investors.

Pump and dump. A type of online stock fraud that uses the Internet to artificially raise or lower share prices in order to make a profit.

Pyramid scheme. A type of investment fraud that relies on investors recruiting more people into the scheme.

Quarantine. Placing a file that has been infected by a virus in a special location on the user's hard disk in order to prevents the virus from reinfecting the computer.

Reactive stalking. A type of cyberstalking (or stalking) carried out by former stalking victim.

Recovery fraud. Contacting victims of 419 fraud by criminals posing as officials who are investigating the crime. The victims are told that it may be possible for them to recover their money if they are willing to pay a fee. See also *419 fraud.*

Response rate. The number of people who respond to an offer or advertisement, usually expressed as a percentage.

Reverse scamming. See *Scam baiting.*

Ripper. A person who produces a pirated version of a movie, music album, or other media. Can also refer to the software used to convert CDs and DVDs into a format suitable for use with a personal computer.

Scam baiting. A humorous response to e-mail fraud that involves tricking con men into wasting time, effort, and money by pretending to fall for the fraud. See also *419 fraud.*

Script. A simple type of computer program normally created using English-like commands.

Script kiddies. A derogatory term for a would-be virus writer with limited programming skills.

Secure Web server. A Web server that encrypts any data sent or received, providing a high level of security for financial transactions.

Security policy. See *Formal security policy*.

Shareware. Software that is supplied on a "try before you buy" basis. After an evaluation period, users must delete the software from their systems or pay a registration fee to continue using the program. Shareware programs are usually priced significantly lower than commercial packages.

Shill. A person who bids at an auction in order to raise the price of the item.

Shoulder surfing. Looking over someone's shoulder as they enter a password.

Signature. A set of characteristics that can be used to identify a specific virus.

Social engineering. A way of exploiting human psychology in order to trick people into revealing confidential information that can be used to access a computer system.

Software audit. The process of cataloguing all of the software and data stored on a personal computer or a network with the aim of identifying any unauthorized items.

Software license. An outline of the conditions under which a piece of software can be used. Buying a piece of software normally means buying a software license that grants the right to make use of the program. The program itself, all installation media, documentation, and other materials remain the property of the software company.

Software piracy. Copying software illegally.

Spam. Unsolicited or unwanted e-mail. Can also describe advertising indiscriminately sent to newsgroups, message boards, guest books, and other public forums.

Spammer. A person who sends out unsolicited e-mail, usually in bulk.

Spear phishing. A form of phishing that targets a specific company or domain.

Spyware. A type of software designed to capture and record confidential information without a user's knowledge or consent.

Stalking-by-proxy. Using third parties to harass a victim.

Stealth virus. A type of virus designed to avoid detection by antivirus software.

Suicide club. An online group that provides people with the information and advice needed to take their own lives.

Technobabble. The use of language containing so much technical jargon that it becomes incomprehensible to anyone unfamiliar with the subject.

Threat assessment. A systematic study intended to identify vulnerabilities and determine the level of risk they pose.

Throwaway. An e-mail account or other service that can be obtained cheaply or free of charge and discarded when no longer needed.

Time bomb. See *Logic bomb*.

Trojan. A form of malicious software that is disguised as a legitimate program in order to gain access to a computer system.

URL (Uniform resource locator). A Web address given in a human-friendly format, e.g., www.greenwood.com. See also *IP address*.

Usenet. A global collection of discussion groups. See also *Newsgroup*.

Viral marketing. A marketing technique that exploits social networks in order to promote a product. Essentially, viral marketing relies on the fact that people will share interesting or useful information with friends, colleagues, and relatives. This creates a kind of "epidemic" where the information spreads throughout the population very rapidly. Companies tend to make use of viral marketing by offering free services (e.g., e-mail) or free content, such as funny video clips, or interesting stories. Passing on a video clip or story also passes on the company's message. Viral marketing has become extremely popular in a very short time because it offers a cheap and highly effective form of advertising.

Virus. A small computer program that attempts to copy itself from one computer to another. Most viruses are destructive in nature, intended to damage or delete data on infected systems.

Virus construction kit. A program that can be used to create computer viruses quickly and easily.

Virus hoax. Fake warnings about viruses that frequently circulate around the Internet. See also *Chain e-mail*.

Virus scanner. A computer program designed to detect and identify viruses.

Visa fraud. Obtaining a visa through fraud, forgery, or other unlawful means in order for someone to enter or stay in the country.

Warez. Any type of pirate material, e.g., software, music, or movies.

Web browser. A program that can be used to view Web pages. Examples of Web browsers include Internet Explorer, Mozilla, and Opera.

Webcam. A camera that can be connected to a personal computer and used to transmit images via the Internet. Webcams are often used for live two-way communications, such as video conferencing and instant messaging, since they allow people to see and hear each other in real time.

Web log. See *Blog*.

White knight syndrome. A term used by Internet users to describe a man who wishes to "rescue" a woman from difficult circumstances. Sometimes refers to a woman who is looking for someone to "rescue" her.

Whitelist. A list of trusted e-mail addresses from which messages will be accepted. A message originated from an address not on the whitelist will be automatically rejected. See also *Blacklist*.

Worm. Similar to a computer virus in that it attempts to copy itself from one computer to another. Worms also carry out similar functions to computer viruses, such as deleting data. However, unlike a computer virus, a worm does not attach itself to programs or data files and exists as a separate entity. All worms should be considered destructive.

Zombie. A type of Trojan capable of taking the full or partial control of a computer when activated by the author. A machine infected with a zombie program will periodically check the Internet for instructions. When these instructions are received, the zombie will begin to generate e-mail or Web traffic directed towards a specific company. Fleets made up of thousands of zombies are usually used to launch a distributed denial of service attack against a company or other organization. See also *Distributed denial of service (DDoS)*.

Notes

CHAPTER 1

1. Berinato, 2002.
2. Ibid.
3. Illett, 2005; Evers, 2003.
4. Reuters, 1998.
5. Illett, 2005.
6. Weimann, 2004a, p. 1; Denning, 2001, p. 284.
7. Berinato, 2004.
8. Denning, 2000; Conway, 2002.
9. Denning, 2000.
10. For instance, see Ballard, Hornik, and McKenzie, 2002; Weimann, 2004.
11. Denning, 2001, p. 259.
12. See http://www.psycom.net/iwar.1.html.
13. National Commission on Terrorist Attacks upon the United States, 2004.
14. Woods, 2005.
15. See http://csrc.nist.gov/CryptoToolkit/aes/aesfact.html.
16. Woods, 2005.
17. Ballard, Hornik, and McKenzie, 2002, p. 1007.
18. Zimm, 2001, p. 52.
19. Web addresses for sites such as these are not provided for obvious reasons.
20. Conway, 2002.
21. Weimann, 2004b, p. 9.
22. National Commission on Terrorist Attacks upon the United States, 2004, pp. 157–158.
23. National Commission on Terrorist Attacks upon the United States, 2004, p. 222.
24. Burke, 2004.
25. Detailed information concerning the search terms used, Web sites visited, and so on, is not provided for obvious reasons.
26. Smith, 2004.
27. Ibid.

28. See http://www.answers.com/topic/eric-harris-and-dylan-klebold for a full account of the Columbine High School killings.

29. Farah, 2004.

30. Aft, 2004.

31. Emerson, 2002, pp. 3–4.

32. Weimann, 2004b, p. 7.

33. The Editors, 2004, p. 92.

34. Aft, 2004.

35. Weimann, 2004b, p. 1.

36. Ibid., p. 8.

37. Anti-Defamation League, 2002, p. 6.

38. Anti-Defamation League, 2002, p. 13.

39. Ibid., p. 20.

40. The Editors, 2004, pp. 91–92.

41. Weimann, 2004b, p. 8.

42. The Editors, 2004, p. 92.

43. Ibid.

44. Borland, 2004.

45. Weimann, 2004b, p. 7.

46. Weimann, 2004b, pp. 6–7.

47. See http://maps.google.com/.

48. See the following web sites or live video feeds: New York (http://www.earthcam.com/usa/newyork/timessquare/), London (http://www.earthcam.com/uk/england/london/); Paris (http://www.abcparislive.com/).

CHAPTER 2

1. Green, 2002.

2. Verton, 2002.

3. Vatis, 2001, p. 21.

4. NISCC is roughly equivalent to the U.S. Computer Emergency Response Team (US-CERT), which is tasked with protecting the country's information infrastructure. See http://www.us-cert.gov/ and http://www.niscc.gov.uk.

5. Keizer, 2005a.

6. A full copy of the briefing is available from http://www.niscc.gov.uk/niscc/docs/ttea.pdf.

7. Keizer, 2005a.

8. Böttler, 2002.

9. Sources: Böttler (2002), Christensen (1999), Denning (2001, p. 273), Nagpal (2002), Berinato (2002), Federal Emergency Management Agency (www.fema.gov).

10. Böttler, 2002.

11. Green, 2002.

12. Weimann, 2005, p. 9.

13. Lawrence, 2005.

14. Higgins, 2003, p. 5.

15. See www.boran.com/security.

16. Higgins, 2005, p. 9.

17. Williams, 2003.

18. *BBC News,* January 29, 2004.

Chapter 3

1. Viruses may have appeared on other platforms prior to 1985. Viruslist.com (www.viruslist.com), for instance, reports that the Creeper virus appeared on ARPA-NET in the early 1970s. Creeper was shortly followed by the first antivirus, Rabbit, designed to destroy the Elk Cloner virus, which appeared on the Apple II in 1982 (Tynan, 2003).

2. Kehoe, 1992.

3. Ibid.

4. Overill, 1997.

5. Bocij et al., 2005, p. 707.

6. Ward, 2004.

7. See www.sarc.com/avcenter/calendar.

8. Leyden, 2004b.

9. Roberts, 2005.

10. Zeller, 2005.

11. Miller, 2004.

12. Wearden, 2005.

13. See http://www.microsoft.com/technet/prodtechnol/office/officeexp/maintain/xpsec.ms x.

14. Bridwell, 2004, p. 13.

15. Bridwell, 2004, p. 4.

16. See http://www.californiadatarecovery.com/content/adr_loss_stat.html.

17. See the *2001 Cost of Downtime Survey* published by Eagle Rock Alliance Ltd. and available online at http://www.contingencyplanningresearch.com/2001%20Survey.pdf.

18. National Cyber Security Alliance, 2004.

19. ConsumerReports.org, 2003a; 2003b.

20. Leyden, 2001.

21. For example, see Kephart, Chess, and White, 1993; White, 1998.

22. See http://www.virusthreatcenter.com/lifecycleexplanation.aspx.

23. Most of what is written here does not apply to Open Source software. This is because the software development process is open to scrutiny by many different developers, making it almost impossible to insert malicious code into an application.

24. Bocij et al., 2005, p. 705.

25. Delio, 2001.

26. *CNN.com*, March 19, 2003.

27. Zetter, 2000.

28. Ibid.

29. Gordon, 1994a, 1994b.

30. Zetter, 2000.

31. Ibid.

32. Reynolds Lewis, 2003.

33. Zeller, 2005.

34. Ibid.

35. Thompson, 2004.

36. See http://pages.cpsc.ucalgary.ca/~aycock/spam.html.

37. Reynolds Lewis, 2003.

38. Some examples can be viewed at http://www.cio.com/archive/060101/outbreak_sidebar_1.html and http://vx.netlux.org/lib/static/vdat/ivstarze.htm.

39. Delio, 2001.
40. Farrell, 2005.
41. Cluley, 2000.
42. Anderson, 2000.
43. Delio, 2001.
44. Sophos, 2004.
45. Wakefield, 2004.
46. Anderson, 2000.
47. Cluley, 2000.
48. *The Age,* March 23, 2003.
49. Kotadia, 2004; Schwartz, 2003.
50. Wakefield, 2004; Cluley, 2000.
51. Cluley, 2000.
52. See http://vmyths.com/rant.cfm?id = 124&page = 4.
53. Wakefield, 2004.
54. Blincoe, 2001.
55. Hyppönen (1995); BBC News (5 September 2003); Leyden (2003).
56. Meserve, 2001.
57. Brenner, 2004.
58. Zetter, 2000.
59. Reynolds Lewis, 2003.
60. Reynolds Lewis, 2003.
61. Lyman, 2005.
62. Acohido and Swartz, 2004.
63. Dunn, 2005.
64. Acey, 2005.
65. Leyden, 2004a.
66. Sturgeon, 2004.
67. Smith, 2002.
68. See http://www.soci.niu.edu/~crypt/other/quant.htm.

CHAPTER 4

1. Saliba, 2001; *Wired News,* January 10, 2000.

2. Poulsen, 2004; *New York Times,* August 29, 2005.

3. It is accepted that some producers of adware have objected to their products being described as spyware. However, since this discussion concerns issues surrounding crime and personal privacy, it is considered appropriate to cover adware within the broad context of malware and spyware. Note that the text does not single out any particular product or company and merely reports the (published) views of others.

4. Wehner, 2005.

5. Sullivan, 2005.

6. Keizer, 2005b.

7. Lysecki, 2005.

8. Hulme and Claburn, 2004.

9. Delio, 2004.

10. Hines, 2005.

11. Full details of the survey can be found in *State of Spyware,* a report published by Webroot and available online at www.webroot.com.

12. America Online and National Cyber Security Alliance, 2004.

13. Hulme and Claburn, 2004.

14. Thompson, 2004, p. 4.

15. Ibid.

CHAPTER 5

1. Boal, 2004.

2. Caslon Analytics, 2005.

3. Finch, 2003, pp. 89–90.

4. Newman, 2004, p. 15.

5. Morris, 2004, p. 8.

6. Hupp, 2001.

7. Newman and McNally, 2005, p. 27.

8. See http://www.citibank.com/uk/personal/banking/info/aboutcitibank/background.htm.

9. Sullivan, 2004.

10. Bank, 2005.

11. It is important to remember that all of the software used to support phishing scams has many legitimate uses. Bulk e-mail programs, for instance, can be used to mail out newsletters to members of clubs and societies.

12. Bank, 2005.

13. Sullivan, 2004.

14. smh.com.au.

15. Unisys, 2006.

16. See http://www.privacyrights.org/ar/idtheftsurveys.htm.

17. The National Law Enforcement and Corrections Technology Center, 2004.

18. *CNET News.com,* September 29, 2004.

19. See http://www.antiphishing.org.

20. The National Law Enforcement and Corrections Technology Center, 2004.

21. Margalit, 2005.

22. Wagner, 2004.

23. Sullivan, 2004.

CHAPTER 6

1. Hastings and Syal, 2001.

2. U.S. Department of State, 1997.

3. U.S. Department Of State, 1997, p. 8.

4. See http://www.secretservice.gov/alert419.shtml.

5. U.S. Department of State, 1997, p. 8.

6. De Bruin, 2004.

7. It is worth noting that a number of conflicting figures have been published over the past decade. Some suggest far smaller losses while others suggest much larger losses. As an example, some estimates suggest losses of as little as $300 million annu-

ally in the United States, while others give claim that more than $1.5 billion is lost each year.

8. Smith, Holmes, and Kaufmann, 1999, p. 3.

9. Reich, 2004.

10. Festa, 2003.

11. See, for example, http://www.crimes-of-persuasion.com/Crimes/Business/nigerian.htm.

12. McUsic, 2006.

13. Rosenberg, 2006.

14. Reich, 2004.

15. See http://www.419legal.org/pages.php?p = 12.

16. Reich, 2004.

17. *BBC News,* July 10, 2001.

18. Logan, 2004.

19. Reich, 2004.

20. *Info Please Almanac* produced by Pearson Education Inc., http://www.infoplease.com.

21. See http://home.rica.net/alphae/419coal/index.htm.

22. The population of Nigeria was estimated at approximately 132 million as of 2006 by the *Info Please Almanac* produced by Pearson Education Inc. (http://www.infoplease.com/ipa/A0107847.html).

23. See http://urbanlegends.about.com/library/blthreat.htm for further information.

24. See, for example, http://www.vmyths.com/hoax.cfm_id = 257&page = 3.htm.

25. See www.petitionspot.com, www.ipetitions.com. and www.gopetition.com.

26. See, for example, https://www.swiftvets.com/swift/petition.php.

27. See the Interactive Return Web site at http://www.interactivereturn.com/casestudies.html.

CHAPTER 7

1. See http://pages.ebay.co.uk/aboutebay/thecompany/companyoverview.html.

2. Kong, 2000.

3. O'Malley, 2006.

4. Enos, 2001.

5. National Consumers League, 2004.

6. Steiner and Steiner, 2002.

7. American Diabetes Association, http://www.diabetes.org/diabetes-statistics/complications.jsp.

8. See http://www.medic8.com/healthguide/articles/stjohnswort.html and http://www.consumerlab.com/results/sjw.asp.

9. Gardner, 2005.

10. *CBC News,* January 17, 2006.

11. Gardner, 2006.

12. *CBC News,* 2006.

13. Christianson, 2005.

14. U.S. Department of State Bureau of Consular Affairs, 2005.

15. See http://www.brides-4u.com/information/fraudsters.

16. Baranikas, 2003.
17. National Consumers League, 2000.
18. National Consumers League, 2006.
19. *CBS News,* May 10, 2004.
20. Armour, 2003.
21. There is an unspoken assumption that the visitor to the site is not a young person using a parent's credit card.
22. Smith, 2004.
23. A more detailed account of Ponzi's life and the various frauds he perpetrated can be found at http://home.nycap.rr.com/useless/ponzi/.
24. Berensen, 2000.
25. Grice and Ard, 2000.
26. Bocij, 2002.

CHAPTER 8

1. Mohammed, 2004.
2. Ibid.
3. Messaging Pipeline, January 7, 2005.
4. See http://www.radicati.com/news/facts.asp.
5. See http://spam-filter-review.toptenreviews.com/spam-statistics.html.
6. Ibid.
7. Latta, 2006.
8. See http://www.spamhaus.org/statistics/countries.lasso.
9. Latta, 2006.
10. See http://spam-filter-review.toptenreviews.com/spam-statistics.html.
11. Keizer, 2005b.
12. Tynan, 2002.
13. Lopez, 2004.
14. Chang, 2003.
15. Keizer, 2005.
16. Rowland, 2003.
17. Chang, 2003; Rowland, 2003.
18. Sturgeon, 2004.
19. Keizer, 2005b.
20. See http://www.commtouch.com/site/ResearchLab/calculator.asp.
21. Rowland, 2003.
22. Chang, 2003.
23. Tynan, 2002.
24. Ibid.
25. Other estimates suggest that an even smaller response rate of 0.0001 percent may be sufficient to generate a profit for some spammers (Chang, 2003).
26. Rowland, 2003.
27. Chang, 2003.
28. Spring, 2003.
29. Ibid.
30. See http://www.ftc.gov/spam/.
31. See http://spamcop.com.

32. *BBC News,* August 10, 2005.

33. *Guardian Unlimited,* August 10, 2005.

34. All of this depends on various factors, such as the user's security settings. If the precautions advised by computer security experts are used, this technique will not work.

CHAPTER 9

1. Most computer users own a newsreader program capable of downloading materials from newsgroups. Outlook Express, for instance, can act as a newsreader and is distributed as part of Windows 95, 2000, and XP.

2. Bocij et al., 2005.

3. Changes in the way the report was produced appear to have resulted in somewhat lower figures than previous reports.

4. Business Software Alliance and International Data Corporation, 2005, p. 2.

5. Hermida, 2005.

6. Business Software Alliance, 2003.

7. International Federation of the Phonographic Industry, 2005a.

8. Motion Picture Association of America, 2004.

9. Ibid.

10. International Federation of the Phonographic Industry, 2005b, p. 3.

11. See www.iipa.com.

12. *News24.com,* July 16, 2003.

13. *Hindu,* November 25, 2003.

14. Lamy and RIAA, July 13, 2005.

15. Menta, 2002.

16. Blackburn, 2004.

17. Liebowitz, 2004.

18. Byrne, 2005.

19. Gibson, 2005.

20. Knight, 2004.

21. Tanaka, 2004.

22. *BBC News,* May 15, 2003.

23. *BBC News,* September 9, 2003.

24. *BBC News,* November 22, 2005.

25. *PC Pro,* March 2006.

CHAPTER 10

1. A more comprehensive definition and an accompanying discussion are given in Bocij (2004).

2. Reno, 1999.

3. For example, see Petherick, 1999; Burgess and Baker, 2002.

4. Bocij and McFarlane, 2003.

5. Bocij, 2004.

6. Reno et al., 1998.

7. Ibid.

8. Budd and Mattinson, 2000.

9. Bocij, 2004, p. 42.

10. Reno, 1999.
11. Koch, 2000.
12. Dean, 2000.
13. See www.haltabuse.org.
14. Zona, Sharma, and Lane, 1993.
15. Mullen et al., 1999.
16. Spitzberg, 2002, p. 262.
17. At this writing, the figures for 2005 could be accessed at http://www.haltabuse.org/resources/stats/index.shtml.
18. Bocij, 2003.
19. Katz, 2005.
20. Addley, 2000.
21. *BBC News*, September 2, 2005.
22. *BBC News*, December 22, 2004.
23. Katz, 2005.
24. Brown, 2005.
25. Raymond, 2005.
26. Bocij, 2005.
27. One type of reactive stalking, called offensive stalking, can involve an intention to harm other people. Sometimes, reactive stalking is used as a preemptive measure, enabling a "first strike" against a perceived threat. In other cases, stalking is used as a deterrent or in retaliation for a real or perceived attack. Even if a stalker recognizes that her actions have harmed an innocent person, there may be little guilt, since this may be seen as acceptable "collateral damage."

CHAPTER 11

1. See http://www.census.gov/.
2. Ellwood and Jencks, 2002.
3. Hall and Havens, 2006.
4. U.S. Congress, Office of Technology Assessment, 1993, p. 17.
5. U.S. Department of Commerce, Economics, and Statistics Administration, 1997.
6. Austin, 2003, p. 4.
7. See http://www.nua.ie/surveys/how_many_online/.
8. Pew Internet & American Life Project (see http://www.pewinternet.org/trends/DemographicsofInternetUsers.htm).
9. National Statistics, February 2004 data set, "Adults who have used the Internet in the 3 months prior to interview by sex/age (Great Britain)." See http://www.statistics.gov.uk/.
10. Hughes, 2001, p. 16.
11. Pew Internet & American Life Project (see http://www.pewinternet.org/trends/Daily_Activities_4.23.04.htm).
12. Caslon Analytics, 2003.
13. See http://www.meetic.co.uk/.
14. See http://www.stanford.edu/group/siqss/Press_Release/press_detail.html.
15. Sanders, 2000.
16. Schnieder, 2000.

17. McKenna and Bargh, 2000, p. 63.

18. Bradley and Poppen, 2003.

19. *BBC News,* July 21, 2003.

20. Ibid.

21. See the online version of the Cambridge Advanced Learner's Dictionary at http://dictionary.cambridge.org.

22. See investorwords.com at http://www.investorwords.com/5306/white_knight.html.

23. http://agencychick.typepad.com/ad_hoc/2004/03/tuesday_7_days_.html.

24. http://www.solvedating.com/dating-tips-needs.html.

25. http://www.globalpsychics.com/lp/love_advice/falling_in_love.htm#3.

26. http://www.voy.com/86426/3760.html.

27. http://blogs.salon.com/0001811/2004/07/21.html.

28. There is nothing to suggest that white knights must always be male, or that the people they rescue must always be female. However, in order to improve clarity, I refer to white knights as males and those they rescue as females.

29. See http://www.mangosauce.com/archives/000027.html.

30. See http://www.channels.nl/knowledge/21586.html.

31. See Bocij, Bocij, and McFarlane, 2003, for an account of such an incident.

32. *ABCNews,* June 12, 2003.

33. Kleinfield, 2003.

34. *ABCNews,* June 12, 2003.

35. Kleinfield, 2003.

36. *ABCNews,* June 12, 2003.

37. Ibid.

38. Capitol Hill Blue, 2004.

39. Whitty, 2003.

40. Whitty, 2002, p. 352–353.

41. See http://www.infidelitycheck.org.

42. See http://www.saferdating.com.

43. Wiltz, 2002.

44. Ibid.

45. Bocij and McFarlane, 2002.

46. Fortgang, 1999.

47. Smith, 1998; Tyson, 1998.

48. U.S. Fire Administration, 2003, p. 3.

49. Price, 1996.

50. Downey, 2003.

51. Hanley, 1996.

52. Downey, 2003.

53. Hanley, 1996; Nelan, 1996.

54. Bocij, Bocij, and McFarlane, 2003.

55. Bocij, 2004, p. 68–70.

56. Ibid.

CHAPTER 12

1. Since the term "cult" often carries negative connotations, some people prefer to use the term "New Religious Movements" or NRMs. However, in order to maintain clarity, the more well-known term is used throughout.

2. Kjaerland, Alison, and Lundrigan, 2003.

3. See also the discussion of cyberterrorism, which points out that terrorist groups have started to adopt this method for use in their recruitment campaigns.

4. See www.watchman.org.

5. Taylor, 2002.

6. Ibid.

7. Ray and Marsh, 2001; Hunt, 1999.

8. Lee and Leets, 2002.

9. Schafer, 2002; B'nai Brith Canada, 1999.

10. Not his real screen name.

11. For example, see Rollman, Krug, and Parente, 2000; Rollman and Parente, 2001.

12. Most chat room environments use a variety of techniques to prevent people from using inappropriate or offensive language during conversations or as part of a screen name.

13. There are number of well-known security flaws within the application used to create the chat room environment. One of these weaknesses can be exploited to make the program ignore attempts to close it. The program can be terminated, but only by identifying and ending the specific Windows process it uses. This solution is often beyond most novice computer users.

14. The Anti-Defamation League (2000) states: "The eighth letter of the alphabet is "H." Eight two times signifies 'HH,' shorthand for the Nazi greeting, 'Heil Hitler.' "88" is often found on hate group flyers, in both the greetings and closing comments of letters written by neo-Nazis, and in e-mail addresses."

15. Schafer and Navarro, 2003.

16. Ibid.

17. Ibid.

18. Ibid.

19. These programs allow users to assign long passages of text to an abbreviation chosen by the user. When the user types the abbreviation, it is automatically replaced by the expanded version of the text. As an example, a user might specify that whenever "ty" is typed, it should be replaced by "Thanking you in anticipation."

20. Haines, 2004b.

21. Craig, 2003.

22. *BBC News,* February 12, 2005.

23. Scheeres, 2003.

24. Ibid.

25. Haines, 2003.

26. Cobain, 2005.

27. DeAngelis, 2000.

28. Holmes, 2006.

29. Kershaw, 2005.

30. However, at least one study has reported that most Internet addicts are women.

31. DeAngelis, 2000.

32. Holmes, 2006.

33. DeAngelis, 2000.

34. Greene, 1998.

35. Greene, 1998.

36. Greene, 1998.

37. *Deutsche Welle,* August 8, 2003.
38. Vance, 2004.
39. Demick, 2005.
40. Whang, 2003.
41. Demick, 2005.
42. Jacobs, 2003.
43. Gluck, 2002.
44. Demick, 2005; *GameSpot News,* December 22, 2005.
45. Kim, 2005.
46. Ying, Han, and Chen, 2006.
47. http://groups.google.co.uk/googlegroups/about.html.
48. Ko, 2001.
49. Haines, 2004a.
50. Sparks, 2004.
51. Crabb, 2006.
52. Hall, 2004b.
53. Harding, 2004.
54. Crabb, 2006.
55. *BBC News,* 3 December 2003.
56. Harding, 2004.
57. Hall, 2004a.
58. *Guardian Unlimited,* January 30, 2004.

Bibliography

As might be expected with a subject that deals with modern technology, many of the information sources used are located on the Internet. Unfortunately, Internet sources are sometimes unreliable, since pages may be moved or deleted whenever a Web site is updated. Readers unable to locate an Internet resource listed here are invited to contact the author via the publisher for further information.

ABCNews. 2003. "Serial Proposer" [online]. ABCNews, June 12, 2003. Available at: http://abcnews.go.com/sections/GMA/Relationships/GMA030612Cassanova_colonel.html.

Acey, M. 2005. "UK's Critical Infrastructure Under Trojan Attack" [online]. TechWorld.com, June 16, 2005. Available at: http://www.techworld.com/networking/news/index.cfm?NewsID = 3863.

Acohido, B. and J. Swartz, 2004. "Are Hackers Using Your PC to Spew Spam And Steal?" [online]. *USA Today,* September 9, 2004. Available at: http://www.usatoday.com/tech/news/computersecurity/2004–09–08-zombieuser_x.htm.

Addley, E. 2000. "Mobile Phone Bullies Drove Teenager to Suicide" [online]. *Guardian Unlimited,* October 13, 2000. Available at: http://www.guardian.co.uk/internetnews/story/0,7369,381908,00.html.

Aft, A. 2004. "Terror Groups Exploit Internet for Communications, Recruiting, Training" [online]. Jewish Institute for National Security Affairs. Available at: http://www.jinsa.org/articles/articles.html/function/view/categoryid/1930/documentid/2621/history/3,2359,2166,1930,2621.

The Age. 2003. "'Hacktivists' Wage Iraq War Online" [online]. The Age Company Ltd., March 23, 2003. Available at: http://www.theage.com.au/articles/2003/03/29/1048653892300.html.

America Online and National Cyber Security Alliance. 2004. "AOL/NCSA Online Safety Study" [online]. America Online and National Cyber Security Alliance, October 2004. Available at: http://www.staysafeonline.info/pdf/safety_study_v04.pdf.

Anderson, K. 2000. "Why Write Computer Viruses?" [online]. BBC News, November 6, 2000. Available at: http://news.bbc.co.uk/1/hi/sci/tech/738348.stm.

Anti-Defamation League. 2000. "A Visual Database of Extremist Symbols, Logos and Tattoos" [online]. New York: Anti-Defamation League. Available at: http://www.adl.org/hate_symbols/default.asp.

Anti-Defamation League, 2002. "Jihad Online: Islamic Terrorists and the Internet." New York: Anti-Defamation League. Available at: http://www.adl.org/Learn/internet/jihad.asp.

Armour, S. 2003. "Diploma Mills Insert Degree of Fraud into Job Market" [online]. *USA Today*, September 28, 2003. Available at: http://www.usatoday.com/money/workplace/2003–09–28-fakedegrees_x.htm.

Association for Computing Machinery Committee on Computers and Public Policy. 1987. *The Risks Digest* [online]. December 7, 1987. Association for Computing Machinery. Available at: http://catless.ncl.ac.uk/Risks/5.71.html#subj1.

Austin, J. 2003. "Sole Parent Carers." Deakin, Australia: Carers Australia. Available at: http://www.carersaustralia.com.au/documents/Sole%20Parent%20Carers.pdf.

Ballard J., J. Hornik, and D. McKenzie, 2002. "Technological Facilitation of Terrorism." *American Behavioral Scientist* 45, no. 6, pp. 989–1016.

Bank, D. 2005. "'Spear Phishing' Tests Educate People About Online Scams" [online]. *The Wall Street Journal Online*, August 29, 2005. Available at: http://online.wsj.com/public/article/SB112424042313615131-z_8jLB2WkfcVtgdAWf6LRh733sg_20060817.html?mod = blogs.

Baranikas, I. 2003. "Russian Scam without Borders [online]." *CDI Russia Weekly* 258 (May 2003), 21–27. Washington, DC: Center for Defense Information. Available at: http://www.cdi.org/russia/258–10.cfm.

BBC News. 2001. "Warning Over Nigerian Mail Scam" [online]. *BBC News*, July 10, 2001. Available at: http://news.bbc.co.uk/1/hi/uk/1431761.stm.

BBC News. 2003. "German Cannibal Tells of Fantasy" [online]. *BBC News*, December 3, 2003. Available at: http://news.bbc.co.uk/2/hi/europe/3286721.stm.

BBC News. 2003. "Apple Doubles Online Music Sales" [online]. *BBC News*, May 15, 2003. Available at: http://news.bbc.co.uk/1/hi/business/3029613.stm.

BBC News. 2003. "Apple Sells 10m Tunes on the Net" [online]. *BBC News*, September 9, 2003. Available at: http://news.bbc.co.uk/1/hi/technology/3092542.stm.

BBC News. 2003. "Computer Worm Targets Blair" [online]. *BBC News*, September 5, 2003. Available at: http://news.bbc.co.uk/2/hi/technology/3083192.stm.

BBC News. 2003. "Cyber Sex Lures Love Cheats" [online]. *BBC News*, July 21, 2003. Available at: http://news.bbc.co.uk/2/hi/technology/3083173.stm.

BBC News. 2004. "Q&A: The Mydoom virus" [online]. *BBC News*, January 29, 2004. Available at: http://news.bbc.co.uk/newswatch/ukfs/hi/feedback/default.stm.

BBC News. 2004. "Sex-case Delhi Schoolboy Bailed" [online]. *BBC News*, December 22, 2004. Available at: http://news.bbc.co.uk/2/hi/south_asia/4118503.stm.

BBC News. 2005. "Downloads Enter US Singles Chart" [online]. *BBC News*, February 7, 2005. Available at: http://news.bbc.co.uk/1/hi/entertainment/music/4242571.stm.

BBC News. 2005. "'Happy Slap' Pupil Found Hanged" [online]. *BBC News*, September 2, 2005. Available at: http://news.bbc.co.uk/1/hi/england/merseyside/4209632.stm.

BBC News. 2005. "Itunes 'Outsells' US Music Stores" [online]. *BBC News,* November 22, 2005. Available at: http://news.bbc.co.uk/1/hi/entertainment/4459312.stm.

BBC News. 2005. "Man 'Set Valentine Suicide Pact'" [online]. *BBC News,* February 12, 2005. Available at: http://news.bbc.co.uk/2/hi/americas/4259079.stm.

Berensen, A. 2000. "Investigators Arrest a Suspect in Stock Manipulation Case" [online]. *New York Times,* September 1, 2000. Available at: http://www.nytimes.com/library/financial/090100emulex-plunge.html.

Berinato, S. 2002. "The Truth About Cyberterrorism" [online]. *CIO Magazine,* March 15, 2002. Available at: http://www.cio.com/archive/031502/truth.html.

Berinato, S. 2004. "The Future Of Security" [online]. *CIO.com,* June 2, 2004. Available at: http://www.cio.com.au/index.php/id;1039367795;fp;512;fpid;6.

Blackburn, D. 2004. "On-line Piracy and Recorded Music Sales" [online]. Harvard University. Available at: http://www.economics.harvard.edu/~dblackbu/papers/blackburn_fs.pdf.

Blincoe, R. 2001. "Kournikova Virus Kiddie Gets 150 Hours Community Service" [online]. *Register,* September 27, 2001. Available at: http://www.theregister.co.uk/2001/09/27/kournikova_virus_kiddie_gets/.

B'nai Brith Canada, 1999. "1999 Audit of Anti-Semitic Incidents" [online]. League for Human Rights of B'nai Brith Canada. Available at: http://www.bnaibrith.ca/publications/audit1999/audit1999-04.html.

Boal, M. 2004. "The Identity Addict" [online]. *Playboy.com.* Available at: http://www.playboy.com/magazine/article/identity_addict/.

Bocij, P. 1992. *Software For Free: A Guide To Low-Cost PC Software.* Pangbourne, Berkshire: Kuma Publishing Limited.

Bocij, P. 2002. "Corporate Cyberstalking: An Invitation To Build Theory" [online]. *First Monday* 7, no. 11. Available at: http://firstmonday.org/issues/issue7_11/bocij/index.html.

Bocij, P. 2003. "Victims Of Cyberstalking: An Exploratory Study Of Harassment Perpetrated Via The Internet" [online]. *First Monday* 8, no. 10. Available at: http://www.firstmonday.dk/issues/issue8_10/bocij/index.html.

Bocij, P. 2004. *Cyberstalking: Harassment in the Internet Age and How to Protect Your Family.* Westport, CT: Praeger Press.

Bocij, P. 2005. "Reactive Stalking: A New Perspective on Victimisation." *British Journal of Forensic Practice* 7, no. 1, pp. 23–34.

Bocij, P. and L. McFarlane. 2002. Online Harassment: Towards a Definition of Cyberstalking. *Prison Service Journal* 139, pp. 31–38.

Bocij, P. and L. McFarlane. 2003. "Seven Fallacies About Cyberstalking." *Prison Service Journal* 149, pp. 37–42.

Bocij, P., H. Bocij, and L. McFarlane. 2003. Cyberstalking: A Case Study Concerning Serial Harassment in the UK. *British Journal of Forensic Practice* 5, no. 2, pp. 25–32.

Bocij, P., D. Chaffey, A. Greasley, and S. Hickie. 2005. *Business Information Systems: Technology, Development and Management for the E-business,* 3rd ed., London: Financial Times and Prentice Hall.

Borland, J. 2004. "Are P2P Networks Leaking Military Secrets?" [online]. *ZDNet News.* Available at: http://news.zdnet.com/2100–1009_22–5285918.html.

Böttler, J. 2002. *Threats Posed by Cyber Terror and Possible Responses of the United Nations.* December 2002. Amsterdam: United Nations International Student Conference of Amsterdam, First Committee on Disarmament and International Security.

Bradley, N. and W. Poppen. 2003. Assistive Technology, Computers and Internet May Decrease Sense of Isolation for Homebound Elderly and Disabled Persons. *Technology and Disability* 15, pp. 19–25.

Brenner, B. 2004. "Fast-Moving Zafi-B Disables Firewalls, Spreads Political Message" [online]. SearchSecurity.com, June 15, 2004. Available at: http://search-security.techtarget.com/originalContent/0,289142,sid14_gci970143,00.html?offer = LGss605.

Bridwell, L. 2004. "ICSA Labs 9th Annual Computer Virus Prevalence Survey" [online]. ICSA Labs. Available at: https://www.icsalabs.com/icsa/docs/html/library/whitepapers/VPS2003.pdf.

Brown, C. 2005. "Mobile-Phone Bullying 'An Epidemic'" [online]. *Scotsman.com,* November 19, 2005. Available at: http://news.scotsman.com/topics.cfm?tid = 519&id = 2265612005.

Budd, T. and J. Mattinson. 2000. "Stalking: Findings From the 1998 British Crime Survey" [online]. *Research Findings* 129, pp. 1–4. London: Home Office Research, Development and Statistics Directorate. Available at: http://www.homeoffice.gov.uk/rds/pdfs/r129.pdf.

Burgess, W. A. and T. Baker. 2002. "Cyberstalking." In J. Boon, et al. (eds.), *Stalking And Psychosexual Obsession: Psychological Perspectives For Prevention, Policing And Treatment*, pp. 201–219. London: John Wiley & Sons.

Burke, J. 2004. "Al-Qaeda Launches Online Terrorist Manual" [online]. *Guardian Unlimited*, January 18, 2004. Available at: http://observer.guardian.co.uk/international/story/0,6903,1125877,00.html.

Business Software Alliance and International Data Corporation. 2005. "Second Annual BSA and IDC Global Software Piracy Study." May 2005. Washington, D.C.: Business Software Alliance and International Data Corporation. Available online at: http://www.bsa.org/globalstudy/upload/2005-Global-Study-English.pdf.

Business Software Alliance. 2003. "Proving The Connection: Links Between Intellectual Property Theft And Organised Crime." London: Business Software Alliance. Available online at: http://www.bsa.org/uk/upload/Proving-the-Connection2.pdf.

Byrne, S. 2005. "Study Finds the Youth Harm Music Sales in Long Term with P2P" [online]. RankOne Media Group, November 30, 2005. Available at: http://www.cdfreaks.com/news2.php?ID = 12747.

Capitol Hill Blue. 2004. "Womanizing Colonel Penalized by Army" [online]. Capitol Hill Blue, February 3, 2004. Available at: http://www.capitolhillblue.com/artman/publish/article_3749.shtml.

Carabott, M. 2005. "'Happy Slap' Murder of Former Malta Resident" [online]. *Independent Online,* July 7, 2005. Available at: http://217.145.4.56/ind/news.asp?newsitemid = 18383.

Caslon Analytics. 2003. "Caslon Analytics Profile: Email, SMS, IM & Chat" [online]. Caslon Analytics. Available at: http://www.caslon.com.au/emailprofile4.htm.

Caslon Analytics. 2005. "Caslon Analytics Profile: Identity Theft, Identity Fraud" [online]. Caslon Analytics Pty. Ltd.. Available at: http://www.caslon.com.au/idtheftprofile.htm.

CBS News. 2004. "Top Officials Hold Fake Degrees" [online]. *CBS News*, May 10, 2004. Available at: http://www.cbsnews.com/stories/2004/05/10/evening-news/main616664.shtml.

CBC News. 2006. "Cross-border Rx" [online]. *CBC News*, January 17, 2006. Available at: http://www.cbc.ca/news/background/drugs/.

Chang, R. 2003. "Could Spam Kill Off E-Mail?" [online]. *PCWorld.com*, October 22, 2003. Available at: http://www.pcworld.com/news/article/0,aid,113061, 00.asp.

Christensen, J. 1999. "Bracing for Guerrilla Warfare in Cyberspace" [online]. *CNN Interactive*, April 6, 1999. Available at: http://edition.cnn.com/TECH/specials/hackers/cyberterror/.

Christianson, L. 2005. "Online Baby Scams on the Rise" [online]. *Exploring Adoption*, June 8, 2005. Available at: http://adoptionblogs.typepad.com/adoption/adoption_fraud/.

Cluley, G. 2000. "Who Writes Viruses?" [online]. *SearchSecurity.com*, September 11, 2000. Available at: http://searchsecurity.techtarget.com/tip/1,289483,sid14_gci493274,00.html?bucket=ETA.

CNET News.com. 2004. "Good news: 'Phishing' Scams Net Only $500 Million" [online]. *CNET News.com*, September 29, 2004. Available at: http://news.com.com/Good+news+Phishing+scams+net+ionlyi+500+million/2100-1029_3-5388757.html.

CNN.com. 2003. "Looking into the Mind of a Virus Writer" [online]. *CNN.com*, March 19, 2003. Available at: http://www.cnn.com/2003/TECH/internet/03/19/virus.writers.reut/.

Cobain, I. 2005. "Clampdown on Chatrooms after Two Strangers Die in First Internet Death Pact" [online]. *Guardian Unlimited*, October 11, 2005. Available at: http://technology.guardian.co.uk/online/news/0,12597,1589332,00.html.

Cohen, F. 1987. "Computer Viruses—Theory and Experiments." *Computers and Security* 6, no. 1, pp. 22–35. (This paper was originally presented at the DOD/NBS 7th Conference on Computer Security in 1984.)

Computer Economics Inc. 2003. "Virus Attack Costs On the Rise—Again" [online]. Computer Economics Inc., September 2003. Available at: http://www.computereconomics.com/article.cfm?id = 873.

Connolly, K. 2006. "An Unhappy Export" [online]. *Daily Telegraph*, March 13, 2006. Available at: http://www.telegraph.co.uk/news/main.jhtml?view = BLOGDETAIL&grid = P30&blog = berlin&xml = /news/2006/03/13/blberlin13.xml.

ConsumerReports.org. 2003a. "Cyberspace Invaders" [online]. ConsumerReports.org. Available at: http://www.consumerreports.org/static/0206com0.html.

ConsumerReports.org. 2003b. "Readers Report on Home Computer Security" [online]. ConsumerReports.org. Available at: http://www.consumerreports.org/static/0206com5.html.

Conway, M. 2002. "Reality Bytes: Cyberterrorism and Terrorist 'Use' of the Internet" [online]. *First Monday* 7, no. 11. Available at: http://www.firstmonday.org/issues/issue7_11/conway/.

Crabb, A. 2006. "The Cannibal & His Copyright" [online]. *The Age*. Available at: http://www.theage.com.au/news/world/the-cannibal—his-copyright/2006/03/04/1141191883394.html?page = fullpage#contentSwap3.

Craig, O. 2003. "Chatmates Watched Internet Suicide" [online]. *Telegraph.co.uk*, February 9, 2003. Available at: http://www.telegraph.co.uk/news/main. jhtml?xml = %2Fnews%2F2003%2F02%2F09%2Fwsuic09.xml&secureRefresh = true&_requestid = 108966.

Dean, K. 2000. "The Epidemic Of Cyberstalking" [online]. Wired Digital Inc. May 1, 2000. Available at: http://www.wired.com/news/politics/0,1283,35728,00. html.

DeAngelis, T. 2000. "Is Internet Addiction Real? " [online]. *Monitor on Psychology* 31, no. 4. Available at: http://apa.org/monitor/apr00/addiction.html.

De Bruin, P. 2004. "SA cops, Interpol Probe Murder" [online]. *News24.com*, December 31, 2004. Available at: http://www.news24.com/News24/South_ Africa/News/0,,2-7-1442_1641875,00.html.

Delio, M. 2001. "A Worm Writer's Worst Friend" [online]. *Wired News*, May 29, 2001. Available at: http://www.wired.com/news/print/0,1294,43839,00. html.

Delio, M. 2004. "Spyware Infiltrates the Enterprise." *InfoWorld* 40, October 4, 2004, pp. 35–41.

Dell Inc. 2004. "Dell Launches Campaign to Build Awareness of PC Security Issues" [online]. Dell Inc., July 20, 2004. Available at: http://www1.us.dell.com/con-tent/topics/global.aspx/corp/pressoffice/en/2004/2004_07_20_rr_000?c = us&l = en&s = dhs&cs = 19.

Demick, B. 2005. "Fear of Excessive Game-Playing on Net Rises in S. Korea" [on-line]. New York Times Company, August 31, 2005. Available at: http://www. boston.com/news/world/asia/articles/2005/08/31/fear_of_excessive_ game_playing_on_net_rises_in_s_korea/.

Denning, D. 2000. "Cyberterrorism" [online]. Georgetown University. Available at: http://www.cs.georgetown.edu/~denning/infosec/cyberterror-GD.doc.

Denning, D. 2001. "Activism, Hacktivism, And Cyberterrorism: The Internet As A Tool For Influencing Foreign Policy." In Arquilla, J. et al. (ed.), *Networks and Netwars: The Future of Terror, Crime, and Militancy*, pp. 239–288. Santa Monica: Rand.

Deutsche Welle. 2003. "German Kids Go to Camp for Internet Addiction" [online]. *Deutsche Welle*, August 8, 2003. Available at: http://www.dw-world.de/dw/ article/0,,943281,00.html.

Downey, M. 2003. "City and Nation Never Apologized to Jewell" [online]. *MontereyHerald.com*, May 31, 2003. Available at: http://www.montereyherald. com/mld/montereyherald/sports/5987061.htm.

Dunn, J. 2005. "World's Largest Trojan Fraud Uncovered" [online]. Techworld. com, May 31, 2005. Available at: http://www.techworld.com/security/news/ index.cfm?NewsID = 3764.

Eagle Rock Alliance Ltd. 2001. "2001 Cost Of Downtime Survey 8/01-DR," West Orange, NJ: Eagle Rock Alliance, Ltd. Available at: http://www.contingency-planningresearch.com/2001%20Survey.pdf.

The Editors. 2004. "Dot-Com Terrorism: How Radical Islam Uses the Internet to Fight the West." *New Atlantis* 5 (Spring 2004), pp. 91–3.

Ellwood, D. and C. Jencks. 2002. "The Spread of Single-Parent Families in the United States since 1960" [online]. John F. Kennedy School of Government, Harvard University. Available at: http://www.ksg.harvard.edu/inequality/ Seminar/Papers/ElwdJnck.pdf.

Emerson, S. 2002. Fund-Raising Methods and Procedures for International Terrorist Organizations, February 12, 2002. Washington D.C.: House Committee on Financial Services (Subcommittee on Oversight and Investigations). Available online at: http://financialservices.house.gov/media/pdf/021202se.pdf.

Enos, L. 2001. "Online Auctions Top FBI Net Fraud List" [online]. ECT News Network, July 3, 2001. Available at: http://www.crmbuyer.com/story/7986.html.

Evers, J. 2003. "Does Cyberterrorism Pose a True Threat?" [online]. *PC World*, March 14, 2003. Available at: http://www.pcworld.com/news/article/0,aid,109819,00.asp.

Farah, J. 2004. "How Jihadists Use Net to Kill, Maim, Destroy" [online]. *WorldNetDaily.com*. Available at: http://www.worldnetdaily.com/news/article.asp?ARTICLE_ID = 40517.

Farrell, N. 2005. "Trojan Converts Porn To Islam" [online]. *Inquirer*, September 6, 2005. Available at: http://www.theinquirer.net/?article = 25960.

Festa, P. 2003. "419 Scams Clean Out Gullible US Victims" [online]. Computer Crime Research Center. Available at: http://www.crime-research.org/news/2003/04/Mess1105.html.

Finch, E. 2003. What a Tangled Web We Weave: Identity Theft and the Internet. In Y. Jewkes, ed., *Dot Cons: Crime, Deviance, and Identity on the Internet*, pp. 86–104. Collompton, England: Willan Publishing.

Fortgang, L. Berman. 1999. The Hero Syndrome. *Innovative Leader* [online], 8, no. 5. Available at: http://www.winstonbrill.com/bril001/html/article_index/articles/401-450/article401_body.html.

GameSpot News. 2005. "Couple's Online Gaming Causes Infant's Death" [online]. *GameSpot News*, December 22, 2005. Available at: http://www.gamespot.com/news/6127866.html.

Gardner, A. 2005. "Prescription Drugs Cheaper on Canadian Internet Sites" [online]. *ABC News*, September 19, 2005. Available at: http://abcnews.go.com/Health/Healthology/story?id = 1141058.

Gibson, O. 2005. "Online File Sharers 'Buy More Music'" [online]. *Guardian Unlimited*, July 27, 2005. Available at: http://arts.guardian.co.uk/news/story/0,11711,1536886,00.html.

Gluck, C. 2002. "South Korea's Gaming Addicts" [online]. *BBC News*, November 22, 2002. Available at: http://news.bbc.co.uk/1/hi/world/asia-pacific/2499957.stm.

Goodman, J., D. Heckerman, and R. Rounthwaite. 2005. "Stopping Spam" [online]. *ScientificAmerican.com*, March 28, 2005. Available at: http://www.sciam.com/article.cfm?chanID=sa006&colID=1&articleID=000F3A4B-BF70-1238-BF7083414B7FFE9F.

Gordon, S. 1994a. "The Generic Virus Writer" [online]. IBM. Available at: http://www.research.ibm.com/antivirus/SciPapers/Gordon/GenericVirusWriter.html.

Gordon, S. 1994b. "The Generic Virus Writer II" [online]. IBM. Available at: http://www.research.ibm.com/antivirus/SciPapers/Gordon/GVWII.html.

Gordon, S. 2000. "Virus Writers: The End of the Innocence?" [online]. IBM. Available at: http://www.research.ibm.com/antivirus/SciPapers/VB2000SG.pdf.

Green, J. 2002. "The Myth of Cyberterrorism" [online]. *Washington Monthly*, November 2002. Available at: http://www.washingtonmonthly.com/features/2001/0211.green.html.

Greene, R. W. 1998. "Is Internet Addiction for Worrywarts or a Genuine Problem?" [online]. *CNN.com,* September 23, 1998. Available at: http://edition.cnn.com/TECH/computing/9809/23/netaddict.idg/.

Grice, C. and S. Ard. 2000. "Hoax Briefly Shaves $2.5 Billion off Emulex's Market Cap" [online]. CNET Networks Inc., August 25, 2000. Available at: http://news.com.com/2100–1033–244975.html?legacy = cnet.

Guardian Unlimited. 2004. "German Cannibal Gets Eight-and-a-Half Years" [online]. *Guardian Unlimited,* January 30, 2004. Available at: http://www.guardian.co.uk/germany/article/0,2763,1135135,00.html.

Haines, L. 2003. "Internet Suicide Chat Room Killer Held" [online]. *Register,* January 27, 2003. Available at: http://www.theregister.co.uk/2003/01/27/internet_suicide_chat_room_killer/.

Haines, L. 2004a. "Internet Rape Fantasy 'Game' Goes Horribly Wrong" [online]. *Register,* April 5, 2004. Available at: http://www.theregister.co.uk/2004/04/05/internet_rape_fantasy_game_goes/.

Haines, L. 2004b. "Seven Dead In Net Suicide Pact" [online]. *Register,* October 12, 2004. Available at: http://www.theregister.co.uk/2004/10/12/net_suicide_pact/.

Hall, A. 2004a. "Cannibal Sentenced to Eight Years" [online]. *Scotsman,* January 31, 2004. Available at: http://thescotsman.scotsman.com/international.cfm?id = 121512004.

Hall, A. 2004b. "Cannibal's Video of 'Victim's' Final Hours Played to Court" [online]. *Scotsman.com,* December 9, 2003. Available at: http://news.scotsman.com/index.cfm?id = 1349282003.

Hall, M. and B. Havens. 2006. "The Effect of Social Isolation and Loneliness on the Health of Older Women" [online]. Prairie Women's Health Centre of Excellence. Available at: http://www.uwinnipeg.ca/admin/vh_external/pwhce/effectSocialIsolation.htm.

Hanley, C. 1996. "'Hero' Guard Focus of FBI" [online]. *The Standard-Times,* July 31, 1996. Available at: http://www.s-t.com/daily/07-96/07-31-96/a01wn010.htm.

Harding, L. 2004. "Cannibal Who Fried Victim in Garlic Is Cleared of Murder" [online]. *Guardian Unlimited,* January 31, 2004. Available at: http://www.guardian.co.uk/germany/article/0,2763,1135725,00.html.

Hastings, C. and R. Syal. 2001. "Briton Kidnapped by Nigerian Gang in Cash Fraud" [online]. *Telegraph.co.uk,* July 15, 2001. Available at: http://www.telegraph.co.uk/news/main.jhtml?xml = /news/2001/07/15/nkid15.xml.

Hermida, A. 2005. "Software Piracy 'Seen As Normal'" [online]. *BBC News,* June 23, 2005. Available at: http://news.bbc.co.uk/1/hi/technology/4122624.stm.

Higgins, M. (ed.). 2003. "Symantec Internet Security Threat Report," Volume 3, February 2003. Available at: http://www.securitystats.com/reports.html

Hindu. 2003. "Piracy racket may 'aid' terrorists: Ribeiro" [online]. *Hindu,* November 25, 2003. Available at: http://www.hinduonnet.com/thehindu/2003/11/25/stories/2003112504481300.htm.

Hines, M. 2005. "Research: Spyware Industry Worth Billions" [online]. *CNET News.com,* May 3, 2005. Available at: http://news.com.com/2100–1029–5693730.html?tag = tb.

Holmes, L. 2006. "What is 'Normal' Internet Use?" [online]. About.com, March 11, 2006. Available at: http://mentalhealth.about.com/cs/sexaddict/a/normalinet.htm.

Hughes, D. 2001. *The Impact of the Use of New Communications and Information Technologies on Trafficking in Human Beings for Sexual Exploitation: A Study of the Users.* Strasbourg, Switzerland: Committee for Equality between Women and Men/Council of Europe.

Hulme, G. and T. Claburn. 2004. "Tiny, Evil Things" [online]. *Information Week,* April 26, 2004. Available at: http://www.informationweek.com/story/showArticle.jhtml?articleID = 19200218.

Hunt, N. 1999. "Hate Groups Seek to Recruit through Internet" [online]. *Reuters.* Available at: http://www.rickross.com/reference/hate_groups/hategroups79.html.

Hupp, S. 2001. "Woman Charged in E-mail Case" [online]. *The Des Moines Register,* August 29, 2001. Available at: http://www.mailutilities.com/news/archive/74/1440.html.

Illett, D. 2005. "Security Guru Slams Misuse Of 'Cyberterrorism'" [online]. *CNET News.com,* April 26, 2005. Available at: http://news.com.com/Security+guru+slams+misuse+of+cyberterrorism/2100–1029_3–5685500.html?part = rss&tag = 5685500&subj = news.

International Federation of the Phonographic Industry. 2005a. "One in Three Music Discs Is Illegal But Fight Back Starts to Show Results" [online]. International Federation of the Phonographic Industry, June 23, 2005. Available at: http://www.ifpi.org/site-content/antipiracy/piracy-report-current.html.

International Federation of the Phonographic Industry. 2005b. "The Recording Industry 2005 Commercial Piracy Report." June 2005. London: International Federation of the Phonographic Industry. Available online at: http://www.ifpi.org/site-content/library/piracy2005.pdf.

Jacobs, T. 2003. "Video Gamers Play On As Their Lives Fall Apart" [online]. *Columbia News Service,* June 22, 2003. Available at: http://www.jrn.columbia.edu/studentwork/cns/2003–06–22/282.asp.

Katz, L. 2005. "When 'Digital Bullying' Goes Too Far" [online]. *CNET News.com,* June 22, 2005. Available at: http://news.com.com/When+digital+bullying+goes+too+far/2100–1025_3–5756297.html.

Kehoe, B. 1992. "Zen and the Art of the Internet" [online]. Indiana University. Available at: http://www.cs.indiana.edu/docproject/zen/zen-1.0_toc.html.

Keizer, G. 2005a. "UK Under Cyberattack" [online]. *Information Week,* June 15, 2005. Available at: http://www.informationweek.com/story/showArticle.jhtml?articleID = 164900307.

Keizer, G. 2005b. "Worst Spyware Down, Infected Sites Up" [online]. *TechWeb,* May 2, 2005. Available at: http://www.techweb.com/wire/security/162100621.

Kephart, J., D. Chess, and S. White. 1993. "Computers and Epidemiology [online]." *IEEE SPECTRUM,* May 1993. Available at: http://www.research.ibm.com/antivirus/SciPapers/Kephart/Spectrum/Spectrum.html.

Kershaw, S. 2005. "Hooked on the Web: Help Is on the Way" [online]. *NYTimes.com,* December 1, 2005. Available at: http://www.nytimes.com/2005/12/01/fashion/thursdaystyles/01addict.html?ex = 1142744400&en = 925d059c20cfc9f5&ei = 5070.

Kim, V. 2005. "Video Game Addicts Concern S. Korean Gov't" [online]. *Breitbart.com,* October 6, 2005. Available at: http://www.breitbart.com/news/2005/10/06/D8D2BBTO2.html.

Kjaerland, M., L. Alison, and S. Lundrigan. 2003. "A Comparative Study of Persuasion and Recruitment Techniques Exhibited by Organized Groups on the Internet" [online]. University of Liverpool and Victoria University of Wellington. Available at: http://www1.his.no/vit/oks/kjarland/pdf/Cult%20paper.pdf.

Klein, P. 2004. "Losses From Viruses Reach 5-Year High Swell" [online]. *Information Week,* October 25, 2004. Available at: http://www.informationweek.com/story/showArticle.jhtml?articleID = 51000347.

Kleinfield, N. R. 2003. "Slap on the Wrists for Serial Wooer" [online]. *Sydney Morning Herald,* December 22, 2003. Available at: http://www.smh.com.au/articles/2003/12/21/1071941612448.html?from=storyrhs.

Knight, W. 2004. "Net Music Piracy 'Does Not Harm Record Sales'" [online]. *NewScientist.com,* March 30, 2004. Available at: http://www.newscientist.com/article/dn4831.html.

Ko, M. 2001. "Still in a Hi-tech Closet—Barely." *Report,* June 11, 2001, pp. 34–36.

Koch, L. 2000. "Cyberstalking Hype." *Inter@ctive Week 7,* no. 21, p. 28.

Kong, D. 2000. "Internet Auction Fraud Increases" [online]. *USA Today,* June 23, 2000. Available at: http://www.usatoday.com/money/wealth/consumer/mcw071.htm.

Kotadia, M. 2004. "Virus Linked to al-Qaida" [online]. *Silicon.com,* July 19, 2004. Available at: http://software.silicon.com/malware/0,3800003100,39122359,00.htm.

Lamy, J. and Recording Industry Association of America, 2005. "RIAA's Annual Commercial Piracy Report Shows Trafficking in Pirated Music Increasingly Sophisticated, Closer Ties to Criminal Syndicates" [online]. top40-charts.com, July 13, 2005. Available at: http://top40-charts.com/news.php?nid = 16184.

Latta, J. 2006. "January Virus and Spam Statistics: 2006 Starts with a Bang" [online]. *AlwaysOn Network.* Available at: http://www.alwayson-network.com/comments.php?id=14063_0_4_0_C.

Lawrence, J. 2005. "Fake Degree Can Be Deadly" [online]. *The Sunday Mail.* Available at: http://www.thesundaymail.news.com.au/common/story_page/0,5936,12731425%255E2765,00.html.

Lee E. and L. Leets. 2002. Persuasive Storytelling by Hate Groups Online. *American Behavioral Scientist 45,* no. 2, pp. 927–57.

Lemos, R. 2003. "Counting the Cost of Slammer" [online]. *CNET News.com.* Available at: http://news.com.com/Counting+the+cost+of+Slammer/2100–1001_3–982955.html.

Leyden, J. 2001. "Hardware-trashing Virus Spreads by Email" [online]. *Register,* March 14, 2001. Available at: http://www.theregister.co.uk/2001/03/14/hardwaretrashing_virus_spreads_by_email/.

Leyden, J. 2002. "Lies, Damned Lies and Anti-Virus Statistics" [online]. *Register,* January 16, 2002. Available at: http://www.theregister.co.uk/2002/01/16/lies_damned_lies_and_antivirus/.

Leyden, J. 2003. "New Worm Tries to Bring Down Downing Street Website" [online]. *Register,* September 4, 2003. Available at: http://www.theregister.co.uk/2003/09/04/new_worm_tries_to_bring/.

Leyden, J. 2004a. "Belgian Police Arrest Female Virus Writer" [online]. *Register,* February 16, 2004. Available at: http://www.theregister.co.uk/2004/02/16/belgian_police_arrest_female_virus/.

Leyden, J. 2004b. "Viruses: Up Or Down?" [online]. *Register.* Available at: http:// www.theregister.co.uk/2004/06/01/virus_stats/.

Liebowitz, S. 2004. "Pitfalls in Measuring the Impact of File-Sharing" [online]. Social Science Research Network. Available at: http://papers.ssrn.com/sol3/papers. cfm?abstract_id = 583484.

Logan, T. 2004. "Lure of Black Money Scam" [online]. *BBC News,* March 1, 2004. Available at: http://news.bbc.co.uk/2/hi/technology/3494072.stm.

Lopez, J. 2004. "Mounting Business Losses Boost Anti-Spam Market" [online]. *CIO Today,* April 6, 2004. Available at: http://www.cio-today.com/story.xhtml?story_ title=Mounting_Business_Losses_Boost_Anti_Spam_Market&story_id=23613 &category=entcmpt.

Lyman, J. 2005. "Profile of a Virus Writer: Pride to Profit" [online]. *ECT News Network,* October 6, 2005. Available at: http://www.technewsworld.com/ story/NAD0DHhKr056aU/Profile-of-a-Virus-Writer-Pride-to-Profit. xhtml.

Lysecki, S. 2005. "Spyware Reaches New Threat Level" [online]. Transcontinental Media Inc., June 22, 2005. Available at: http://www.itbusiness.ca/it/client/ en/home/News.asp?id = 1703.

Margalit, Y. 2005. "Combating the Scourges of Identity Theft and Phishing" [online]. SecurityStockWatch.com. Available at: http://www.securitystockwatch.com/ aladdin-05–09–26.html.

Martin, Emilie. 2005. "Top Tips to Stop Spam" [online]. *Computeract!ve,* April 28, 2005. Available at: http://www.vnunet.com/computeractive/ features/2014133/top-tips-stop-spam.

McKenna, K. and J. Bargh. 2000. Plan 9 From Cyberspace: The Implications of the Internet for Personality and Social Psychology. *Personality and Social Psychology Review* 4, no. 1, pp. 57–75.

McUsic, T. 2006. "Program Lists Top Internet, Telephone Scams of 2005" [online]. *Star-Telegram.com,* February 6, 2006. Available at: http://www.mercurynews. com/mld/dfw/business/local/13803275.htm?source = rss&channel = dfw_ local.

Menta, R. 2002. "Ipsos-Reid: More Americans Taste Tunes on Net" [online]. *MP3Newswire.net,* December 7, 2002. Available at: http://www.mp3newswire. net/stories/2002/tunetaste.html.

Meserve, J. 2001. "New 'Injustice' Virus Spreads Political Message" [online]. Network World Fusion, March 20, 2001. Available at: http://security.itworld. com/4340/itwnws_3–19–01_injustice/page_1.html.

Messaging Pipeline. 2005. "New Radicati Study Shows E-Mail Growth" [online]. *Messaging Pipeline,* January 7, 2005. Available at: http://www.messagingpipe-line.com/trends/trends_archive/57300283.

Miller, J. 2004. "First Pocket PC Virus Uncovered" [online]. PDAStreet.com, July 19, 2004. Available at: http://www.pdastreet.com/articles/2004/7/2004-7-19-First-Pocket-PC.html.

Mitnick, K. and W. Simon. 2002. *The Art Of Deception.* Indianopolis: Wiley Publishing Inc.

Mohammed, A. 2004. "Can Spam Really Be Wiped Out in Two Years?" [online]. *Computer Weekly,* July 19, 2004. Available at: http://www.cw360.com/ Articles/2004/07/19/203869/Canspamreallybewipedoutintwoyears.htm.

Morris, R. 2004. "The Development of an Identity Theft Offender Typology: A Theoretical Approach [online]." *Research in Educational Leadership* 2004 (3). Available at: http://www.shsu.edu/~edu_elc/journal/research%20online/researchex04.html.

Motion Picture Association of America. 2004. "2004 Piracy Fact Sheets: U.S. Overview." November 2004. Washington, DC: Motion Picture Association of America. Available online at: http://www.mpaa.org/USPiracyFactSheet.pdf.

Mullen P., M. Pathé, R. Purcell, and G. Stuart. 1999. "A Study of Stalkers." *American Journal of Psychiatry* 156, pp. 1244–9.

Nagpal, A. R. 2002. "Cyber Terrorism in the Context of Globalization." UGC-Sponsored National Seminar on "Globalization and Human Rights," September 7–8, 2002. Mumbai, India: University Grants Commission.

National Commission on Terrorist Attacks Upon the United States. 2004. *Final Report of the National Commission on Terrorist Attacks Upon the United States* (a.k.a. *The 9/11 Commission Report*). Washington DC: National Commission on Terrorist Attacks Upon the United States. Available at: http://www.9–11commission.gov/report/index.htm.

National Consumers League. 2000. "Jan-Sept 2000 Internet Fraud Statistics" [online]. National Consumers League. Available at: http://www.fraud.org/internet/lt00stat.htm.

National Consumers League. 2004. "Online Auction Fraud Complaints Still Rising, Says Consumer Watchdog" [online]. National Consumers League, March 31, 2004. Available at: http://www.nclnet.org/pressroom/03intfraudstats.htm.

National Consumers League. 2006. "Telemarketing Scams January—December 2005" [online]. National Consumers League. Available at: http://www.fraud.org/2005_fraud_trend_report.pdf.

National Cyber Security Alliance. 2004. "Largest In-Home Study of Home Computer Users Shows Major Online Threats Perception Gap." October 25, 2004. National Cyber Security Alliance. Available at: http://www.staysafeonline.info/pdf/NCSA-AOLIn-HomeStudyRelease.pdf.

National Hi-Tech Crime Unit. 2004. *Hi-Tech Crime: The Impact On UK Business.* London: National Hi-Tech Crime Unit and NOP World.

National Law Enforcement and Corrections Technology Center. 2004. "It's Phishing Season" [online]. *TechBeat,* Fall 2004. Rockville, MD: National Institute of Justice. Available at: http://www.nlectc.org/techbeat/fall2004/PhishingSeason.pdf.

Nelan, T. 1996. "FBI Searches Jewell's Home" [online]. *Time Online Edition,* August 4, 1996. Available at: http://www.time.com/time/olympic_bombing/begin.html.

New York Times. 2005. "The Rise of the Digital Thugs" [online]. *New York Times,* August 29, 2005. Available at: http://www.securityinfowatch.com/online/Corporate—and—Office-Parks/The-Rise-of-the-Digital-Thugs/5406SIW329.

Newman, G. 2004. *Identity Theft.* Problem-Oriented Guides for Police Problem-Specific Guides Series, No. 25, November 2004. Washington DC: U.S. Department of Justice. Available at: http://www.cops.usdoj.gov/mime/open.pdf?Item = 1271.

Newman, G. and M. McNally. 2005. "Identity Theft Literature Review." No. 210459, July 2005. Washington DC: US Department of Justice. Available at: http://www.ncjrs.gov/pdffiles1/nij/grants/210459.pdf.

News24.com. 2003. "Piracy Linked To Terrorism" [online]. *News24.com,* July 16, 2003. Available at: http://www.news24.com/News24/Technology/ News/0,,2–13–1443_1388359,00.html.

O'Malley, J. 2006. "Web Auctions Fertile Ground For Criminals" [online]. *Reno-Gazette Journal,* January 26, 2006. Available at: http://news.rgj.com/apps/ pbcs.dll/article?AID = /20060126/NEWS10/601260345/1016/.

Overill, R. 1997. "Computer Crime: An Historical Survey." *Defence Systems International* 98, Autumn 1997, pp. 102–3.

Patent Office. 2005. "Annual Enforcement Report 2004." London: The Patent Office. Available online at: http://www.patent.gov.uk/about/enforcement/ annreport04.pdf

PC Pro. 2006. "Thanks a Billion." *PC Pro* 139, March 2006, p. 31. London: Dennis Publishing.

Petherick, W. 1999. "Cyber-stalking: Obsessional Pursuit and the Digital Criminal" [online]. (s.n.). Available at: http://www.crimelibrary.com/criminology/ cyberstalking/index.html.

PicturePhoning.com. 2005. "Rape Caught On Cameraphone" [online]. Picture-Phoning.com, March 18, 2005. Available at: http://www.textually.org/pic-turephoning/archives/2005/03/007581.htm.

Poulsen, K. 2004. "Wi-Fi Hopper Guilty of Cyber-Extortion" [online]. *Register,* June 26, 2004. Available at: http://www.theregister.co.uk/2004/06/26/ wifi_hopper_extortion/.

Price, S. L. 1996. "Stained Games" [online]. *Sports Illustrated.* Available at: http:// sportsillustrated.cnn.com/events/1996/olympics/weekly/960805/tragedy. html.

Ray, B. and G. Marsh. 2001. Recruitment by Extremist Groups on the Internet. *First Monday* [online], 6, no. 2. Available at: http://www.firstmonday.dk/issues/ issue6_2/ray/.

Raymond, E. 2005. "InfoTrends/CAP Ventures Releases Camera Phone Ownership Study" [online]. DigitalCameraInfo.com, January 27, 2005. Available at: http://www.digitalccamerainfo.com/content/InfoTrends-CAP-Ventures-Releases-Camera-phone-Ownership-Study—.htm.

Reich, P. 2004. "Advance Fee Scams In-Country and Across Borders." Crime in Australia: International Connections, November 29–30, 2004. Melbourne, Australia: Australian Institute of Criminology.

Reid, R. 2005. *Facility Manager's Guide to Security: Protecting Your Assets.* Lilburn, GA: The Fairmont Press Inc.

Reiter, A. 2005. "Saudi Arabia Sentences Rapists Using Camera Phones to Prison, Flogging" [online]. *Reiter's Camera Phone Report,* January 7, 2005. Available at: http://www.cameraphonereport.com/.

Reno, J. 1999. *Cyberstalking: A New Challenge for Law Enforcement and Industry.* Washington, DC: U.S. Department of Justice. Available at: http://www.usdoj. gov/criminal/cybercrime/cyberstalking.htm.

Reno, J., L. Robinson, N. Brennan, and K. Schwartz. 1998. *Stalking and Domestic Violence: The Third Annual Report to Congress under the Violence Against Women Act.* Washington, DC: Office of Justice Programs. Available at: http://www.ojp. usdoj.gov/vawo/grants/stalk98/welcome.html.

Reuters. 1998. "Is Cyberterrorism a Real Threat?" [online*]. CNET News.com,* June 8, 1998. Available at: http://news.com.com/2100–1023–212007.html?legacy = cnet.

Reynolds Lewis, K. 2003. "Changing Motives of Virus Writers Make Them Harder to Catch, Experts Say" [online]. *Newshouse News Service*, August 27, 2003. Available at: http://www.newhousenews.com/archive/lewis082803.html.

Roberts, P. 2005. "Creative MP3 Players Shipped with Windows Virus" [online]. *eWEEK.com*, August 31, 2005. Available at: http://www.eweek.com/article2/0,1895,1854724,00.asp.

Rollman, J., K. Krug, and F. Parente. 2000. The Chat Room Phenomenon: Reciprocal Communication in Cyberspace. *CyberPsychology & Behavior* 3, no. 2, pp. 161–66.

Rollman, J. and F. Parente. 2001. Relation of Statement Length and Type and Type of Chat Room to Reciprocal Communication on the Internet. *CyberPsychology & Behavior* 4, no. 5, pp. 617–22.

Rosenberg, E. 2006. "Nigeria Scam Grabs Dollars of Gullible" [online]. *MiamiHerald.com*, January 1, 2006. Available at: http://www.miami.com/mld/miamiherald/business/personal_finance/13520351.htm.

Rowland, R. 2003. "Spam, Spam, Spam: The Cyberspace Wars" [online]. *CBC News Online*, November 24, 2003. Available at: http://www.cbc.ca/news/background/spam/.

Saliba, C. 2001. "Russian Hackers Blackmail U.S. E-Commerce Sites" [online]. *E-Commerce Times*, March 9, 2001. Available at: http://www.ecommercetimes.com/story/8063.html.

Saunders, R. 2005. "Happy Slapping: Transatlantic Contagion or Home-Grown, Mass-Mediated Nihilism? [online]" *Static* 1. Available at: http://static.london-consortium.com/issue01/saunders_happyslapping.html.

Schafer, J. 2002. Spinning the Web of Hate: Web-Based Hate Propagation by Extremist Organizations. *Journal of Criminal Justice and Popular Culture* 9, no. 2, pp. 69–88.

Schafer, J. and J. Navarro. 2003. "The Seven-Stage Hate Model: The Psychopathology of Hate Groups" [online]. Federal Bureau of Investigation, (from the FBI Law Enforcement Bulletin, March 1, 2003). Available at: http://www.rickross.com/reference/hate_groups/hategroups355.html.

Scheeres, J. 2003. "A Virtual Path To Suicide" [online]. *San Francisco Chronicle*, June 8, 2003. Available at: http://www.sfgate.com/cgi-bin/article.cgi?file = /c/a/2003/06/08/MN114902.DTL.

Schnieder, J. 2000. A Qualitative Study of Cybersex Participants: Gender Differences, Recovery Issues, and Implications for Therapists. *Sexual Addiction & Conipulsivity* 7, pp. 249–78.

Schwartz, J. 2003. "Cyberterrorists Sharpening Their Tools for Online Warfare" [online]. Computer Crime Research Center. Available at: http://www.crime-research.org/news/2003/03/Mess2101.html.

Smith, G. 2002. "From Joke to Alkahest" [online]. *SecurityFocus*, March 18, 2002. Available at: http://online.securityfocus.com/columnists/68.

Smith, G. (ed.). 2004. "National Security Notes" [online]. February 20, 2004. GlobalSecurity.org. Available at: http://www.globalsecurity.org/org/nsn/nsn-040220.htm.

Smith, R., 1998. "Arson motives may vary but the result is the same" [online]. *News-Journal Online*, July 1, 1998. Available at: http://www.news-journalonline.com/special/fire98/98Jul/1fire6.htm.

Smith, R., M. Holmes, and P. Kaufmann. 1999. "Nigerian Advance Fee Fraud." *Trends and Issues in Crime and Criminal Justice* 121 (July 1999). Canberra, Australia: Australian Institute of Criminology.

Smith, S. 2004. "Man Charged With Internet Gay Sex Blackmail" [online]. *365Gay.com.* Available at: http://www.365gay.com/newscon04/05/052104blackmail.htm.

Smith, W. J. 2003. "www.s-u-i-c-i-d-e.com" [online]. *National Review Online,* June 12, 2003. Available at: http://www.nationalreview.com/comment/comment-smith061203.asp.

Sophos Plc. 2003. "University Course For Virus-Writing Is Irresponsible, Says Sophos" [online]. Sophos Plc., May 23, 2003. Available at: http://www.sophos.com/pressoffice/news/articles/2003/05/va_calgary.html.

Sophos Plc. 2004. "Computer Virus Writer: 'Netsky Worm Made Me The Hero Of My Class'" [online]. Sophos Plc., June 18, 2004. Available at: http://www.sophos.com/pressoffice/news/articles/2004/06/va_netskyhero.html.

Spain Herald. 2006. "Two Arrested In Barcelona For 'Happy Slapping'" [online]. *Spain Herald,* January 19, 2006. Available at: http://www.spainherald.com/2006–01–19news.html.

Sparks, J. 2004. "Cannibal Guilty Of Manslaughter" [online]. *Channel 4,* January 30, 2004. Available at: http://www.channel4.co.uk/news/2004/01/week_4/30_eatme.html.

Spitzberg, B. 2002. "The Tactical Topography Of Stalking Victimization And Management." *Trauma, Violence & Abuse* 3, no. 4, pp. 261–88.

Spring, T. 2003. "Spam Slayer: Unite against Spam" [online]. *PCWorld.com,* September 29, 2003. Available at: http://www.pcworld.com/news/article/0,aid,112654,00.asp.

Steiner, I. and D. Steiner. 2002. "Online Escrow Fraud Hits eBay Members [online]." *AuctionBytes* 421, October 25, 2002. Available at: http://www.auctionbytes.com/cab/abn/y02/m10/i25/s01.

Stokes, P. 2000. "Teenage Victim of Phone Bullies Died Clutching Mobile" [online]. *Telegraph.co.uk,* August 19, 2000. Available at: http://www.telegraph.co.uk/news/main.jhtml?xml = /news/2000/08/19/ndani19.xml.

Stuart, A. 2003. "There's a Virus Going Around" [online]. *Inc.com,* March 2003. Available at: http://www.inc.com/articles/2003/03/25286.html.

Sturgeon, W. 2004. "Alleged Belgian Virus Writer Arrested" [online]. *CNET News.com,* February 17, 2004. Available at: http://news.com.com/Alleged+Belgian+virus+writer+arrested/2100–7355_3–5160493.html.

Sullivan, B. 2004. "Consumers Still Falling For Phish" [online]. *MSNBC,* July 28, 2004. Available at: http://www.msnbc.msn.com/id/5519990/.

Sullivan, B. 2005. Spyware Firms Targeting Children [online]. *MSNBC.com,* May 5, 2005. Available at: http://www.msnbc.msn.com/id/7735192/.

Svensson, P. 2006. "Computer Addiction? Nah, Probably Just Modern Life" [online]. *ABC.com,* February 14, 2006. Available at: http://www.abcnews.go.com/Business/story?id = 1603466&page = 1&business = true.

Tanaka, T. 2004. "Does File Sharing Reduce Music CD Sales? A Case of Japan." Conference on IT innovation, December 13, 2004. Tokyo: Hitotsubashi University.

Taylor, C. 2002. "Fighting Online Racism" [online]. *NUA.* Available at: http://www.nua.ie/surveys/analysis/weekly_editorial/archives/issue1no320.html.

Thompson, C. 2004. "The Enemy Within" [online]. *Observer*. Available at: http://observer.guardian.co.uk/review/story/0,6903,1153305,00.html.

Thompson, R. 2004. "Minimizing Liability and Productivity Risks: How to Control the Impacts of Spyware, Hacker Tools and Other Harmful Applications" [online]. Computer Associates, October 2004. Available at: http://www3.ca.com/Files/WhitePapers/etrust_pp_roi_white_paper.pdf.

Tynan, D. 2002. "Spam Inc." [online]. *PC World*, August 2002. Available at: http://www.pcworld.com/howto/article/0,aid,101769,00.asp.

Tynan, D. 2003. "Viral Scourge 101" [online]. *PC World.com*, October 29, 2003. Available at: http://www.pcworld.com/news/article/0,aid,113177,00.asp.

Tyson, W., 1998. "Motives For Arson" [online]. Tyson Fire Investigations. Available at: http://www.tysonfire.com/motives.html.

Unisys. 2006. "Banks Vs. Identity Thieves: Who Will Win?" [online]. Unisys. Available at: http://www.unisys.com/financial/insights/insights__compendium/banks__vs__identity__thieves__d0__who__will__win.htm.

U.S. Congress, Office of Technology Assessment. 1993. *International Health Statistics: What the Numbers Mean for the United States—Background Paper*. OTA-BP-H-1 16. Washington, DC: U.S. Government Printing Office.

U.S. Department of Commerce, Economics and Statistics Administration. 1997. *Census Brief: Children with Single Parents—How They Fare*. CENBR/97-1. Washington, DC: US Department of Commerce, Economics and Statistics Administration. Available at: http://www.census.gov/prod/3/97pubs/cb-9701.pdf.

U.S. Department of State. 1997. "Nigerian Advance Fee Fraud." April 1997, Report No. 10465. Washington, DC: U.S. Department Of State, Bureau Of International Narcotics And Law Enforcement Affairs.

U.S. Department of State Bureau of Consular Affairs. 2005. "Consular Information Sheet" [online]. U.S. Department of State Bureau of Consular Affairs. Available at: http://travel.state.gov/travel/cis_pa_tw/cis/cis_1006.html.

U.S. Fire Administration. 2003. "Firefighter Arson." USFA-TR-141/January. Emmitsburg, Maryland: United States Fire Administration.

U.S. Trade Representative. 2005. "2005 Special 301 Report." Washington, DC: U.S. Trade Representative. Available online at: http://www.ustr.gov/assets/Document_Library/Reports_Publications/2005/2005_Special_301/asset_upload_file195_7636.pdf.

Vance, A. 2004. "Internet Addicts Sent Home From Finnish Military" [online]. *Register*, August 3, 2004. Available at: http://www.theregister.co.uk/2004/08/03/internet_addicts_finland/.

Vatis, M. 2001. *Cyber Attacks During The War On Terrorism: A Predictive Analysis*. Hanover, NH: Institute For Security Technology Studies, Dartmouth College.

Verton, D. 2002. "Talk of Iraq Conflict Raises Cyberattack Fears" [online]. *Computerworld*, September 27, 2002. Available at: http://www.pcworld.com/news/article/0,aid,105479,00.asp.

Wagner, M. 2004. "The Password Is: Chocolate" [online]. *Information Week*. Available at: http://informationweek.com/story/showArticle.jhtml?articleID = 18902123.

Wakefield, J. 2004. "Firm Justifies Job For Virus Writer" [online]. *BBC News*, September 23, 2004. Available at: http://news.bbc.co.uk/1/hi/technology/3677774.stm.

Ward, M. 2004. "Cyber Crime Booms In 2004" [online]. *BBC News*. Available at: http://news.bbc.co.uk/2/hi/technology/4105007.stm.

Wearden, G. 2005. "Latest Smart Phone Virus Targets Symbian" [online]. ZDNet UK, April 6, 2005. Available at: http://news.zdnet.co.uk/internet/security/0,39020375,39194129,00.htm.

Wehner, R. 2005. "How Secure Is Your Computer?" [online]. Latis Networks Inc.. Available at: http://www.stillsecure.com/docs/StillSecure_Denver-Post_Honeypot.pdf. Originally published in *The Denver Post*, February 28, 2005.

Weimann, G. 2004a. "Cyberterrorism: How Real Is the Threat?" [online]. *Special Report 119*, December 2004. U.S. Institute of Peace. Available from: http://www.usip.org/pubs/specialreports/sr119.html.

Weimann, G. 2004b. "www.terror.net: How Modern Terrorism Uses the Internet [online]." *Special Report 116*, March 2004. U.S. Institute of Peace. Available from: http://www.usip.org/pubs/specialreports/sr116.html.

Weimann, G. 2005. "Cyberterrorism: The Sum of All Fears?" *Studies in Conflict & Terrorism* 28, pp. 129–49.

Whang, L. S. 2003. "Online Game Dynamics in Korean Society: Experiences and Lifestyles in the Online Game World." *Korea Journal* 43, no. 3, pp. 7–34.

White, S. 1998. "Open Problems in Computer Virus Research." Virus Bulletin Conference, October 1998. Munich, Germany: Virus Bulletin Ltd. Available at: http://www.research.ibm.com/antivirus/SciPapers/White/Problems/Problems.html.

Whitty, M. 2002. Liar, Liar! An Examination of How Open, Supportive and Honest People Are in Chat Rooms. *Computers in Human Behavior* 18, pp. 343–52.

Whitty, M. 2003. Pushing the Wrong Buttons: Men's and Women's Attitudes toward Online and Offline Infidelity. *CyberPsychology & Behavior* 6, no. 6, pp. 569–79.

Williams, M. 2003. "Slammer Was Fastest Spreading Worm Yet" [online]. *IDG News Service*, February 3, 2003. Available at: http://www.pcworld.com/news/article/0,aid,109163,00.asp.

Wiltz, S. M. 2002. "*Kansas v. Robinson*: Internet 'Slavemaster' Murder Trial" [online]. *CourtTV.com*, September 22, 2002. Available at: http://www.courttv.com/trials/robinson/background.html.

Wired News. 2000. "Hacker Posts Credit Card Info" [online]. *Wired News*, January 10, 2000. Available at: http://www.wired.com/news/technology/0,1282,33539,00.html?tw = wn_story_related.

Woods, R. 2005. "Shattered: Carnage And Chaos A Hundred Feet Down" [online]. July 10, 2005. Times Newspapers Ltd. Available at: http://www.timesonline.co.uk/article/0,,22989-1688888,00.html.

Yaukey, J. 2002. "How to Avoid Online Auction Fraud" [online]. *USA Today*. Available at: http://www.usatoday.com/tech/columnist/2002/05/07/yaukey.htm.

Ying, S., S. Han, and P. Chen. 2006. "The Death of a Young Online Game Player" [online]. *EastSouthWestNorth*, March 4, 2006. Available at: http://www.zonaeuropa.com/20060304_1.htm.

Zeller, T. 2005. "A Virus Writer Tests the Limits in Cellphones" [online]. *New York Times*, October 31, 2005. Available at: http://www.nytimes.com/2005/01/24/technology/24virus.html?ex = 1264222800&en = 479d2eb863672542&ei = 5088&partner = rssnyt.

Zetter, K. 2000. "What Makes Johnny (and Jane) Write Viruses?" [online]. *PC World,* November 15, 2000. Available at: http://www.pcworld.com/news/article/0,aid,34405,pg,1,00.asp.

Zimm, A. 2001. "A Causal Model Of Warfare." *Military Review.* January–February 2001, pp. 47–53.

Zona, M., K. Sharma, and J. Lane. 1993. "A Comparative Study of Erotomanic and Obsessional Subjects in a Forensic Sample." *Journal of Forensic Sciences* 38, no. 4, pp. 894–903.

Index

About the Author

PAUL BOCIJ is a published writer of numerous computer training titles and has published articles on various cybercrimes in journals such as *The Criminal Lawyer* and *Prison Service Journal*. He is the author of *Cyberstalking* (Praeger, 2004).